THE NEW PORTUGAL

Portugal

MINHO

• Braga

TRAS-OS-
MONTES

• Oporto

BEIRA

Aveiro

• Coimbra

Lisbon •

Setubal

• Evora

ALENTEJO

ALGARVE

50   100 km

THE NEW PORTUGAL

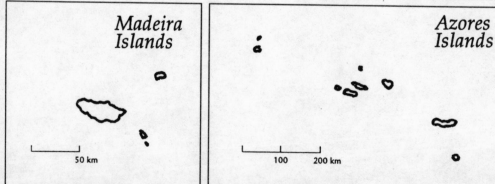

Madeira
Islands

Azores
Islands

50 km

100   200 km

RESEARCH SERIES / NUMBER 86

The New Portugal:

Democracy and Europe

Richard Herr, Editor

University of California at Berkeley

Library of Congress Cataloging-in-Publication Data

The New Portugal : democracy and Europe / Richard Herr, editor.
    p. cm. — (Research series ; no. 86)
    ISBN 0-87725-186-X : $15.50
    1. Portugal—Politics and government—1974-   2. Representative
government and representation—Portugal—History—20th century.
I. Herr, Richard. II. Series: Research series (University of California,
Berkeley. International and Area Studies) ; no. 86.
DP681.N49 1992
946.904'4—dc20   92-34235
                                                            CIP

Printed in the United States of America

CONTENTS

ACKNOWLEDGMENTS

This volume is based on the proceedings of the conference "Portugal since the Revolution," held at the University of California, Berkeley, 21–23 September 1990. The conference was organized by the Iberian Studies Group of the Center for Western European Studies on the Berkeley campus, and for one of its sessions it enjoyed the hospitality of the Supreme Council of the União Portuguesa do Estado da California in San Leandro. The Fundação Luso-Americana para o Desenvolvimento, the Fundação Calouste Gulbenkian, and the Luso-American Education Foundation of Oakland contributed precious financial support to the conference. Additional help came from the University of California Center for German and European Studies and the following organizations of the Berkeley campus of the University of California: the Provost for Research, the Office of International Affairs, and the Divisions of the Humanities and of the Social Sciences of the College of Letters and Science.

International and Area Studies (IAS) of the University of California at Berkeley provided for the publication of this volume, thanks to the good offices of its dean, Albert Fishlow. David Szanton, executive director of IAS, arranged for the publication. The volume benefits from the supervision and fine editing of Bojana Ristich of IAS Publications.

The editor also wishes to thank Dr. António Costa Pinto, without whose help on the spot in Lisbon neither the organization of the conference nor the preparation of this volume would have been possible.

R. H.

NOTES ON CONTRIBUTORS

RICHARD HERR is Professor of History Emeritus and former chair of the Iberian Studies Group, University of California at Berkeley.

MANUEL BRAGA DA CRUZ is Professor of Political Institutions, Instituto Superior de Ciências do Trabalho e da Empresa (ISCTE), Lisbon, and a member of the Instituto de Ciências Sociais, Universidade de Lisboa.

CAROLINE B. BRETTELL is Professor of Anthropology at Southern Methodist University, Dallas.

JOÃO CAMILO DOS SANTOS is Professor of Spanish and Portuguese at the University of California at Santa Barbara.

JOÃO CARLOS ESPADA is a member of the Instituto de Ciências Sociais, Universidade de Lisboa, and was political adviser to President Mário Soares, 1986–90.

MARIA CARRILHO is Professor of Political Sociology at the ISCTE, Lisbon.

ANTÓNIO COSTA PINTO is a Lecturer in Modern European History at the ISCTE, Lisbon.

JAIME GAMA is leader of the Socialist Party in the Assembly of the Republic and former Foreign Minister of Portugal.

ANTÓNIO GOUCHA SOARES is a member of the Faculty of Economics, Universidade Nova de Lisboa.

JOÃO DE PINA-CABRAL is Professor of Social Anthropology, ISCTE, Lisbon, and a member of the Instituto de Ciências Sociais, Universidade de Lisboa.

JAIME REIS is Professor of Economic History at the Universidade Nova de Lisboa.

JOSÉ GUILHERME REIS LEITE is a member and former president of the Regional Legislative Assembly of the Azores.

DOUGLAS L. WHEELER is Professor of History at the University of New Hampshire, Durham, and Coordinator of the International Conference Group on Portugal.

INTRODUCTION:
THE LONG ROAD TO DEMOCRACY AND EUROPE

Richard Herr

The papers in this volume came out of a conference held in Berkeley, California, in September 1990 entitled "Portugal since the Revolution." Because the authors relate to contemporary Portugal in many different ways, they weave a rich tapestry of the country and its recent history. Some are Portuguese scholars—a political scientist, Manuel Braga da Cruz; a political sociologist, Maria Carrilho; a contemporary historian, António Costa Pinto; a social anthropologist, João de Pina-Cabral; an economic historian, Jaime Reis; and an economist, António Goucha Soares. Three authors are professors at U.S. universities who have dedicated their lives to Portuguese studies—the anthropologist Caroline Brettell, the student of literature João Camilo dos Santos, and the historian Douglas L. Wheeler. While these persons draw on their skills as representatives of different scholarly disciplines, three men involved in the art of governing provide a complementary insight into the Portugal of today. Jaime Gama is the leader of the Socialist Party in the Assembly of the Republic and a former foreign minister of Portugal. At the time of the conference José Guilherme Reis Leite was president of the Regional Legislative Assembly of the Azores, and João Carlos Espada draws on his experience as an adviser to President Mário Soares of Portugal. In their papers they reveal the reality of today's Portugal not just as trained observers, but also as participants making statements of their own.

The authors met after the event to evaluate the lessons of the conference. Joining them around the table were, among others, former deputy prime minister Rui Machete, who as president of the Fundação Luso-Americana para o Desenvolvimento was largely responsible for the funding of the conference; Afonso de Barros, an agricultural economist and then president of the Instituto Superior

1

de Ciências do Trabalho e da Empresa (ISCTE), whose name veils its importance in the Portuguese academic world; and Philippe Schmitter, Professor of Political Science and chair of the Center for European Studies at Stanford University.

As convener, I remarked that the theme suggested to me by the papers was that contemporary Portugal has undergone two revolutions, a radical "Revolution of the Flowers," from 25 April 1974 to the establishment of the Constitution of 1976, and a second one since then that has undone the first revolution but is not a counterrevolution—a failed revolution of the 1970s and an ongoing revolution of the 1980s. My proposal met wide opposition among the group. Indeed several persons found that the title, "Portugal since the Revolution," misrepresents the developments that were the subject of the conference. Listening to their objections as recorded at the meeting is a good way into this volume.

Philippe Schmitter: It's not revolution; this is the wrong term, it encourages the wrong idea of what was really at stake. Portugal was backward with respect to the rest of Europe and had a colonial vocation. It has been coming to terms with the fact that it is a European country. This has been happening not only to small peripheral countries like Portugal, but also to central ones like Germany and France.

Maria Carrilho: It seems that if we use the term revolution, we are perhaps confined too much to a certain kind of "problematic." It does not seem to me that the beginning of the Portuguese process, which we can call democratization better than revolution, started with a revolutionary program. It was a program for the acquisition of certain mechanisms typical of democracies, the formation of political associations, holding elections, and the like. I think it is better to abandon the thread of revolution—failed revolution, successful revolution—in favor of the major theme of democratization.

Carlos Espada: I would prefer not to speak about a revolution that has failed and another that has been successful because I think we have one single process of trying to escape from the dictatorship and build a new liberal democratic society. Even the problem of European integration could be seen as part of this effort to build an open society.

João de Pina-Cabral: I would like to give an anthropological slant to this process and say, "Look, we have much more than democratization; what we have is a transformation." The process of transformation has manifested itself in the legal structure, the political structure, the economic structure, and also in the ways people live. It has manifested itself in forms that political scientists and sociologists don't always necessarily observe, but they are really important ways. For example, we have in Portugal at the moment an enormous religious creativity in the form of heterodox religious practices. It is a process of transformation within continuity that has been permitted by the liberalization. Not only is Portugal integrating itself into Europe, but it is also realizing a lot of potentials that were implicit.

Jaime Gama: I fully agree with the idea of banishing from American studies of Portuguese society the concept of revolution. We have now a normalized political society because we have achieved three points. Democracy is never a perfect society in the sense of a Marxist Communist society. First, we have withdrawn all the armed forces from the political scene. Second, we now have a stable political situation because we have for the first time an existing legal Communist Party much reduced in influence. And finally, we now have a president of center-left origin who works as a symbol for integration of all the left and center left, and at the same time we have a government of the right and for the right, which had always been suspicious of democracy and democratic institutions. This is important for stabilizing and normalizing democracy because from now on nobody can move out of a democratic scenario. All the political actors in Portugal, both civilian and military, are condemned to work in that way. For that reason, I fully agree with banishing the notion of revolution.

Schmitter: I don't agree with the democratization theme alone; that's too restrictive. I have my profound doubts about the degree of democratization in Portuguese society. Portuguese society is becoming more liberal, open, competitive, and tolerant, but I don't know that it has become more democratic in any real restrictive sense of that term. It isn't becoming more like the United States, but there are many other conceivable models, many varieties of democracy.

Portugal has experienced a change of orientation toward Europe. Before it was oriented toward its colonies, toward a different universe. The genius of the European integration process is that it has generated even greater diversity. It's not an accident that within this framework subnational regions—Catalonia or Brittany or Corsica—are becoming increasingly active. Converging toward a European norm doesn't necessarily imply the abolition of cultural, linguistic, and other peculiarities. It would be very interesting to capture what it is that Portugal is giving up and pooling with the Europeans and what will remain distinctively Portuguese.

Jaime Reis: The conference has been more about the revolution than what people are now trying to say. Most of the papers have an enormous amount on the revolution. This conference has been very much, in a sense, an exorcism of the revolution, pushing it back, back. Now we're in the nineties and we don't have to worry about the revolution, and many people here have been trying to explain why the revolution is no longer a problem. That was a crisis, we're over the crisis, but it's there in the conference. And if you try to hide it, the reader is going to feel he's been cheated when he opens the book.

Afonso de Barros: Curiously I have noticed that no one has referred to one of the aspects in which was manifested what is perhaps one of the greatest transformations of our history. It was not a transition from dictatorship to democracy; it was a transition from an extroverted country, a colonial country tied to an overseas problem, into a country that came to focus its gaze upon itself. It is a country that has come to port in Europe and has before it a sea without end, the vast Atlantic, with you on the other side. This return to our frontiers and the realization that this island is really tied to a European continent must be kept in mind as we seek to understand the process toward a democracy in Portugal and the process of integration into Europe.

2

From overseas colonial vocation to European country, from dictatorship to democracy, profound social transformation within continuity, our chapters will develop these themes. To appreciate them better the reader may welcome a reminder of the essentials of Portugal's past, both recent and more distant.

Janus-like, Portugal has since its early days looked over its shoulder at Europe and seaward toward lands outside. After throwing off allegiance to the crown of Leon-Castile in the twelfth century, Christian Portugal had to complete the expulsion of Muslim rulers from its present territory in Europe. Crusading zeal and hatred of the Muslims goes far to explaining Portugal's embarcation on empire. In the early fifteenth century, seeking a way to get at the Arabs of north Africa from behind, Prince Henry the Navigator sponsored the famous series of voyages that rounded the bulge of west Africa. Half a century later Vasco da Gama passed the Cape of Good Hope and reached India in 1497, putting substance into the title to half the world awarded Portugal by the Treaty of Tordesillas made with Castile in 1494. The rulers of Portugal were responding with anxiety to Columbus' claim for the crown of Castile of lands to the west.

For centuries Spain represented the threat from Europe. At Aljubarrota in 1383 Portuguese arms defeated the attempt of King John I of Castile, son-in-law of the late king of Portugal, to seize the Portuguese crown. In the next centuries the rulers of both countries vied to see which one could effect such a union at the expense of the other. Finally Philip II of Spain was able in 1580 to enforce his claim to the throne of Portugal through his mother. In the next sixty years Portugal discovered that Europe would not let it enjoy the benefits of empire unimpeded. The Dutch used the opportunity of their war of independence from the kings of Spain and Portugal to dismember the Portuguese empire. Only by throwing off allegiance to the rulers of Spain after 1640 was Portugal able to retake Brazil and protect its remaining holdings in Africa, India, China, and the East Indies.

From early in its history Portugal thus had to look in one direction at Spain and Europe and in the opposite one toward the Atlantic to maintain the role it had embraced. Both of these tensions were to mark the long road to democracy that began with the nineteenth century.

Like most of Europe, Portugal entered a new era as the result of the French Revolution and Napoleon. Because Portugal was an ally of Britain, Napoleon plotted with the rulers of Spain to take it over. Terrified by the approach of a French army in 1807, Prince Regent João embarked his aged and insane mother, Queen Maria, and much of the Portuguese court for a refuge in Brazil. In the fierce Peninsular War that ensued, British, Portuguese, and Spanish troops eventually drove the Bonapartist forces out of the Iberian peninsula, but the Portuguese empire and monarchy would never be restored to their former state.

The royal stay in Rio de Janeiro was to lead to the secession of that country from Portuguese sovereignty. The prince regent, who became King João VI after the death of his mother in 1816, tarried in Rio after Napoleon had been defeated. Eventually he returned to Lisbon in 1821, and a year later his son Pedro, whom he had left in charge in Rio, proclaimed himself Emperor of Brazil. João and his Portuguese subjects lacked the resources to challenge this act, so Brazil attained its independence virtually without firing a shot.

Since the early eighteenth century Brazil had laid more golden eggs for its mother country than the other colonies—literally, since gold was Brazil's main commercial product (followed by diamonds and sugar). Henceforth, Portugal would have to turn its attention back to Asia and Africa. But in the nineteenth century these possessions paled by comparison with the glory that had been Brazil. Only Angola, which continued to be a source for slaves for Brazil and the West Indies, provided a meaningful income, and this was to dry up as the countries of America one by one abolished slavery.

So the nineteenth century was to see Portugal's attention centered on finding its answer to the ideologies and political changes that were sweeping Europe. The British general William Beresford had remained in command of the Portuguese army after 1814, with effective authority over the country, to the dismay of many Portuguese officers. In 1820 a military coup established a constitutional monarchy in Spain. Portuguese army officers, following this example, staged a revolt and brought about the adoption the next year of a constitution, and King João hurried back from Brazil to accept it and protect his crown.

This proved to be the beginning of the long struggle for liberal constitutional government that finally ended—permanently, one can believe—with the Third Portuguese Republic of 1976. The example of other European countries was constantly before the Portuguese leaders, but developments in the empire became influential at critical junctures. The nineteenth century was consumed by the search for an acceptable political system. In 1823 the conservative European powers forced both Portugal and Spain to give up their constitutions, but João VI promised to grant his subjects a constitutional charter providing for limited representative government. Upon his death in 1826, his son and heir Pedro from Brazil fulfilled his father's plan, setting up his own daughter Maria II as constitutional ruler. Although Pedro's brother Miguel took up arms against the charter in alliance with the defenders of absolutism among the wealthy landholders and members of the clergy, Portugal has lived ever since under some form of written fundamental law, longer than any European country except France and a few minor states.

The Charter of 1826 attracted the moderate center among the mercantile and landowning classes. During the next decades they were threatened and at times defeated by the partisans of clerical absolutism on the right and radical liberalism on the left, but after 1852, the charter, amended to give broader authority to the responsible classes, was the law of the land until the Revolution of 1910. Power was in the hands of the elites, and they maintained control by a system known as *caciquismo* that allowed them to dominate the lower classes through corruption and managed elections. Nevertheless Portugal, like other European countries, was experiencing the apprenticeship of democracy.

Meanwhile, the rulers struggled to modernize the economy. They developed road and rail transportation, and they abolished restrictions on the sale of noble lands and sold off the properties of the church. The Portuguese economy, however, fell further and further behind those of the leading Western nations, as Jaime Reis points out in his essay in this volume. Relying on recent studies, including his own, Reis brings into question the explanations for Portugal's economic backwardness that blame its traditional agriculture and its economic dependence on Britain. The constitutional monarchy itself was partly at fault, Reis points out, for its economic policies hindered investment in productive sectors, and its failure to implement public education meant that the modernization of both agriculture and industry suffered from an illiterate labor force. One might add that illiteracy also contributed to the failure to develop a solid constitutional regime.

The reappearance of the empire in the public attention was the catalyst for political change. Portugal, as the oldest European colonizer of Africa, could not but become involved in the race for the dark continent that developed among the European powers after 1870. Because Portugal had for centuries held settlements along the coast of Angola and Mozambique, it felt entitled to a band of land across southern Africa from the Atlantic to the Indian Ocean. Its claim, publicized in a "rose colored map" in 1886, ran immediately into British ambitions to control a strip of Africa from the Cape of Good Hope to Cairo. In 1890 an ultimatum forced the Portuguese to accept British authority over the region that now includes Zimbabwe, to the dismay of the Portuguese public, who believed the nation's honor was at stake. Portugal's international impotence was a severe blow to the monarchy, which seemed more than ever merely a vassal of the British crown. Although there had been no fighting, the effect was not unlike that felt in Spain from its defeat by the United States in 1898 and loss of its last colonies in America and Asia. In both countries the constitutional monarchy was henceforth doomed, although it took years before the final collapse.

The end of the Portuguese monarchy came in 1910. A military coup chased the youthful king Manuel II out of the country and established the First Portuguese Republic. The republic was a valiant attempt to create a liberal parliamentary democracy, but it proved to be no permanent solution, in large part because Portugal could not escape its relations with Europe.

Portugal's participation in World War I ended in a rout by the German army. The liberal republic suffered discredit, and an authoritarian, protofascist movement called Lusitanian Integralism began to win followers on the right, while on the left, news of the Bolshevik Revolution in Russia aroused hopes of a proletarian revolution among the small urban working class. The two extremes fed on each other in Portugal in the 1920s, as they did elsewhere.

Corruption and the instability of the republic's governments seemed to justify the denunciations of the system's critics on the left and the right. Few were prepared to defend the democratic republic when General Manuel Gomes da Costa, the World War I commander, rose on 26 May 1926 against the government, dissolved the parliament, and established a ministry made up largely of military officers. Very rapidly a more forceful general, António Oscar de Carmona, forced Gomes da Costa aside. By 1928 Carmona was president and de facto military dictator of Portugal, while many members of the middle class who had backed the republic welcomed his strong hand. In his essay in this volume António Costa Pinto analyzes the forces that brought about the overthrow of the republic. Taking issue with those authors who have identified them as fascist, he stresses their conservative and Catholic nature.

Carmona remained president until his death in 1951. Not he, however, but his chosen minister of finance, the professor of political economy António de Oliveira Salazar, was to give form to the new regime. With conservative economic policies, Salazar balanced the budget and made the escudo a strong international currency, solving a problem that had plagued the country since the nineteenth century. In 1932 Salazar became prime minister. Thereupon he submitted a constitution of his making to a national referendum, which accepted it, although a high rate of abstention suggests that many people were opposed. The constitution created the Estado Novo (New State) and gave the government dictatorial powers. The nature and accomplishments of Salazar's dictatorship have been subject to controversial interpretations. In this volume both António Costa Pinto, discussing the political and ideological structure of the regime, and Jaime Reis, reevaluating its achievements in the economic sphere, explain the issues involved in the debates and reach their own conclusions. The regime, they show, was less fascist and achieved greater national economic growth than its enemies have maintained.

Salazar glorified the Patria, and with it the colonies, whose agricultural and mineral resources were a strong factor in Portugal's financial strength after World War II. The dictator claimed that Portugal had no empire, for the territories in Africa and Asia were merely Overseas Provinces of Portugal (Ultramar Português). In fact many Portuguese emigrants had settled in the African territories, Goa on the coast of India, Macao off the coast of China, and other Portuguese-speaking lands. In 1960 all inhabitants of Angola, Guinea, and Mozambique became full Portuguese citizens. Official maps proclaimed that "Portugal is not a small country" and showed the overseas territories superimposed impressively across Europe, of which they covered a great part.

Both white and native overseas populations became restive after 1950, however, observing how Britain, France, and Belgium were giving up their empires or being forced out by wars of independence. The revolt of the overseas Portugal brought on the death of Salazar's New State, although not until after the death of Salazar himself. India seized Goa from the Portuguese in 1961. News of the loss of Goa, combined with France's surrender to the rebellion in Algeria, brought on left-wing military risings in Angola, Mozambique, and Guinea. Receiving support from the Soviet Union and Communist China, the risings aimed at social revolution as well as political independence. Salazar was determined to preserve the territories at all costs, and the Portuguese army became embroiled in interminable wars which promised no solution. By 1970 the cause of the rebels was finding sympathy among some Portuguese officers, who began to see the real enemy not in the local insurgents but in the government in Lisbon. Their plotting led eventually to the Revolution of 25 April 1974 that overthrew the New State.

In September 1973 a clandestine meeting of army officers near Evora established the Movement of the Armed Forces (MFA), which soon made contact with dissatisfied officers in Africa. They looked to General Antonio de Spínola, an experienced leader of the African war. Spínola had recently published a book entitled *Portugal and the Future,* in which he called for negotiations with the African rebels. After a first attempt at revolt in March 1974 failed, a better organized one succeeded in moving tanks into Lisbon in the early morning of 25 April. Crowds welcomed them, and the prime minister, Marcelo Caetano, who had succeeded Salazar as head of the government when Salazar suffered a stroke in 1968, surrendered and handed over the government to Spínola. Thus was reborn the democratic Portuguese Republic, the third republic counting Salazar's New State as the second.

Although the MFA had carried out the coup, Spínola promised free elections, and the leaders of political parties, who had been in hiding, in exile, or in prison, rapidly appeared. In May Spínola, as president of Portugal, established a government that included members of the Communist and Socialist parties and the moderate Popular Democratic Party (PPD). The "Revolution of the Flowers" (people in the streets on 25 April gave the soldiers red carnations) became a contest for control between the leaders of the armed forces and the political parties. The outcome was certainly not foregone, and for a year and a half, the MFA appeared to have a commanding hold over the future of Portugal.

In July 1974 General Vasco Gonçalves, a left-wing leader of the MFA, became prime minister and remained in this position until September 1975. His rule was accompanied by violence in the cities and regions of large rural estates and strikes by the organized workers. During this period the government carried through a radical restructuring of the Portuguese economy: banks and insurance companies were nationalized, the large estates of the Alentejo were expropriated and placed under collectivist committees, and labor unions were incorporated into a single organization, the Intersindical. In these measures the Communist Party gave Gonçalves full support, and in return it obtained controlling influence in both the agricultural collectives and the labor unions.

The formation of Gonçalves's ministry inaugurated the ascendency of the supporters of a radical revolution. The MFA, and within the MFA its left wing, closely allied with the Communists, appeared to be in control of both the ministry and the armed forces movement. Dismayed by these developments, President Spínola spoke out against the imposition of a collectivist revolution. Supporters of Spínola's moderate position planned a large demonstration in Lisbon for 28 September 1974. The left-wing revolutionaries, fearing a fascist counterrevolution, prevented it by building barricades to halt their march. The demonstrators were justified in expecting the protection of the COPCOM, a new military force that Spínola had established to maintain order. Its commander was Brigadier Otelo Saraiva de Carvalho, the popular hero and main organizer of the 25 April coup. He did not act, however, and the demonstrators had to abandon their march. Spínola resigned, aware that he was powerless to stem the revolution, the last figure with the prestige to resist the government of Gonçalves. In March 1975, after an abortive Spínolist coup, a Council of the Revolution, drawn from the MFA and including Gonçalves, received full power. During this year of turmoil and tension, the eyes of the West were glued on Portugal, fearing a potential ally of Russia among the NATO members.

Although it was not evident at the time, the turning point came a month later, in April 1975, when the Portuguese went to the polls to elect a Constituent Assembly. After a campaign marked by considerable violence, the Socialists obtained 38 percent of the vote, the Popular Democratic Party 26 percent, and the Communists a mere 13 percent. This was a clear popular rebuff to the MFA, one for which the Catholic bishops' instructions to the faithful to vote for parties compatible with Christianity could take some credit. The reaction of Gonçalves and the Communist leaders was to assert that the election had no relevance to the continuation of the revolutionary process. In the Alentejo, revolutionary committees had been occupying and collectivizing the large estates, and this activity now accelerated, while workers' committees aroused revolutionary fervor in the industrial areas. In the north of Portugal strong protests denounced these revolutionary activities, accompanied at times by violence. By the end of the summer the Socialists, led by Mário Soares, and the Popular Democrats under Francisco de Sá Carneiro, with the aid of members of the Council of the Revolution who resented Gonçalves' ties to the Communists, managed to maneuver Gonçalves out of the premiership.

Sensing their declining power in both the government and the Council of the Revolution, the left-wing members of the MFA and their supporters attempted a coup on 25 November 1975. They were crushed by forces that remained loyal to the government, led by General Ramalho Eanes, while the Communists cagily kept out of the fray. More obviously than April 1975, this date marked the halt of the radical revolution. Despite continued violence in the streets caused by extremists on both the left and the right, the Constituent Assembly proceeded with its task, and on 2 April 1976, it approved the Constitution of the Republic, an act that affirmed the primacy of the civilian sector within the political process.

Acceptance of the new constitution meant elections for a regular assembly and president. The first occurred on 25 April 1976, fittingly the second anniversary of the revolution. Repeating with little change in proportions the results of the 1975 elections, it confirmed the Socialists as the largest party, with the Popular Democrats next, the two parties that have commanded the electoral scene ever since. (In 1976 the PPD changed its name to the Social Democratic Party, PSD.) Mário Soares, the Socialist leader, became prime minister, but had to count on the votes of other leftist parties. Two months later, presidential elections returned General Eanes, victor of November 1975, with a commanding majority.

The Constitution left many questions in the air. On the one hand, it incorporated the radical economic measures enacted since April 1974—which meant that it would take a constitutional amendment to modify them—and it maintained the Council of the Revolution, made up of representatives of the armed forces, with the authority to protect the constitution in "the spirit . . . of April 25." But on the other, it provided for an Assembly of the Republic and a president elected by universal suffrage. The President of the Republic was also president of the Council of the Revolution and was to name the prime minister, who would, with his government, be responsible to both the president and to the Assembly. The constitution sought both to preserve the gains of the revolution and to create a balance between the will of the people and the power of the military authors of the revolution. The majority of voters and the radical soldiers had already been shown to be of different minds, however, so that the constitution was an unstable instrument that inevitably would lead to conflict. Very soon the Assembly of the Republic, representing the point of view of the voters, would attempt to undo the collectivist legislation enshrined in the constitution. Although President Eanes had been the victor over the military left on 25 November 1975, he would become the defender of the revolutionary socialism. Henceforth, to this day, the president and the majority of the Assembly have been of different political persuasions. It is to the credit of the Portuguese leaders of all persuasions that these tensions have been resolved peacefully.

3

The structure of present-day Portugal took shape as the forces of moderation slowly obtained political control and then used it to replace the patterns established during the two revolutionary years with a liberal parliamentary democracy and free market economy.

The ostensible motive for the overthrow of the dictatorship had been the fruitless colonial war. From the outset the revolutionaries had promised to end the war with satisfaction for the rebels. Spínola had advocated autonomy within some kind of Lusophone federation; the Socialists and Communists called for outright independence of the colonies. Portuguese armies in the field, by halting military action of their own volition, left the second policy the only possibility, and on 26 July 1974, President Spínola announced that Portugal would recognize the wishes of the colonies for independence. By the end of 1975 Portugal had divested itself of all its colonies in Africa, not without leaving indigenous military forces with rival ideologies in conflict for control of the new countries.

Although Macao off the Chinese coast and Timor in the East Indies remained for the time being within the fold, the empire that had existed for nearly half a millennium was effectively liquidated in less than two years. The legacy of the empire that had been as recently as mid-century a source of prestige and income was to be a grave financial burden. Between half a million and a million refugees (*retornados*) fled to Portugal and had to be found housing and sustenance.

At the same time, the post–World War II period of prosperity and expansion in Western Europe, which Portugal has shared in a modest way, ended in 1973 with the energy crisis brought on by the rise in oil prices enforced by the Organization of Petroleum Exporting Countries (OPEC). Young men and women of Portugal who had been emigrating to northwest Europe in large numbers since the early 1960s, would no longer find work there, and many would come home, adding to the burden of the retornados. By 1977 the country suffered a 30 percent annual rate of inflation, 15 percent unemployment, and a massive balance of payments deficit.

Disillusionment with the revolution was setting in, especially among the intellectuals, who had welcomed it as the end of the bourgeois society behind Salazar's dictatorship, with its stultifying censorship. Profiting from freedom of the press, Portuguese writers poured forth a stream of novels expressing their thoughts about their country, as João Camilo dos Santos shows us in his chapter. By the end of the 1970s, bourgeois society seemed to be again in command, and many intellectuals denounced the revolution as an exercise in "opportunism and mediocrity." The prospect of becoming part of Europe offered no consolation for this intelligentsia because for them Portugal was suffering from its Western nature, an "old, unhappy, agonizing country" when compared to the virile peoples of the former colonies. Caroline Brettell has found a similar disenchantment among the peasantry, who referred to "Lisbon's revolution" and believed that the parties did not represent the masses, only themselves.

The leaders committed to preserving the new Portuguese democracy looked to Europe for support. In May 1977 the government of Portugal applied for admission to the European Economic Community (EC), initiating a lengthy process that António Goucha Soares describes in his chapter. But the European Community would admit

Portugal only if its democratic institutions were stabilized, and the International Monetary Fund would give Portugal help only if it accepted an austere economic program that meant giving up some of the revolutionary measures. Democracy, a freer economy, and a European orientation were to go hand in hand.

The economic crisis brought on a series of political crises that dragged Portugal inexorably away from the left. The Communists and other parties to the left of the Socialists, seeing the revolutionary achievements threatened, withdrew their support from Soares in December 1977. The Socialist leader managed to continue as prime minister but only by an agreement with the relatively conservative Social Democratic Center Party (CDS). This was a stopgap arrangement that lasted only until July 1978, and when a couple of nonparty prime ministers selected by President Eanes could not maintain the support of the Assembly, the president dismissed the Assembly and called for new elections. A newly created Democratic Alliance that included Sá Carneiro's PSD and the CDS of Diogo Freitas do Amaral won a majority of the seats, and in January 1980 Sá Carneiro became prime minister. The Democratic Alliance was openly committed to reversing the socialist aspects of the constitution. Since Eanes, as president, vetoed attempts to modify the constitution, the Democratic Alliance parties put their full efforts into defeating Eanes's candidacy for reelection in December 1980. Three days before the election, Prime Minister Sá Carneiro was killed in an airplane accident while campaigning for the opposing candidate. With Portugal in a state of shock, Eanes won in a landslide, showing that the Portuguese voters of all hues found this apparently colorless military man a trusted father figure in a crisis. Portugal was in a political standoff between a president determined to protect the gains of the revolution and a right-of-center assembly that favored freeing the economy but lacked a popular leader, while inflation and economic hardship continued.

Nevertheless, the reversal of the revolution advanced inexorably. In August 1982 the Assembly by a large majority revised the constitution to abolish the Council of the Revolution, the body of military officers with authority to invalidate unconstitutional acts. President Eanes was constrained by the vote to proclaim the amendment, although he did so with a heavy heart and tears in his eyes. The officers who had fought in the African wars of liberation and had imbibed the collectivist message of the rebels, formed the last bastion of the leftist revolution, and the Council of the Revolution had been their instrument. Die-hard defenders of armed forces involvement grouped around President Eanes, but in 1986 no military officer ran in the election to replace Eanes as president.

The abolition of the Council of the Revolution led to the gradual restoration of private property and a free market economy. These changes in turn made possible the conclusion of Portugal's entrance into the European Common Market. In 1983 Soares again became prime minister, with right-of-center support, and on 12 June 1985, his government signed the Treaty of Accession into the European Community. One of the signers, Jaime Gama, then foreign minister of Portugal, is among the authors of this volume. On 1 January 1986 Portugal officially became a member, along with its neighbor Spain.

Soares resigned a few days after the Treaty of Accession was signed, blamed for Portugal's continuing economic crisis. President Eanes dissolved the Assembly and called for elections in October 1985. The Social Democrats became the largest party in the Assembly, and their leader, Anibal Cavaco Silva, who had succeeded Sá Carneiro, became prime minister. Yet in the presidential election held in January and February 1986, with Eanes not running, Mário Soares was voted in, the first civilian president of Portugal since the coup of May 1926. Again the president and the prime minister were of different political orientations. João Carlos Espada, who for several years was a postdoctoral research fellow in the president's office, explains in his chapter how Soares as president exercised what he styled a "magistrature of influence," unlike his predecessor and more like a constitutional monarch, taking a nonpartisan position and in the process contributing heavily to the stabilization of the democratic system. The test came in April 1987, when Cavaco Silva lost a vote of confidence. Instead of giving a leader of the left the opportunity to form a government, as those who had voted him into office expected, Soares dissolved the parliament and held new elections. This time the Social Democrats won an outright majority in the Assembly, and Cavaco Silva returned as prime minister, unshakable so long as his party remained united.

Soares's action won the affection and admiration of the majority of the Portuguese people, grudgingly perhaps on the right of center, but among many of them also nevertheless. They established the pattern of politics that still holds. The Social Democrats supported Soares for reelection in January 1991, and he obtained an impressive 70 percent of the votes. In October 1991, parliamentary elections gave Cavaco Silva's Social Democrats slightly over 50 percent of the vote, and assured them another term with an absolute majority in the assembly. The Socialists, who came in second, had 29 percent, and the Communist share fell to only 9 percent. During the years of Cavaco Silva's government and Soares's presidency, compromise has become the watchword of Portuguese politics instead of confrontation.

Since both the European Community and the majority of the Portuguese people favored the course that replaced the political role of the military with a European-style parliamentary democracy (Portugal is, however, one of the few countries of the European Community with a unicameral parliament), the success of the Assembly now seems to have been almost inevitable. It did not seem so at the time. (In February 1981, a Spanish military force had seized its parliament in an attempt to destroy its new democracy, and the example seemed close to home.) A reading of Maria Carrilho's essay makes understandable the process whereby the parliamentary parties succeeded in easing the army out of its political role after the constitutional revision of 1982.

The evolution of Portuguese society has also played a major role in the turn away from the revolutionary agenda. Douglas Wheeler in his chapter points out that one of the major differences between the First and Third Portuguese Republics consists of the better education of the people. The political class in the latter is more professional, more cultured, more open to the outside world than it was in the former.

At a lower level Portuguese society has been radically altered during the transition since 1974, also contributing to the solidification of democracy. Braga da Cruz in our roundtable discussion stressed the importance of what he terms a "tertiarization of Portuguese society," a flight of the population from the primary economic sector of agriculture into the the service or tertiary sector. By 1990, according to Braga da Cruz's investigations, Portugal's primary sector had declined to little more than 15 percent of the total active population, while the tertiary sector was approaching or passing 50 percent. Most of the flight from agriculture is going neither into the manufacturing sector nor into the cities of the littoral, but into the commercial and service sectors and into the small cities of the interior that are now becoming big urban centers. This is a major revolution in Portuguese society.

Outside the armed forces, the strongest supporters of socialist legislation had been the industrial workers, organized by the Communists into the giant union, the Intersindical, and the laborers on the large estates of the Alentejo, which under Communist leadership had been collectivized in the heady years of the revolution. The collectives had not been an economic success, and one of the main objectives of the Democratic Alliance was to return the estates to their former owners. The relative decline of agriculture and the old urban centers after 1974 weakened the forces defending the collectivist legislation. At the same time the loss of influence by the Communist Parties throughout Western Europe, reflecting the breakup of Communist Eastern Europe, has also had its effect in Portugal.

What resistance there was on the left after 1980 took the form of street violence, bank robberies, and bombings of foreign embassies and similar targets. In 1987 Otelo Saraiva de Carvalho, the hero of 25 April 1974, was convicted of leading the terrorists, who called themselves the Popular Forces of the 25th of April. Two years later the Supreme Court released him because of irregularities in his trial. The terrorist activities were futile gestures, for the rapid changes in Portuguese society have made unthinkable a return to the collectivist spirit of 1974.

The flight from the countryside was accelerated by Portugal's entry into the EC. As one of the poorest countries in the Common Market, it has received much financial aid and foreign investment, about which Douglas Wheeler's chapter speaks. The European Community has sent some $5 billion in aid, largely for highways and public works that provide the infrastructure for a modern economy. At the same time, investment has flowed in from multinationals attracted by low Portuguese wages. Urbanization, the mechanization of agriculture, and the modernization of manufacture had all been advancing under Salazar. After a hiatus caused by the revolution and the economic crisis that followed it, the vast infusion of capital has revived and accelerated the economic transformation. This is destroying some of the unique charm of Portugal, but it is improving the economic lot of many of its citizens. Cavaco Silva's victory at the polls in October 1991 shows that a majority of the Portuguese welcome these developments.

Having left behind its empire, Portugal has successfully achieved both a democratic system and membership in the European Community. The country has reached the end of the long road to Europe and democracy.

I

The Transition

DEMOCRACY AND THE ARMED FORCES IN PORTUGAL: FROM REVOLUTION TO ROUTINE

Maria Carrilho

INTRODUCTION: THE PORTUGUESE MILITARY IN THE 1990s

Portugal's young democracy is at present a consolidated regime. While this means that the uncertainty which characterizes transition is over, it does not imply that the political system is fixed and static.[1] For example, public discussion and controversies over the present electoral system are now going on smoothly and are not seen as a destabilizing factor. The same thing is happening with the restructuring of the armed forces and the terms of military service. It is a fact that we now live in a situation where political transformation and innovation can be pursued without military interference. The definition of the concept of regime consolidation is not a matter for this paper, but one of the major problems involved in this concept is how to test the success of consolidation.[2] A political system's capacity for innovation (including that of the military) can be considered a main indicator of a consolidated democracy. In any case, civil-military relations in Portugal now follow a democratic pattern, whether we consider as a democratic guarantee the effective "objective" civil control through a network of fixed and precise norms and rules, or we assert that the major support for democracy is a "self-regulative" or "subjective" civil control through the internalization of a democratic culture by the military.[3] The constitution and the law define and ensure democratic civilian control of the armed forces. Police and public order are separated from military functions.

For their part, Portuguese officers today reveal themselves to be in tune with democratic goals, as we found in a recent enquiry.* The majority of them seem to be receptive to social and organiza-

*Mail-in questionnaire to a sample of 1992 officers from the army, navy, and air force. The response rate was more than 75 percent.

tional innovations. Opinions about the opening up of the armed forces and the military hierarchy to women and the principle of equal career opportunities can be considered significant indicators given the military's history as a closed, male-dominated institution. Almost all officers accept the integration of women into the armed forces (85.3 percent in the army, 91.4 percent in the navy, and 94.8 percent in the air force), and the percentage who think that women should become officers is similar. A woman in a command position would be accepted either without any difficulty or with only initial difficulty, according to 79 percent of officers in the army and navy and 83 percent in the air force.

As for international issues, Portuguese officers seem easily to accept new assignments (more than 72 percent in the army and navy and 78 percent in the air force). The majority expressed their readiness to serve in UN peacekeeping forces, but the proportion was larger in the army (67.9 percent) and air force (65.8 percent) than in the navy (51.9 percent). Most officers follow European issues and consider Portugal to have a "better future perspective with European integration" than without. And they believe that Europe will become stronger in the world context (72.6 percent in the army, 77.8 percent in the air force, and 84.3 percent in the navy).

In terms of military careers, it can be said that the same trend identified by Charles Moskos in developed democratic societies— i.e., the importance of the professional-occupational versus the institutional-traditional component—is also evident in Portugal.[4] The officers canvassed greatly value professional commitment to "activity to which one's talents are suited." This comes first on a scale where "to serve the national interest" comes second.

The above situation does not necessarily point to widespread satisfaction with military issues either within the military ranks or outside of them. Successive governments continue trying to reduce defense budgets, young men contest the draft, and officers feel themselves misunderstood by the very society to which they belong. This latter attitude can be seen through the open-ended questions in the above-mentioned questionnaire. However, though apparently accentuated in Portugal, these are, after all, the same difficulties that are seen in other European democracies.

When one considers that the Portuguese armed forces went through a colonial war and a revolution, how is it that we have arrived at such a state of democratic "normality" and "routine?" The purpose of this chapter is to shed some light on this question by focusing on the role of the military in the democratization process. The worldwide questioning and redefining of the functions and legitimacy of the military is also taking place in Portugal and will be discussed in a subsequent work.

In our research, we started off with some fundamental hypotheses, subsequently confirmed. The consolidation process is deeply marked by the events and modalities of transition: a) the main problems emerging during democratic consolidation can be understood only if we take into account the events of the transition period; b) during the consolidation period a number of characteristics that would eventually identify the democratic regime took shape; c) when the main protagonists of transition and consolidation were not the same, they entered into competition among themselves for forming part of and shaping the political class of the new democracy.

In what concerns periodization, it is worth mentioning that in the Portuguese case we can identify the fundamental stages of the democratization process—though we are not trying to generalize in this matter. From a comparative standpoint, much of the interest in the Portuguese case lies in its *visibility*, in its almost symbolic expression of certain mechanisms. This visibility results from the very nature of the principal protagonist of the events—the military. The dedication to formality and clear definition; the value given to straightforward position-taking; the honor accorded to the spoken word; the internalization and the taste for the symbolic and for ritual—all these have become recognizable characteristics of the military identity and self-image. Of course this is in addition to the inevitably high visibility that weaponry gives the military's performance.

1. REVOLUTIONARY TRANSITION (1974–76)

MILITARY PROTAGONISM AND MASS MOBILIZATION

The beginning of the democratization process in Portugal came with the military coup of 25 April 1974, led by the Movimento das Forças Armadas (MFA). Explanations for the unusual purpose of the event—i.e., democratization—accumulate from the first moment. We shall not develop this point, but our previous research allows us to summarize the main factors.[5] In the first place we should note that traditionally Portuguese political culture had always allowed for a certain degree of military participation. In this century, previous changes of regime had been accompanied by military intervention: from monarchy to republic on 5 October 1910; from democratic republic to dictatorship on 28 May 1926. Antonio de Oliveira Salazar, who built a system of civil-police control, never forgot to involve the upper military hierarchy; the members of the military were also allowed to participate in the corporativist structures without retiring from the armed forces. At the same time, it seems remarkable that the most critical moments for the authoritarian regime were spearheaded by military opponents.

However, events at the end of the regime came to be determinant. At the level of civil-military relations, a growing tension between the military and government authorities resulted from the insistence of the latter on a military solution to the colonial conflict; at the institutional level, government actions looking quickly to enlarge the officers' corps—which consequently affected the professional interests and prestige of the military institution at the time—brought the situation to the breaking point. Indeed only by overthrowing the authoritarian regime was the path opened for the resolution of these complex problems.

In this context, the MFA's program, which guided the military intervention, looked to the removal of the old regime's leading figures and the abolition of its support organizations (such as the feared political police); the release of political prisoners and the end of censorship; the guarantee of free political organization; and the finding of a "political and nonmilitary solution to the wars overseas." All these statements pointed clearly to a democratization process. But the initial prudence of the program, resulting from negotiations between the two main groups of the MFA, was quickly surpassed by the events caused by the enormous popular participation.* In a way, the very modality of the beginning of democratization—a military coup (i.e., an undisciplinary act)—facilitated the liberation of social forces

---

*One group of the MFA, led by General António de Spínola, was more cautious about independence for the colonies; the other, dominated by young MFA officers, wanted to grant independence to those territories as soon as possible.

that could not be contained without violating the liberating image of the MFA. The apparent strength of the social movements contributed to the reinforcement of the MFA's left wing.

At the time, the formal power structure established by the MFA was headed by the Junta of National Salvation, made up of senior officers and chaired by General António de Spínola. Those assumed to be the most influential political parties were asked by the MFA to take part in the Provisional Governments. Even so, the relationship between the military and the parties became quite difficult. On the political scene, the process leading from the military's prominence during the transition to its substitution by the political parties in the consolidation phase is rather intricate. We must take into consideration the circumstances of the main political parties and the groups at the beginning of the democratization process to make this development understandable. From the early days of liberation, it became clear that the structure and organization of the political associations and parties was not at all suitable, and the parties were certainly not prepared, to lead the installation process of the new democracy. Indeed in the period before elections for the Constituent Assembly, the only group able to act as an interlocutor with the military was the Communist Party, which was more organized and cohesive than the others. This helped it to gain an advantageous position in relation to the other parties.

In sum, with the old regime deposed, the political parties began to find the conditions for their establishment in the society, but they had neither sufficient strength nor legitimacy for any one of them to take control of the process. Inevitably, it came to look like the military had succeeded in doing what the opposition politicians had not. And so a significant phenomenon came to pass: all the parties looked to strengthen their ties to the military and gain its support as a means toward enhancing their own political influence. The effect of the involvement of the military in politics was twofold: on the one hand, it contributed to the political instability; on the other, it destroyed the cohesion and esprit de corps within the armed forces (and also the MFA, where different tendencies, from radical to moderate, had emerged). Its latent function, however, came to be the validation of the civilian party system.

POLITICAL UNCERTAINTY AND INSTITUTIONAL TURBULENCE

The period leading up to the 1976 elections is marked by a continuous uncertainty at the political level and deep organizational disturbance at the military level. Not only did economic and social changes contribute to the political uncertainty in Portugal, but international factors played a role as well. We have to bear in mind that in those years, the two superpowers were living in a state of cold-war tension. The American military intervention in Vietnam had ended the year before, and in Eastern Europe the "limited sovereignty" doctrine ruled. The United States and USSR were faced with the redefinition of their zones of influence. In this context the international orientation of the new African states coming from Portugal's decolonization took on great importance. In other words, the Portuguese transition process involved not only the future of Portugal, but also that of a great part of Africa (Angola, Mozambique, Guinea-Bissau, the Cape Verde Islands, and the island of São Tomé). The officers of the MFA were quite aware of this international game, but different perspectives and strategies existed among them—orientations toward the West, the East, and the Third World.

Under the pressure of events in Africa during May and June 1974 (intensification of guerrilla action by the independence movements on the one side, and urban terrorism by white groups on the other) and the widening gaps among various social, political, and economic forces in Portugal, the relationship between the two wings of the MFA became more complicated. The first crisis took place in July 1974 and ended with the replacement of the Provisional Government and the creation of conditions for the MFA to force General Spínola to accept a law which bound the Portuguese state to recognize definitively the right of the African peoples to their independence.

The evolution of the African situation was complex, however, and the need for a Portuguese military presence to oversee the decolonization process contributed greatly to the continued relevance of the MFA in national politics. Differences between the two principal factions of the MFA grew sharper during the summer of 1974, when a "war of documents" began. It was a form of expression and political action adopted by the military—in line with the above-mentioned characteristic of visibility—which deserves further study. This kind of action consisted in the elaboration and publication by officers of documents taking positions, issuing petitions, and proferring criticism. Throughout the revolutionary period this kind of action had a greater public impact than the parties' own declarations and congresses, to such a degree that it came to be a way of "counting the rifles," which at the time was more important than taking public opinion polls. One document—the Documento Hugo dos Santos–Engrácia Antunes (named for two of its promoting officers)—made public in August 1974 and containing close to two hundred officers' signatures, showed the already worrisome effects at the institutional level of the political involvement of the military.

The rising social tension, in which groups aligned with the old regime played a part, led to the crisis of 28 September 1974 that marked an important step for the military and civilian left. Close to seventy people were imprisoned, accused of participation in a rightist plot. General Spínola handed in his resignation as president, and the Junta of National Salvation designated General Francisco de Costa Gomes as his successor.

The following months were characterized by a growth of the demands of social movements (led by the Communist Party and leftist groups), increasing international involvement (though not explicit), and the delineation of the available political options.

On 11 March 1975, a confrontation between military factions took place, resulting in a new shift to the left. This date marks the beginning of the most dynamic period of the revolutionary process. A number of prominent figures in Portuguese finance and business were detained; the nationalization process was accelerated; more improvements in salaries, social security, and retirement benefits were introduced; and a movement to occupy the land in the latifundia regions grew.

At the same time, alterations of prime importance occurred at the organizational levels of political power, enhancing the military's influence. The institutionalization of the MFA was affirmed through two key bodies: the Council of the Revolution—CR (the former Council of the Twenty, a sort of political bureau of the MFA)—and the MFA Assembly. Until the publication of the new constitution the CR assumed constituent powers, as well as legislative control over economic and military matters. The latter had until then been the responsibility of the Junta of National Salvation, which was now abolished. Having previously functioned in an ill-defined manner, the MFA Assembly became the representative body of the MFA. Its jurisdiction covered the "elaboration, discussion, and approval of proposals before the CR" and the "analysis of the evolution of national politics, and the issuing of recommendations on the same." It was made up of 240 representatives elected from the three branches of the armed forces, including not only officers, but also sergeants and enlisted men.

Already in existence (since August 1974) was the Continental Operational Command (COPCON), led by Major (now General) Otelo Saraiva de Carvalho and charged with the preservation of public order in continental Portugal. It is worth stressing that the creation of COPCON went against a century-long trend in Western armies (including Portugal's)—i.e., the progressive separation between the functions of the military and those of the maintenance of public order.

The new MFA public relations department (Fifth Division) spread the idea of a "People-MFA Alliance" and took on innovative tasks: "civic action" and "cultural dynamization" designed to give technical and organizational aid to the population and to imbue them with the objectives of the new socialist society under construction.

It should be clear by now that at that time the Portuguese armed forces were organized along radically different lines from their NATO counterparts, even coming to assume clearly revolutionary tones. This turn of events was the cause of great apprehension in NATO circles, and certain discreet measures were taken to influence the Portuguese process. NATO had ceased to count on the Portuguese armed forces in its defense planning and even foresaw the use of foreign units on Portuguese soil (namely in the Azores). This fact was not public at the time, but some Portuguese officers were aware of it. These circumstances contributed to generating an institutional and patriotic reaction among some important military officers against the revolutionary and populist sectors.

At the level of internal political organization, a contradictory process was beginning to take shape: on the one hand, the political parties were becoming more entrenched, though not yet strong enough to control the transition process; on the other, the political involvement of the military was becoming routine and even institutionalized. Just before the elections for the Constituent Assembly, the MFA-Parties' Constitutional Platform was signed by the MFA and all the parties. This platform, also known as the First MFA-Parties Pact, was to ensure "the continuation of the political, economic, and social revolution begun on the 25th of April 1974, through political pluralism, and in freedom, but without sterile interparty battles—a common project of national reconstruction." This would put the country on an "original road toward a Portuguese socialism." This agreement was to be included in the constitution to be approved by the Assembly. A transition period of three to five years was established during which "military power would maintain itself independent from civil power." This independence was ensured by the presence of the CR and the MFA Assembly alongside the other branches of power (president of the republic, government, and Legislative Assembly).

As it turned out, however, the April 1975 Constituent Assembly election results changed the balance in the political ring. The Socialist Party was the big winner, and the Communists were not as strong in the polls as their capacity for mobilization had led people to believe. As for the center-right parties, although in the minority, they revealed themselves to be effective. While these results did not directly affect the composition of the government, it is certain that they legitimized the military and civil opposition (led by the Socialist Party) to that part of the military seen as linked to the Communist Party. This discrepancy between the electoral representation of the parties and their influence on government policies is evidence of what Juan Linz and Alfred Stepan call "the dangerous dynamics of the provisional governments" in the transition process.[6]

For its part, the MFA Assembly had become a sort of parallel parliament. It issued the "Guiding Document of the People-MFA Alliance." In addition to covering political and economic issues (development of the state sector, support for agrarian reform, and production control by the workers), the document drew the lines for great changes in the traditional manner of policy-making. A fundamental role was attributed to the "popular-based organizations," which would form "local assemblies" by region and then culminate in the organization of a National Popular Assembly. The MFA was supposed to take part in this organization at various levels, specifically through its Unity Assemblies, and the CR was to become the "supreme body of national sovereignty." Inspired by COPCON, this plan for the organization of "people's power" excited various groups on the extraparliamentary European left, while at the same time it contributed to a feeling of anxiety and even open hostility in international political circles. At the domestic level, the parties clearly foresaw the devaluation of their role. The Constituent Assembly, the only elected body, became the target of certain hostile attitudes emanating from the MFA Assembly and also the Revolutionary United Front (FUR), composed of leftist groups including the Communists.

Portugal's political future became more and more uncertain. The one clear thing was that whatever the country's political future might be, the road to it would be a military one. Within the armed forces, organizational and institutional agitation was spreading throughout the ranks. The reality was that two conflicting organizational structures had come to exist side by side: the traditional chain of command and a parallel hierarchy, promoted by the MFA's left wing. This situation put one of the most basic foundations of military organization—i.e., discipline—to the test. The issue became a sensitive one, and the attempt to introduce democratic mechanisms like elections and assemblies in the armed forces encountered a great deal of opposition from within the military itself.

August 1975 saw the publication of the "Document of the Nine," signed by nine high MFA officials on the moderate left (some of them belonging to the CR). It contained explicit criticisms of government policies, including the orientation of the decolonization process, and warned of the danger of new forms of totalitarianism. Other public positions were soon taken by individual officers and groups within the MFA via documents, speeches, and interviews.

The clouds on the social and political horizon thickened to the point that the possibility of armed conflict or even a civil war was seriously broached (as would later be revealed). In this context semiclandestine organizations preparing for armed resistance had been growing. The most significant was an enlisted men's revolutionary organization, the Soldados Unidos Vencerão (SUV). Its program pointed clearly to the dismantling of what remained of the traditional organization of the armed forces by "imposing elections for Unity Assemblies in the barracks; the calling of soldiers' Plenary Assemblies whenever we want"; and by giving incentives for "the linking up of the organs of popular power—i.e., the residents' commission, workers' commissions, and village councils."[7] The SUV even began organizing press conferences with masked speakers and publishing an underground paper, and it distributed pamphlets in various barracks as well. Some elements of the Portuguese revolutionary vanguard began to seek links to international terrorist groups, especially the IRA, the Basque ETA, and the Red Brigades in Italy.*

During labor troubles in November 1975 we witnessed the sequestration of the Constituent Assembly by workers and other demonstrators on the street. A few days later most of the government's ministers decided to suspend their functions, saying that there were not enough security guarantees.

Once again it was a military movement that would redefine the objectives of the democratization process on 25 November 1975. A paratroopers' revolt led to the involvement of the revolutionary and moderate sectors of the MFA. Military units tied to MFA moderates, commanded by General António Ramalho Eanes, revealed an operational capacity much superior to those following the revolutionary line and easily controlled the situation. The most relevant officers belonging to the revolutionary line, like Carvalho, were detained. It became clear that at the end of 1975 the revolutionary period was over and the military institution was once again moving back to its traditional identity.

2. FORMAL TRANSITION AND GUIDED CONSOLIDATION (1976–82)

THE CONSTITUTIONAL REDISTRIBUTION OF POWER

The period that official documents of the time refer to as the "transition" was typified by a contradictory situation. There was a programmed withdrawal of the armed forces from the political scene while at the same time the process of consolidation of the mechanisms of parliamentary democracy was marked by the protective presence of the military. This presence took on certain somewhat state-oriented features in opposition to the partisan-oriented policies seen by the military to be so prevalent among the political parties. Here we note the neopatrimonialist heritage that character-

---

*There is no documentation available on this information, but it circulated in the foreign press at the time. The author herself was a correspondent for an Italian newspaper.

ized Portuguese political society at the time of the April 1974 military coup.[8]

Having carried through the decolonization process that ended just before 25 November 1975, the officers who had been at the head of events driving the country to democratic "normalcy" nevertheless still found themselves with real responsibilities. The MFA had to oversee the situation until the promulgation of the constitution and the legislative elections, meaning that their position would have to be maintained until at least April 1976. At the same time, the existence of social and political forces betting on the comeback of the previous regime was a real fact. It should be recalled that many interests, whether on Portuguese or African soil, had been affected by the decolonization. In just a few months, beginning in mid-1975, returnees from Africa had caused Portugal's population to rise by nearly 9 percent. The social situation became explosive. By early 1976 the level of violence had intensified.*

We can say that the military's continued presence on the political scene was legitimated by its interventions on 25 April 1974 and 25 November 1975 in favor of pluralistic democracy, as well as by the precarious state of public order. This is the context in which the military renegotiated a compromise with the political parties—the Second MFA-Parties Pact, signed on 26 February 1976. It would replace the first pact, and it made it clear that the parties would compete for the organization of political power while the administrative and legislative autonomy of the armed forces would be maintained. The MFA would thus continue to serve as the vigilant eye guaranteeing the party system, free elections, and the socialist-democratic direction of the transition process.

The constitution approved on 2 April 1976 saw the military's role maintained principally through two bodies: the presidency of the republic and the CR, the latter recognized as a sovereign body as well. The CR retained the functions of advisor to the president and guarantor of the fulfillment of the constitution, as well as being the legislative body for military matters (Art. 142). In practice it functioned as a sort of constitutional court and at the same time was responsible for the elaboration of laws and regulations on the orga-

---

*A press memorandum from the public relations office of the Communist Party, distributed on 29 January 1976, mentioned "more than 300 actions of fascist violence" since the previous May.

nization, functions, and discipline of the armed forces (Arts. 146 and 148).

To the president of the republic (elected by universal suffrage) were conferred powers (including the right to veto) which could define the system as semi-presidentialist (Arts. 136, 137, 139).[9] Although the constitution did not specify anything regarding the origin of the next president, it was obvious at that time that he could come only from the military ranks. Ramalho Eanes, military chief of the 25 November action, supported by the Socialists and the center-right parties, obtained a majority of 56 percent in the first round of the 27 June 1976 presidential election.

THE MILITARY AND THE POLITICAL CLASS

The form of political organization that the 1976 constitution foresaw reflected the power levels attained by the various political players of the time and their "contractual" relationship. We can say that the military was then recognized as retaining a somewhat "Caesarist" status, embodied by the CR and the president.[10]

The situation, however, became favorable to the parties as the democratic mechanisms—especially elections—continued functioning. The results of the first parliamentary elections on 25 April 1976 confirmed the permanence of the main political orientations shown in the 1975 elections. In brief, however, the ensuing process of formal democratization brought about the incompatibility of the objectives and arrangements established by the constitution and the dominant trends at the economic and social levels. In other words, the CR and the president were very soon tied to the defense of an inadequate constitution, one to which only the Communist Party showed real attachment. At the same time, however, the successive elections and governmental crises resulted in a democratic exercise in conflict resolution, which served to strengthen the party system. In this sector, in other words, the very practices, both formal and informal, of representative democracies were being routinized and consolidated.

Civil-military relations faced a somewhat more problematic evolution. The CR's existence began to be tested and hotly disputed by the center-right parties, which tried to anticipate the revision of the constitution. At the same time, divergent groups existed within the armed forces differing principally—and beyond politico-ideological questions—on the issue of the very role of the military as defined in the constitution. In a 1979 internal analysis, the Institute of National Defense, an official entity beholden to the Joint Chiefs of Staff and the Ministry of Defense, delineated certain "factors of national power, their potentials and vulnerability." It considered that the constitution contained "norms susceptible to controversy" and that there persisted "deficiencies in the organization of the armed forces within the general structure of the state—specifically with respect to connections with the political power." It was also stressed that the existence of the CR contributed to the "formation of a public perception of political instrumentalization of the armed forces" and that the fact that the Joint Chiefs of Staff were subject to the deliberations of the CR constituted a vulnerability in the military organization.[11]

In spite of the fact that many officers preferred to see the military institution removed from the political scene, it is certain that at the time the battles among the different political forces still involved the armed forces. A clear indicator of this reality is that the December 1980 elections were contested by two generals. Left-approved Eanes won decisively over Soares Carneiro, the candidate of the liberal-conservative government (Aliança Democrática—AD). Thus the "cohabitation" of the president and the government became conflictive and contributed to the complexity of the civil-military relationship, with government leaders insisting on slogans like the "need for demilitarizing Portuguese society" and the "liberation of civil society." A side effect of this campaign against President Eanes and the CR was an acceleration in the deterioration of the public image of the armed forces.

The core of the upcoming constitutional revision was precisely the military issue. It is worth noting that over nearly eight years a politically well-prepared elite had developed within the military, and some among them were willing to continue their participation in the political sphere. But with the exception of the Communists, the principal parties remained opposed to this idea. The government and the Socialist Party (in the opposition) laid down an accord that was intended to end the CR's mandate and to disallow any further participation by any of its members in the planned State Council and Constitutional Court.

From all this, the need to redefine civil-military relations emerged clearly—now moving toward a subordination of the military to civilian political control—as did evidence of a latent competition between "civil politicians" and "military politicians." Both groups had an implicit interest in the formation of the political class which in the coming years would step into the various seats of power. In this match, assumed to be a zero-sum game by the civilians, the winners were the civilian politicians, as appears easily predictable in looking back. After all, civil politicians were backed by increasingly stronger parties, and the military politicians were not approved of even within the military institution itself.

3. DEMOCRATIC CONSOLIDATION AND CIVIL CONTROL (1982-86)

Beyond putting an end to the CR, the 1982 constitutional revision confirmed the removal of the military from the visible political scene and took from the presidency its power of nominating the military chiefs of staff. The Superior Council of National Defense was created as a consultative body which could take on administrative powers. The formal structuring of the armed forces within the democratic system was completed a few months later, with the approval of the National Defense and Armed Forces Law. Primary among its guiding principles were the following: a) a concept of national defense clearly limited to defense against external enemies, leaving the armed forces no role whatsoever in the maintenance of public order or as guarantor of state unity; b) the subordination of the armed forces to political power, reinforced by the budgetary control by parliament over the government, whose Ministry of Defense now subsumed the armed forces; c) the strengthening of the Ministry of Defense, the one government department on which it was "incumbent to prepare and execute national defense policy . . . as well as to secure and supervise the armed forces" (Art. 33).

The Defense Law, approved with the votes of the governing AD as well as the Socialists, was coldly received by the military hierarchy. The principal reservations were to the authority to nominate and dismiss military chiefs of staff, which had been passed from the presidency to the government. President Eanes decided to veto the law, which went back to parliament, where the veto was overridden and the law approved with no alterations.

It became clear that the political parties were leading the democratic consolidation and the civilian leaders were pushing the military off the political stage. This process, however, was not easily accomplished in the years following the constitutional revision of 1982. The center of the civil-military tension had passed from the CR to the president. Eanes was not under attack by the liberal and conservative parties, while problems with the Socialist Party were growing. The president was gaining center-left popularity, crowding the Socialists on their own territory. A leadership conflict in fact developed between Eanes and Mario Soares, the prime minister since 1983 and long-time secretary of the Socialist Party.

Eanes had become a reference personality for several groups: those members of the military distanced from politics but willing to play some role; those disenchanted with the parties and especially with the economic austerity of the Soares government; and those politicians aiming to use these tensions as a vehicle for their own greater influence. These circumstances led to the formation in 1985 of a new party—the Partido Renovador Democrático (PRD). The party had been put together by supporters from Eanes' 1981 campaign for the presidency.* Surprisingly, some months later in the legislative elections this party obtained 18 percent of the votes, for the most part Socialist crossovers. The PRD's story is deserving of further study, particularly in relation to the political role of the military in democracy. In a brief analysis, I would point out the following: a) the PRD's existence demonstrates the accomplishments of the democratic parliamentary system: a party, and no longer an organ of the armed forces, became the point of reference for a number of military elements previously linked to the MFA who did not necessarily become formal members of the new party; b) the good showing at the 1985 polls reflected not only disenchantment, but also Portuguese political culture, in which the Caesarist component was still present (here represented by the arbitrating role of progressive members of the military). This involved a kind of contradiction which could not last for long. Caesarism is unbearable within the

*These supporters were organized under the banner of the Comissão Nacional de Apoio à Recandidatura do Presidente Eanes (CNARPE), the campaign organization for the reelection of President Eanes.

routinized context of a democratic party system. In fact, the next elections, in July 1987, marked a dramatic fall for the PRD, whose share of the vote decreased to 4.9 percent.

Using a minimalist definition, we can say that democracy was consolidated beforehand, but with the implementation of the 1982 constitutional revision, 1986 marks the fulfillment of democratic consolidation if we adopt a maximalist definition. The traditional parties showed that they believed Portugal's democracy to be consolidated and without need of any further military protection, even that offered symbolically by a general as president. So it was that there were no military candidates campaigning to succeed Eanes. The election of Mario Soares signaled the complete removal of the military from the visible political scene. It was the first time since the First Republic that the chair was to be occupied by a civilian.

Another major event in 1986—the beginning of integration into the European Community—came to consolidate further the young Portuguese democracy, giving it a European economic and political context, thus stimulating its economy and society. The characteristics and future of the young Portuguese democracy appear to be tightly linked to Europe's. As for Portugal's military, its future is now seen as being part of the much larger problem, the future of European defense.

CONCLUSION

Portugal is now a structured and consolidated democracy characterized by its flexibility and capacity for innovation. Civil-military relations now follow a democratic pattern, with the democratic socialization of the officer corps representing an important aspect, and one not easily attained in other such recent democracies.

In the revolutionary period, the political involvement of the military led to high tensions between the revolutionary and the reformist sectors (the conservative right being out of the game). With the reformists' triumph after the events of 25 November 1975, the armed forces returned to their institutional-traditional role and withdrew from the visible political scene.

During the democratic consolidation period, however, a certain party of the "military-politician" elite competed with the civilian politicians for influence among the rising political class of the new democracy. The military's protective role can be explained by the Portuguese state's previous patrimonialist character. This was favored by the Caesarist-oriented popular political culture

Political parties are everywhere the leading actors in democratic consolidation, and in Portugal as well they have succeeded in shaping the political class. Civil supremacy over the military has even reached the symbolic level since Mario Soares assumed the presidency following the 1986 elections.

NOTES

This paper was produced in the context of a research project entitled Democracy and the Armed Forces in Portugal, sponsored by the Volkswagen Foundation.

1. For the concept of transition and the uncertainty which characterizes it, see Guillermo O'Donnell and Philippe Schmitter, *Transitions from Authoritarian Rule*, vol. 4, *Tentative Conclusions about Uncertain Democracies* (Baltimore, 1986), pp. 3–7.

2. On the concept of consolidation, the discussion is ongoing. See Philippe Schmitter, "The Consolidation of Political Democracy in Southern Europe," unpublished paper, Stanford University and Istituto Universitario Europeo, 1988; Leonardo Morlino: "Consolidamento democratico: Definizione e modelli," *Rivista italiana di scienza politica*, no. 2 (1986): 197–238; and "Democratic Consolidation and Democratic Theory," unpublished paper, conference on "Problems of Democratic Consolidation," Bad Homburg, July 1989; and Giuseppe Di Palma, "La consolidación democrática: Una visión minimalista," *Revista española de investigaciones sociológicas*, no. 42 (1988): 67–92.

3. The first two viewpoints are found in Samuel Huntington, *The Soldier and the State: The Theory and Politics of Civil-Military Relations* (Cambridge, Mass., 1957); Morris Janowitz, *The Professional Soldier*, 2d ed. (New York, 1971); and Samuel E. Finer, *The Man on Horseback: The Role of the Military in Politics*, 3d ed. (Middlesex, 1976). The last is in Claude E. Welch, *No Farewell to Arms? Military Disengagement from Politics in Africa and Latin America* (Boulder, 1987), and Alfred Stepan, *Rethinking Military Politics: Brazil and the Southern Cone* (Princeton, 1987).

4. A discussion on this issue is found in Charles Moskos and Frank R. Wood, eds., *The Military: More than Just a Job?* (Washington, D.C., 1988).

5. See Maria Carrilho, *Forças armadas e mudança política no seculo XX em Portugal* (Lisbon, 1985), part 4.

6. Juan Linz and Alfred Stepan, "Democratic Transition and Consolidation in Southern Europe—With Reflections on Latin America and Eastern Europe," unpublished paper, July 1990.

7. Quotations from the SUV Program.

8. For the concept of neopatrimonialism, see S. N. Eisenstadt, *Revolution and the Transformation of Societies: A Comparative Study of Civilizations* (New York, 1978), pp. 274ff. Eisenstadt considers the Portuguese revolution included in the category of "revolutions in neo-patrimonialist societies."

9. See Maurice Duverger, "La nozione di regime 'semi-presidenziale' e l'esperienza francese," *Quaderni costituzionali* 2 (1983): 99–133.

10. For the concept of Caesarism, see Antonio Gramsci, "Noterelle sulla politica del Machiavelli," in his *Quaderni dal carcere* (Turin, 1975), pp. 1619–22.

11. Quotations from the conclusions of "O país que somos," Estágio Interforças (Lisbon, 1979), reserved document.

DIRECT SOURCES

Documentation on defense at the Instituto de Defesa Nacional, Lisbon.

Enquiry into the Portuguese Officer Corps, 1989–90 (directed by Maria Carrilho).

Semi-directive interviews of fifteen persons (military and civilian) who had participated in the events.

MÁRIO SOARES, THE PRESIDENCY, AND THE DEMOCRACY: THE "MAGISTRATURE OF INFLUENCE"

João Carlos Espada

The first presidential mandate of Mário Soares began on 9 March 1986 and ended five years later, after his reelection to the presidency, with more than 70 percent of the votes cast, on 13 January 1991. It will be remembered as the first mandate of a Portuguese civil president since 1926. In addition, however, Soares's presidency will be remembered for other, less symbolic reasons.

Nowadays the political situation at the time of Soares's election in January 1986 seems to us almost paleolithic. The country was then politically divided over the model of society to build, and that strongly influenced the constitutional debate on the so-called "irreversibility of nationalizations" which had taken place in the revolutionary period of 1974–75. This constitutional debate was only one of several expressions of an archaic political culture in which took place what should have been—but was not—the normal and peaceful competition between the left and right wings.

The right wing saw Soares as "materialist, atheist, and masonic," as Eurico de Melo (at the time the second personality of the Portuguese right-of-center government) put it. For the left wing, then strongly influenced by a Marxist ideology, Soares was seen as a traitor to the workers' cause and as an American instrument. Even the Portuguese adhesion to the European Community was not uncontested. Strongly criticized by the Communist Party (PCP), and accepted only with resignation by the leftist sectors of the Socialist Party (PS), the European cause was not acceptable to the right wing either. After being elected to the leadership of the Social Democratic Party (PSD) in early 1985, Anibal Cavaco Silva firmly warned that he could not subscribe to the "Adhesion Contract" which had been negotiated by the coalition government of the so-called "Bloco Central," under the leadership of Mário Soares, Carlos Mota Pinto, and Rui Machete.

As far as the political system is concerned, the situation was not far better. The chronic instability of the four-party system had been strained by the arrival of a fifth party: the Partido Renovador Democrático (PRD), which had been created by General Ramalho Eanes, the President of the Republic at that time, and which had as its main goal the destruction of Soares's left-of-center leadership of the PS and its alliance with the PCP. (Nowadays, what remains of the PRD proposes a coalition with the PSD, after the next parliamentary elections, although this same party joined the PCP in 1985 in supporting the candidacy of Salgado Zenha for president.) Finally, there had been a great and lasting tension between the president and the several governments. General Eanes ran the presidency as the leader of a political faction in systematic opposition to the government's policies.

Six years later, the general outlook seems very different. First of all, we have for the first time a government with an absolute majority in the parliament, and that government is already the longest lived since the democratic revolution of 1974. This government is based on the PSD, the right-of-center party that had supported the defeated presidential candidate, Freitas do Amaral, against Soares. Nevertheless, there has been strong institutional cooperation between the government and the president.

Defining himself as the president of all the Portuguese people, Soares has avoided becoming the center of political controversies. Indeed he seems to be recognized as a reference point for national stability. This is perhaps one of the most curious differences from the political situation of early 1985: having begun his presidential candidacy with 8 percent in the public opinion polls, Soares has maintained his popularity as president in the range of 65–75 percent, achieving a large consensus in the country. To the surprise of some analysts, even Prime Minister Cavaco Silva announced that he would not support any other candidate if Soares decided to run again for president.

At the same time, it seems that the five-party system is now moving toward what has been called a "double-hegemony system."

This is not exactly a two-party system, as in the Anglo-American democracies, because at least five parties still exist in the parliament. But each half of the political spectrum is now under the hegemony of one main party—the PSD on the right and the PS on the left—and each has a real possibility of attaining power.

Last but not least, the political culture in Portugal seems different nowadays from what it was on the eve of the president's first election. The constitutional debate has ended, as a very mature and balanced revision has taken place. The ideological basis of the constitution—such as the commitment to the construction of socialism, or the "irreversibility of nationalizations"—has been removed. The new text emphasizes the ideal of an open society, with pluralistic and democratic procedures, and leaves the choice of specific policies to the free vote of citizens. This revision, of course, has been possible only with the cooperation of the two main parties, the PSD in the government and the PS in the opposition.

Another important feature of the new political culture is the consensus built around the Portuguese adhesion to the European Community. In spite of some lack of enthusiasm of the prime minister regarding certain European issues, we are now very far from the old days of 1985 when he used to criticize the Portuguese adhesion. Moreover, the European cause has won the strong support of all the PS, and it has been one of the crucial issues that provoked an ideological crisis in the PCP. As Zita Seabra, one of the most important dissenters from the Communist leadership, has declared, Alvaro Cunhal, the Communist secretary-general, was completely wrong, even on the issue of the European Community. Instead of a capitalist backward step, Seabra has said, the Portuguese adhesion to the Common Market has been one of the most important changes since 25 April 1974.

These comparisons will not be very controversial, and I dare say they supply enough evidence for the great political changes Portugal has experienced over the last five years. I do not pretend that these changes are due solely to the president's mandate. One cannot forget the important role played by the prime minister and his majority or that of the PS and its successful new leader, Jorge Sampaio. Moreover, it would be a great mistake to undervalue the role of the civil society: the new entrepreneurs, the young emerging middle class, the opinion-makers, and so forth.

One cannot, however, explain the changes without taking into account the contributions of President Soares. One of the most important has been his interpretation of the presidential role in the Portuguese political system—what he has called the "magistrature of influence." In a seminar at the Institute of Social Sciences at the University of Lisbon (7 March 1990), the president explained his views. After recalling his constitutional powers—to dissolve the parliament, dismiss the prime minister, veto the laws, and be the supreme commander-in-chief of the armed forces—Soares added, "The President's power exists mainly through his political influence." And he underlined that the way this political influence exists depends on the kind of majority there is in the parliament. Soares then explained that he had chosen his own role as the "Moderating President" on political grounds, not on constitutional or juridical ones. "After my election," he said, "the country was politically divided into two halves. I thought I should show both halves that I was going to be the President of all the Portuguese people, including those who had voted against me."

Thus on the very day of his electoral victory, Soares announced that his presidential majority had been dissolved at the very moment that it had become the majority. That meant that the president was not going to be the leader of either the opposition or any other political faction. Unlike his predecessor, Eanes, Soares wanted to be a moderator and guardian of liberal democratic procedures. "I don't believe," the president explained, "that this moderating role reduces or has reduced my own political powers. On the contrary, I believe that the President may have great political power, and that that power will be much greater as his interference into day-to-day government policies declines."

Of course, the power to which the president referred is mainly that of political influence, not of direct intervention. This is what I believe he meant by "the magistrature of influence."

One of the most important issues that the president had to deal with was the fall of Cavaco Silva's first government in April 1987. This government fell after a coalition vote of the left-wing opposition, Socialists and Communists, who seconded a motion of censure presented by the PRD. This anomalous left-wing majority hoped that the president would give them a new government. In fact, there was a formal majority that would allow for a left-wing government, even if in the process the first party in the last elections, the PSD, had to become part of the opposition. The left-wing opposition reminded the president that he had been elected by the left in the presidential runoffs.

In spite of pressures to appoint a new prime minister, the president decided to call for general elections. This was possible only because Soares saw himself as the president of all the Portuguese and refused to act as a leader of a political faction. His decision evoked much criticism from the left, but as time went by, one could see how intelligent was the call for elections.

The left-wing majority that had overthrown the minority right-of-center government was in no condition to reach an agreement on a positive program. It was an abnormal coalition of interests, with strong antagonisms among them. Primary among these was the common desire of the PRD and PCP to destroy the left-of-center PS. Moreover, the small left-wing majority in parliament no longer corresponded to the majority preferences of the voters, as the election was going to show. For the first time since the democratic revolution one sole party, the PSD, got the absolute majority. That was the most expressive evidence that the citizens approved the president's decision to call the elections.

The general elections of 1987 were a product of the president's view of his role in the Portuguese political system. At the same time, these elections and their results strongly influenced the president's commitment to his "magistrature of influence." Furthermore, the elections had a strong influence on the further evolution of the Portuguese political situation.

First of all, the absolute PSD majority opened the way to the so-called "double hegemony system." On the right, the voters have a tendency to maximize their power by giving their votes to the majority party. On the left the same thing occurs: supporters now have much more incentive to vote for the left-of-center PS if they want to oppose effectively the right-of-center government.

Second, the right wing had to adapt to the new political environment brought on by the 1987 elections. After having accused Soares of being "materialist, atheist, and masonic," the PSD moved sharply to the center, and at the center the party won the 1987 elections. Furthermore, the PSD could not deny that the electoral victory had been possible because of the impartial and fair procedure of the president. Thus the PSD became hostage of its own victory; to keep the voters, the party should no longer be aggressive toward the president.

Third, the 1987 elections had a strong impact on the left wing. The PS felt obliged to correct its leftist tendencies and began a strong and (I believe) enduring move to the left of center. The PRD simply disappeared at the elections: from 18 percent in 1985, it fell to no more than 5 percent in 1987. As far as the PCP is concerned, the 1987 elections seem to have contributed heavily to the openness of its most serious crisis.

Finally, the 1987 elections (in my opinion) strengthened Soares's commitment to the "magistrature of influence." Having to deal with a new majority government, Soares had to show dedication to his commitment to fairness and impartiality. This meant he should not attempt to obstruct the government. At the same time, the president should guarantee that the new majority would not and could not subvert the liberal democratic principle of "majority rule, minority rights."

The president has succeeded fairly well. When the new majority gave signs of exaggerating its legitimate power, the president's New Year speech to the nation on 31 December 1988 strongly criticized the abuse of power and appealed to pluralism and the respect for civil rights. I would even say that the president's stress on pluralism and tolerance since 1988 may well have had some influence on the PSD decline and the PS recovery in European and local elections in 1989.

Nowadays Portugal is in a very different situation from 1985. Mário Soares ended his first mandate with great success and ran again for president with the support of the two main parties, his own PS and his formal rival, the PSD, which is led by the prime minister. The strong ideological controversies in Portugal have evaporated. Now the problem seems to be the excessive consensus built around the personality of Soares.

Some analysts say that in the president's second mandate, Soares should be a more active protagonist. In my opinion, this would be a mistake. First, it seems to me that one should not change a winning policy. Second, the president can be a protagonist—as I think this one has been—without becoming the president of a political faction. One can always be the protagonist for the role of moderator and guardian of liberal democratic rules. One conclusion that may be drawn from the last presidential election is that the common sense of the Portuguese voters has led them to understand and to approve Soares's approach to the role of president. Unfortunately, some analysts lack this common sense.

THE PLACE OF PORTUGAL IN THE EUROPEAN UNION

António Goucha Soares

1

The Treaty of Rome, signed on 25 March 1957, establishing the European Economic Community, began a complex process of European integration been has been getting progressively more powerful. Constituted initially of six states (France, the Federal Republic of Germany [FRG], Italy, Belgium, Holland, and Luxembourg), the European Community (EC) has been added to on several occasions.

The first of these additions took place in 1973, encompassing the United Kingdom (UK), Ireland, and Denmark. Norway participated in the negotiations but did not ratify the Treaty of Accession to the European Community as the result of a national referendum. This enlargement, which included only north European states, placed the United Kingdom at the forefront of the movement for European integration. It involved the defeat of continental opposition to British membership after the departure of General Charles De Gaulle from the presidency of the French republic in 1969.

The second enlargement became effective in 1981 with Greece's entrance into the EC. This marks the beginning of the EC's expansion toward southern Europe which characterized the 1980s; during the 1970s it seemed to be a predominantly north European phenomenon. This southern expansion continued with the entrance of Portugal and Spain into the Community in 1986, giving it a greater North/South balance. The EC's enlargement during the 1980s would not have been possible, however, if the states in question—Greece, Portugal, and Spain—had not in the 1970s undergone profound democratic changes in their political structures. It is a reflection of the democratic solidarity of the EC that it was prepared to recognize these three south European states, which, after abandoning right-wing authoritarian regimes, undertook efforts to establish and consolidate democratic governments.

These developments must be seen within the context of the changes that took place in Portugal as a result of the revolution of 1974. The political system that resulted from the constitution of 1976, based on respect for fundamental rights and a pluralist democratic regime, fulfilled the political requirements for membership in the EC. Moreover, the independence of all Portuguese colonies in Africa allowed a refocusing of Portuguese foreign policy in the direction of Europe. As a result, Portugal made its formal request to enter the EC on 28 May 1977. In June 1978, the Council of Ministers of the Community accepted Portugal's application, thus initiating the negotiation process in October of the same year.

The negotiation process was prolonged for seven years, however, due to the political instability that characterized the first years of Portuguese democracy, the social and economic hardships that member states were facing at the time, the institutional barriers prevalent within the Community prior to the Single European Act, and the joint consideration given to Portugal's and Spain's applications. On 12 June 1985, the government of Prime Minister Mário Soares signed the Treaty of Portuguese Integration into the European Community in Lisbon. Portugal became a full member on 1 January 1986.

Given its aim of integrating all European nations, the EC will continue with its policy of enlargement. Formal applications for membership are pending from Austria, Turkey, Malta, Cyprus, and Sweden. In addition, the EC underwent a de facto enlargement as a result of German unification in October 1990 (a fusing of the German Democratic Republic [GDR] into the FRG). The disappearance of the GDR as a political reality and its simultaneous absorption by the FRG automatically made the ex-GDR a member of the EC. The ex-GDR, which today makes up five new *Länder* of the FRG, became a full member of the EC, having been exempted from the restrictions of the transition periods normally imposed by the Community on new members. This event could be an indication of what will happen in the 1990s: a new geographical profile of enlargements. Parallel to the northern and southern expansion of the 1970s and 1980s respectively, we may witness an EC opening to the East as a consequence of democratic changes in the East European countries.

2

There are several ways in which we can classify the states that form the EC in order to define their relative position vis-à-vis the Community as a whole. We shall focus on three aspects which we consider particularly significant. The first is the demographic weight of member states. With this criterion we can identify a nucleus of four large states: the FRG, Italy, France, and the UK. Each of these countries has a population of about 55–60 million. The FRG after German unification has approximately 80 million. Spain comes close to this nucleus with about 40 million. Therefore a group of five states represents 280 million inhabitants of the 340 million that make up the EC. Portugal, with 10 million inhabitants, is clearly a small state within the Community. The strengthening of supranational elements that will probably characterize the coming years may end up benefiting the larger states at the institutional and decision-making levels. This could be detrimental to smaller states if they are not able to find formulas that will bring greater balance to the Community.

The second aspect relates to economic indexes which differentiate between rich and poor states.* Portugal, with Greece at the head of the list of the EC's poorest countries, is in a delicate situation among the European economies.

Closely related to the second point is the differentiation between core and peripheral states within the EC. Despite the arbitrariness of designating a "center" of the Community, it is evident that there is a London-Milan axis where the greater political-social-economic-cultural developments of the EC take place. Portugal, in this regard, occupies a manifestly peripheral position vis-à-vis the Community as a whole.

The characterization of Portugal as a small, poor, and peripheral country corroborates the importance of its entrance into a community that since the 1950s has been experimenting with advanced formulas of economic integration, to which it may soon add a polit-

---

*Take, for example, the Gross Domestic Product of Portugal with reference to the mean of the Community: 1985—52.1 percent; 1990—55.4 percent. The following states are below the Community mean: Greece: 1985—56.8 percent; 1990—53.5 percent; Ireland: 1985—65.1 percent; 1990—57.3 percent; Spain: 1985—71.8 percent; 1990—76.3 percent (data of the Commission of the EC Directorate General, Economic and Financial Affairs).

ical dimension (as we shall see below). It was a natural and obvious option; the alternative would have been isolation and autism in the sphere of international relations. It was also timely in its implementation. Changes in Eastern Europe that occurred after the signing of the Single European Act forced the postponement of other entrance requests and furthermore shifted EC concerns toward Central Europe. These factors confirm the foresight of those who prioritized the European option for Portugal in 1985 and accepted the negotiated terms of the Treaty of Accession, although they aroused great concern among large sectors of Portuguese society.

3

With the aim of establishing a common market among its member states, the EC is an international organization with some very special characteristics. Compared to other international organizations, the principle of sovereignty of the member states, expressed in the way they are represented in the organs of these organizations, as well as in the way the states can be bound by decisions taken by the organizations, is weaker in the EC.

There are three Community institutions: the Parliament, the Commission , and the Court of Justice. In none of these are the member states represented equally. In the composition of these institutions the population, size, and importance of each member state were taken into account, although these criteria were not applied according to the principle of proportionality. Also, in the institution that makes the final decisions on most EC legislation—the Council— a number of decisions are taken by a qualified majority vote and bind all member states, including those that did not agree with the decision. For these reasons, the EC has been considered an international organization with some "supranational" features.

4

In 1986 the member states of the EC signed the most important amendment to the Treaty of Rome: the Single European Act. It is so

called because in the same act member states introduced amend-
ments in the treaties establishing the EC and created the legal
framework for European political cooperation. The Single Act also
established the "magic date"—1992—by the end of which is supposed to be achieved the single European market. This market will
consist of an area without internal frontiers among the twelve member states, and the free movement of goods, persons, services, and
capital will be ensured.

The aim of establishing an internal market by 1992 introduced
a new dynamic into the Community, calling for the adoption of new
legislative measures. The progress made since then has been remarkable, but unfortunately member states have not been implementing
those measures at the national level as fast as they are supposed to.

In the process of achieving the internal market, the Single Act
provided for strengthening economic and social cohesion in the
Community in order to promote its overall harmonious development. This was to be accomplished through a reform of the Community structural funds—regional, social, and agricultural. As a
result of the support provided for in the Treaty of Accession, as well
as that coming from the reform of the structural funds, large
amounts of capital have been coming to Portugal since 1986, giving
rise to considerable changes in the economic and social structure of
the country. This financial support, along with other economic factors, has allowed Portugal to have its largest cycle of economic
growth since the Revolution.

One can foresee the eventual extension of the Community after
1992 to Eastern Europe and (in view of recent Middle East events)
to Turkey, if these countries are politically acceptable. Such an
extension could seriously compromise the level of financial support
that Portugal has been receiving from the EC.

5

The fall of the authoritarian regimes in Eastern Europe by the
end of 1989 and the meaning of this transformation in terms of
European political geography pressed the Community to start thinking about a political dimension to the European integration process.
An intergovernmental conference met in Maastricht, the Nether-

lands, in December 1991. By the agreements reached there, the member states of the EC took steps to establish a closer political union with a common foreign and defense policy and cooperation in the areas of justice and internal affairs. They also agreed on a process for developing a European monetary union.

On these matters, Portugal's interests differ depending on the subject. As a small country with little capacity to intervene in international politics, Portugal would benefit from being a member of a community that—if it succeeds in creating a strong foreign policy—would become one of the world powers. Widening the range of Community powers in the areas of fundamental human rights, social affairs, and environment would establish a legal framework for areas in which the Community has already been active. It does not seem that Portugal would face any difficulty with the extension of such powers.

The most interesting changes, however, will be those connected with the way the Community works. They are not directly linked to the political union, but they will take advantage of the amendment procedure which will have to be established. The first of these changes concerns strengthening the democratic legitimacy of the Community. As pointed out above, the power to make decisions belongs to the Council. This institution seats delegates of the member states, each of which is represented by a government minister. The Council is not subject to the political control of the Parliament. The European Parliament is supposed to represent the peoples of the Community. Since 1979, its members have been elected directly. However, the Parliament does not really have a share in the power to make decisions and does not have any political control over the institution to which these powers belong—that is, the Council. For these reasons, the Community has a "democratic deficit." If the Community is to have a political dimension, this lack of democracy has to be resolved.

Compared to the other institutions, in the Parliament the principle of equality of member states is violated. The number of seats for each state is established by taking into account the population and weight of each of them in the whole Community. Although there is not a proportional relationship between these two elements, large member states have a considerably greater number of seats than small member states. Strengthening the powers of Parliament and increasing its participation in the decision-making process would reduce the influence of small member states in the final decisions.

The Portuguese government has already let it be known that it is worried about this and that it would prefer that the Council not share its power with any other institution. This position is justified in that it gives the most support to national interests.

Therefore, a conflict exists between two vital interests: the need for democracy in the way that the Community works and the risk of a relative loss of weight of the small member states. The solution to this problem could be the formation of a second chamber in the Parliament, directly elected, which would represent the member states like a senate. Member states would transfer to this chamber most of the powers that now belong to the Council.

Another issue in the discussion on political union should be the enhanced efficiency of Community institutions. One of the criticisms very often leveled against the Community is the lack of institutional capacity to deal efficiently with the powers conferred to it. The most important issue to be discussed would be the voting system in the Council. For many Council decisions unanimity is still required. In practice, member states have a veto in these matters. The aim would be to accept decisions by the vote of a qualified majority as a general rule. Experience shows that with such a system it is easier to reach consensus among member states and therefore to approve new measures. Some states are not pleased with the idea—e.g., Portugal, whose government has said that major problems could arise in social affairs and in taxation.

Both the strengthening of democracy by an increase in the role of the Parliament and vote by a qualified majority in the Council would enlarge the supranational features of the Community. In our opinion, the European integration process has a strong political-cultural dimension. Trying to avoid supranational developments based on cost-benefit arguments is a short-term perspective. It would increase the peripheral condition of Portugal and prevent it from playing a leading role in the construction of a reality for which in geostrategical terms the country has no other choice.

REFERENCES

Bank of Portugal. 1990. *Relatorio de 1989*. Lisbon.

Commission of the EC. 1989. *Économie européenne*, no. 42. Brussels, November.

Hartley, T. C. 1988. *The Foundations of European Community Law*. Oxford: Clarendon Press.

Joliet, René. 1986. *Le Droit institutionnel des Communautés Européennes*. Liège: Faculty of Law, Economics, and Social Sciences.

Mota de Campos, João. 1989. *Direito comunitario*, vol. 1. Lisbon: Fundação Calouste Gulbenkian.

PORTUGAL, EUROPE, AND LUSOPHONE AFRICA

Jaime Gama

Portugal's European reaccomodation—which constitutes our main foreign policy objective today—simultaneously incorporates a solid policy of cooperation with the Portuguese-speaking countries in sub-Saharan Africa. At the end of the imperial cycle, we have reencountered the European roots of our nationality and absorbed our long-lasting intercontinental experience derived from the discoveries.

The West European and African orientations have a prominent place within our current foreign policy structure. Through its involvement in NATO, the West European Union (WEU), the Council of Europe, and the European Community (EC), Portugal is part of the West European arena. Through a variety of agreements and treaties with Lusophone Africa (reenforced by the Lomé Convention—in which all Lusophone countries participate), Portugal assumes a privileged role in the desired Europe-Africa relationship.

Anchored in geography and history, this doubly oriented Portuguese foreign policy naturally suffers from pressure exerted by various other factors. The West European orientation must confront the changes in East-West relations: the dismantling of the Soviet empire; a new pan-European security order; the economic, political, and diplomatic strengthening of the European Community; the restructuring of the geopolitical map of the old continent; and a new diplomatic model for European-U.S relations. The African orientation must deal with a generalized economic recession, the exhaustion of one-party political models (some inspired by Marxism-Leninism), the USSR's geostrategic withdrawal from the region, and the refocusing of West European priorities toward Central Europe and the Maghreb. Undoubtedly, Portuguese foreign policy is structurally affected by these transformations, be it in the West European or the African sphere.

Portugal cannot afford to ignore these drastic changes and will have to adapt to them constructively if it is to play an active role.

IDEOLOGICAL BALANCE

Europe and Africa play an important role in the ideological balance of Portuguese foreign policy options. Whereas the building of a united Europe has brought to the forefront a number of projects that range from the revitalization of individual nation-states to a complete federalism, the African objective in Portugal has inspired five major foreign policy viewpoints. The first focuses on a hypothetical colonial revival. Despite the lack of any practical content, this viewpoint still plays a significant role in domestic policy-making, government, and public opinion. The second viewpoint—opposed to the first—emphasizes the building of a type of leftist neo-empire which would encompass regimes and political values based on Third World revolutionary creeds. The third stresses a special relationship with a peripheral Africa in order to reenforce an Atlantic-centered rapport with the current world sea power, the United States. The fourth viewpoint sees Africa as autonomous but sharing a common identity with Portugal, a special relationship that shapes Portuguese integration into the EC. The final viewpoint is clearly isolationist: economic rebuilding within the EC and the future single market are too important for the dispersion of Portugal's energies into areas of decline, irreversibly condemned to the margins of our real objectives in contemporary foreign policy.

The multiplicity of perspectives regarding Africa in the definition, structure, and implementation of Portuguese foreign policy has most definitely been influenced by recent historical events. Portugal's increased interterritoriality in relation to Europe has weakened orthodox Atlanticism. This is reflected by Portugal's entrance into the EC and WEU, as well as the inclusion of its national territory in the area of application of the European Council for Security and Cooperation and the transfer of the Azores into Iberlant (one of NATO's new military structures). Notwithstanding, Portugal's entrance into the European Community has stimulated its role in relation to Africa. Through the Lomé Convention and various EC channels of cooperation and development aid, Portugal has been placed at the core of a special link that includes the five Lusophone states (Angola, Mozambique, Cape Verde, Guinea-Bissau, and São Tomé and Príncipe). After the tremendous challenges put forth by German unification, the restructuring of Central and Eastern Europe, and the subsequent shifting of EC resources to new areas, Portugal must concentrate special attention on economic cooperation projects with the Lusophone area. The Euro-African balance through which our difficult foreign policy choices are regulated must find a new and sophisticated framework.

The perceptions that lead us to fear and accept participation and isolation within the international arena will not cease to face contradictions. For some, the fear of becoming diluted within Europe has been reenforced by Spain's vitality, the decrease in EC funding, the explosion in competitiveness, and the focus on Central and Eastern Europe. For others, the possibility of mutual cooperation with Africa will be nearly impossible due to the specter of the expulsion of the Portuguese after 1975, the disorganization of the African economies and governments, and the difficult relationship between African heads of state and Portugal. There will certainly be others, though, who will believe that after the end of the cold war, the real problems will shift from the eastern to the southern flank of the European Community—that is, the Mediterranean basin and the Maghreb. Who will not wonder about Portugal's ambiguous rapport vis-à-vis the United States as recent worrisome events have shown? Practically all components of Portugal's foreign policy's ideological balance have been put into question by unforeseeable developments that have shattered viewpoints, preconceived ideas, rigid analyses, and any type of dogmatism. Will the African role of a country the size of Portugal resist the passage of time, or will such a role become Portugal's salient mark within an international community characterized by indeterminacy?

EUROPEAN MATRIX, AFRICAN PROJECTION

Portuguese foreign policy in regard to its former African colonies presents limitations as well as potential. Among these factors which reduce Portuguese capabilities in relationship to Lusophone Africa we should stress the following:

- The disproportion between a political-diplomatic aspiration and Portugal's economic capacity, as well as the weak Lusophone economies;

- The genesis of the political regimes of the new Lusophone states, which in most cases were the result of a late and violent decolonization process, heavily influenced by the Soviet Union's foreign policy methods and patterns;

- Economic competition from the West and (until recently) ideological competition from the East;

- The scarcity of available resources for a government-sponsored cooperation policy, together with a combination of mere goodwill and uncoordinated actions;

- The tension created by propaganda from business or political interest groups, as well as the tendency to sway public opinion to believe in the mythical Portuguese perennial role in Africa;

- The absence of generational continuity in the interest toward Africa;

- Portugal's role as a third party in policy implementation, as opposed to its being a primary actor of its own policies;

- The latent contradictions between protecting the interests of the large Portuguese emigrant community in the Republic of South Africa and the demands (even rhetorical demands) for a modern African policy.

Portugal's role in Lusophone Africa has a strong potential due to the following factors:

- Common language; in the case of young African states, it is an instrument of national unity and a link to scientific and technical knowledge, as well as to other cultures;

- Portuguese capacity for adaptation to Africa and its knowledge of the area;

- The welcome given to Portuguese cooperation projects that are smaller in scale compared to giant hegemonizing initiatives;

- Portugal's leverage within the European Community and the linguistic decentralization in favor of the Lusophone area, as a result of Portugal's presence within the EC;

- Political changes in Africa in which multi-party systems are being adopted, as well as decentralized market economies;
- Portugal's own development, together with the modernization of its institutions and businesses, which will reenforce the credibility of its cooperation programs.

In managing its foreign policy toward Lusophone Africa, Portugal must contain the negative factors and expand the positive ones. We are aware that an anti-European Africanism or an uncritical Eurocentrism should not be our aims in contemporary Africa. It must also be emphasized that Portugal's entrance into the European Community—its reinsertion into the European matrix—will significantly strengthen its weight in relation to Africa. However, we must not become complacent under such diplomatic reassurance.

To become active in African affairs with clearly defined and dynamic goals within the context of the European Community will be the best path for those who possess precise, flexible, and nuanced insight.

THE AZORES IN THE PORTUGUESE REPUBLIC

José Guilherme Reis Leite

The theme of this contribution, the Azores in the Portuguese Republic, is an authentic one, as well as challenging. Since I have served in political positions in the Azores in the last years, I believe that it will come as no surprise that my discussion will be essentially political.

In order to understand the meaning of the Azores in the Portuguese Republic it must be noted that these Atlantic islands have had a decisive place in the definition of the Portuguese state, through either their geostrategic role in the successive empires, or their contribution to the national economy. With the end of the colonial adventure and the reduction of Portugal to its European dimension, the archipelago of the Azores has come to occupy an even stronger and more influential space in the Portuguese political and cultural system. These islands are often considered, in important sectors of the society, as one of the critical elements in the continuity of Portugal as a nation. Because of them Portugal was able to reach out into the Atlantic, the very extension that, since the later Middle Ages, has ensured the possibility of Portugal's survival as an independent state in the Iberian Peninsula.

From the Azorean point of view, this relationship is seen differently since the idea has developed among the Azoreans that they do not receive the compensation to which they feel entitled in return for their decisive contribution to the nation. Solutions have been proposed—some of them theoretical, some already tried—that could answer the desires and demands of the Azorean society. Here is not the place to discuss the history of these proposals, but I will say that they have ranged from desires for political independence, to a protectorate under the successive maritime powers, to political and administrative autonomy within the Portuguese nation. As background, it should be added that the Portuguese state is essentially an old nation-state of strongly centralizing characteristics that has always been suspicious of decentralization and the sharing of political power, for these have appeared to be solutions that could disintegrate nationality and jeopardize the nation's survival. Only under extreme conditions and the threat of rupture has the center agreed to try decentralization, but always with reservations—or so it seems.

All of this is stated in order to make understandable the political and administrative experience of the islands. The archipelago of the Azores, in fulfillment of the Constitution of 1976 (which is the landmark of the democratic regime), came to be formally an Autonomous Region of the Republic with politico-administrative statutes and organs of self-government integrated into the unitary state.

On this particular issue, doubts and diverse opinions have been expressed, as many people (myself included) believe in the urgent need to review this form of unitary state and replace it by a regional state like Italy, for instance. I even think that the Portuguese state is in fact already a regional state because of the political weight and constitutional prerogatives of the autonomous regions.

Let us go deeper into what the politico-administrative autonomy of the Azores is to be. The essentials are found under Title VII (Autonomous Regions) of the present constitution as revised in 1989. There the conditions that justify the special regime for the Azores and Madeira are detailed, with emphasis on geographic, economic, social, and cultural features, and the historical desire of the islanders to achieve autonomy. It is the most meaningful constitutional chapter on the autonomies since it outlines the background against which they have evolved. It recognizes that in addition to the geographic factors that require administrative decentralization (a point that had already been established in the Constitution of 1933), the Azoreans are a people of distinct economic, social, and cultural characteristics, and that they have long fought to have such individuality recognized and to cease being oppressed by centralizing and personality-reducing forms of government. Thus it was accepted and written into the constitution that the Azoreans are special Portuguese with a culture of their own, a variant of the continental Portuguese mother culture, and that in the course of five centuries they have developed specific ways of regarding the world and defining values. In this way this political text has consecrated the lessons perseveringly compiled by successive generations of intellectuals who have defined the contours of those unique characteristics that entitle the Azoreans to special treatment. Among them, Vitorino Nemésio offered a cultural concept that assembles the ideas on this subject and defines it as *Azoreanity*, or the Azorean way of being.

The cultural question is the most controversial and profound of the debate over the Azores, for everyone (supporters and opponents) agrees that it is the most fundamental justification for the right to special treatment and self-government. The geographic conditioning factors can be attenuated by technology and the economic ones through developmental policies, but with powerful popular support, the social and cultural factors, rather than fading away, assume more solid contours and become more patent with every passing year. It is no wonder then that the most serious battle for autonomy is being fought in this field.

The constitutional text, in vivid wording, states the goals of political and administrative autonomy: the democratic participation of the citizens; economic development; the promotion and protection of regional interests; and the reinforcement of national unity and the ties of solidarity among all Portuguese people. Not all these goals are easy to reach. The democratic participation of the citizens is the basic principle of all democracies, and without it there can be no cultural, economic, or social development. It is from the conscience of each citizen and its active power in society that society advances and improves. However, the economic and social development of the Azores cannot be merely a utopian constitutional goal. The development of a peripheral region—poor, isolated, and surrounded by adverse geographic conditions—is something that requires well thought out and interrelated strategies.

The time is long gone when the Azoreans believed that it was possible to achieve an acceptable rate of progress with only the public wealth created by the Azorean society. Self-sustained development, in my opinion, should not cease to be an aim, but the underdevelopment that the Azorean society has had imposed upon it has produced such a level of necessities that only a strong national and international commitment can break the infernal circle of poverty. In the medium run two stages should be attained: raising Azorean per capita income to the Portuguese average and subsequently raising them both to the European Community average. In order to reach these goals, huge efforts are called for, and only self-government will make them possible. Also indispensable to achieve progress and justice among the Azoreans is a political program that works on various national and international fronts and succeeds in stirring up the interest of potential investors in the Azores, producing private investment in the economic and industrial sector and public investment in infrastructures and social policies.

The constitution sets out a judicious recipe to achieve the proposed goal of economic development and equality among the Portuguese. Article 231 charges national organs, in cooperation with the organs of the regional self-governments, with the economic and social development of the autonomous regions, aiming especially at correcting the inequalities derived from their insularity. This is one of the decisive principles of the concept of autonomy that must be viewed as a national and state issue. It is also, in my opinion, a very hard principle to put into practice because of clear resistance of atavistic Portuguese centralism to fulfilling honestly this constitutional provision.

The political class on the mainland has met with a sort of silent revolt against these democratic decentralizing principles, the contention being that "whoever pays the piper calls the tune," an old formula typical of dominators and dictators. In response, it is necessary to prevent national solidarity from resulting in a reduction of regional political power—which would be against the spirit of the constitution—by providing support for the regional economy. An expedient has been discovered to pass the responsibilities of the state to fulfill this constitutional imposition on to international agencies, like the European Community, disregarding the fact that the external funds available for regional development should complement state funds. Another contention is that the government of the republic should assume responsibility for the autonomous regions' development only through its administrative power, ignoring the fact that this procedure is ruled out even by constitutional logic. Such pretentions will be better understood if we bear in mind that the old centralism looks with fear upon what it considers the risk of the development and progress on the islands, which can lead to emancipation, not believing in the virtues of political decentralization and regional self-government as a form of reinforcement of national unity. The fact is that in this field the Portuguese constitution has adopted progressive and democratic principles that the conservative and lower middle class mentality currently prevailing on the Portuguese political scene, and in much of our culture, overtly rejects. In the future the question of economic support for the autonomous regions will have to be clarified. Solidarity among all the Portuguese people is not an easy task, and recognizing that not all of the Portuguese are the same, either socially or culturally, requires much courage.

The differences that should be viewed as enriching the whole, and as such, stimulating unity, are regarded by many as dangerous elements of dissolution of the national body and evasions from the official pattern. It is a field of thought and action which is still far from harmonious in Portuguese society. No wonder then that diverse opinions and tension-generating actions are taken to prevent the politico-administrative autonomy from affecting the integrity of the state's sovereignty.

Now let us pursue the question of economic development. The Azorean economy is fragile and highly dependent, thus a hard nut to crack. In the first place, it is not much diversified, but rests on dairy production. Dairy products face difficulties entering the European markets into which we are integrating because they are surplus products. Only competitive conditions in price and quality can breathe a little life into this sector, but in order to achieve them, considerable investment in the production structures is necessary and can come only from special funds of the European Community. We can say that a growth-related crisis is evident, and it raises profound questions.

I believe that the main problem of the Azorean economy is that of markets since production seems to be defined by the natural conditions of the islands. Dairy products primarily, followed by fisheries, tourism, and exotic cultivation, make up our production and should make our wealth. Here once more, national solidarity as called for by the constitution should be translated into a complementarity of the national and regional economies, based on a plan of development. It makes no sense that production is artificially stimulated on the mainland for the products of the regions, thus depriving the regions of their natural markets.

The most serious issue is undoubtedly how to draw into the Azores the investment funds needed to improve production and marketing. Only political power can achieve that. The Azores have decided for integration jointly with Portugal into the European Community—a historic decision in many aspects. I believe that the Azores have taken a decisive step toward progress and cannot now be deprived of the means to take their proposals and resolutions to the decision-making organs of the Community. It is not acceptable that a regional presence in the national representation in Brussels be obstructed and the establishment of a regional electoral circle for the European Parliament be denied. Although the Azorean interests may be defended through national channels and the prime minister himself, this is less than the expectations of insular self-government. By the logic of autonomy, an Azorean should be entitled to defend and represent insular questions as part of the national delegation and with obvious attention to Portugal's interests. It is not acceptable that the Azores be deprived of a voice in the European Parliament, especially when the future lies in a reinforcement of the European regions, which will soon challenge the rheumatic organization of the monolithic states of which even today we are unfortunately aware in the old continent. By stubbornly swimming against the current, Portugal is again missing the opportunity to be a pioneer and the leader of a fundamental development, only to adhere later to the same theories as represented by others.

It is moreover true that the Azores give Portugal a dimension in foreign policy that it would not have without their consensus. Europe is far from establishing political mechanisms to put into practice in the area of defense similar to those established for economic development. The recent Gulf crisis gave dramatic evidence of that and provided a response for those who had already announced the end of the geostrategic influence of the Atlantic islands in the new scenario resulting from decreased tensions in Eastern Europe that (they said) would inevitably cast the Azores into a forgotten periphery of an all-powerful central Europe.

That is not happening, for the United States is maintaining the initiative in the defense of Western interests and now sees itself as the only superpower active in such matters. The Azores reappear as indispensable in the scenarios of world military strategy, making it possible for them to maintain their traditional policy of rendering services in the key area of the North Atlantic, not only as a shield for and a way of access to Europe, but also as America's advance guard. I believe that the politico-strategic function of the Atlantic is not in the least questioned, as it is one of the decisive elements of the European world, touching Africa and the Americas, in a scenario where the Azores hold a key position. In this sense, it can be said that the decision to include the Atlantic islands in the European Community brought the Community a trump card as yet not appreciated by many people.

We must consider the international issue as one of the most relevant for the constitutional definition of regional powers, stipulating that the region shall participate in the negotiation of treaties and international agreements directly concerning it, and in benefits therefrom as well. It is on the basis of this principle that the region has participated in international negotiations of major consequence since the most significant Portuguese foreign policies all directly involve the Azores as an element of the republic.

This is one of the most innovative constitutional provisions of the nation's political decentralization, with few parallels in the legislation of other nations. For this reason, it has produced a great outcry in the dialectic between the nation and the region, but the sensible thing is to develop and deepen regional participation in Portuguese foreign relations rather than reduce or even wipe out a prerogative that has proved beneficial for national prestige and regional interests.

As a final point, it is proper to emphasize that the constitutional autonomy of the autonomous Portuguese regions calls for a decentralization of the functions of the state. The constitution stipulates not only mechanisms of decentralized public administration for the Azores, but also a form of self-government that is democratic and representative. The touchstone of this political autonomy is the region's own legislative body, the Regional Legislative Assembly. Legislative power is the most noble function of political power, and in a system of regional self-government, one cannot ignore its parameters. The legislative competence of the Regional Legislative Assembly covers matters of specific interest for the region not reserved to the central government. It is bound by the constitution and the overall laws of the republic. Otherwise, it exercises the regional legislative power and has the right of initiating legislation before the Assembly of the Republic. Its competence also includes the power to tax and to allocate regional revenues—a traditional right of parliaments, as they were originally created to deal with such matters.

It seems clear that the Azores represent, in the Portuguese Republic, a special political entity that exercises state functions in its territory and warrants a special form of self-government for the Azoreans. It is not possible to understand the Portuguese state today without taking these realities into account. Nevertheless, even today, the word in several sectors of Portuguese society is that the autonomies are the last of the revolutionary sins of 25 April that survive in the fundamental law and that it is necessary to strike them out as has been done with the other sins. Let the hope be that the Azoreans will resist such an eventuality by means of the democratic mechanisms at their disposal.

In closing, I must comment on the state's special representative, who has been an apple of discord. The constitution provides that the republic's sovereignty is represented in each autonomous region by a Minister of the Republic, appointed and dismissed by the President of the Republic, on the recommendation of the government and with the advice of the State Council. The constitution assigns to this position the functions of resident minister and delegated functions of the President of the Republic—specifically to review the constitutionality of regional legislation and to approve it. A "proparoxytone" entity (to use the expression of a well-known Portuguese politician) was thus created, and it has played, in my reading, an inauspicious role in the quest for the supreme goal of the autonomy, which is the solidarity and union of all Portuguese people. I believe that it would be best to abolish this entity in the next constitutional revision, thus putting an end to the seemingly colonial concept that the Azores are not an integral part of the nation, but rather a sort of adjacent territory where special laws apply with a need for supplementary supervision. While waiting for the constitutional revision, it is at least desirable that as a sign of mutual trust, this position be filled by a civilian and an Azorean (it has always been filled from the military).* Otherwise, an entity that possibly was established with the intent of endowing the autonomy with special dignity may turn into a source of permanent conflict and suspicion for both sides.

I conclude with the proposition that the Azores have, in the Portuguese republic and in our time, a decisive role in the definition of nationality and give our country a presence in international policy

*Since this was written, the Portuguese government has named a civilian to the position, although not an Azorean. — Editor

that it would not otherwise have. The Azoreans view their importance as an element that enriches the whole but feel entitled to receive dividends from that reality. The revolution of 25 April that set Portugal on the road to democracy and integration into its natural space, Europe, made it possible to stipulate in the Portuguese constitution a set of principles of political and administrative decentralization that gave form to regional self-government. This political formula, called autonomy, is the codification and recognition of the individuality of the Azorean people among the Portuguese and aims to be a way to ensure national unity, enhancing and enriching the whole with the regional experiences.

Today's Portuguese society, however, beating cultural and political paths that are more conservative, regards this experience with some reserve and threatens to push the concepts of political autonomy currently established in the constitution back to less daring limits. The future of the Portuguese constitutional autonomies does not appear to be assured, but I believe that there are political mechanisms providing the Azoreans with the means to resist the siege that is laid upon them. Let us hope they choose to use them.

II

The Background

THE NEW STATE OF SALAZAR: AN OVERVIEW

António Costa Pinto

Salazar's Estado Novo ("New State," 1933–74) presents complex problems when analyzed in a comparative perspective.[1] Authoritarian and fascist regimes were established after World War I in a lasting form and without any significant external pressures in Portugal, Italy, and Germany. Salazar's regime, like that of his neighbor Franco, survived the end of the "Fascist Era," but for the purpose of this chapter, the phases of the regime were not very important.[2]

Whether we consider it as a movement or a regime, fascism varied along a spectrum of authoritarianism in the twentieth century. From a historical perspective, fascism was represented by the Italian and German dictatorships. It was in association with their specific characteristics and with those responsible for the overthrow of the regimes which preceded them that the identifying elements of the fascist paradigm were consolidated. The adoption of maximalist definitions, which were periodically revived in the political field, was not effective in the analysis of other dictatorships which sprang up here and there all over the world, in spite of the fact that some of these regimes took on some of the characteristics.[3]

As a form of political regime, its most obvious feature when we compare fascism with other dictatorships of the same period was the totalitarian tension which pervaded its institutions and its relationship with society.[4] This tension is indissolubly linked with the fact that a fascist party took charge of the transition and consolidation of the new regime. Although all the dictatorships of the period share a considerable common nucleus with fascism and in some cases were inspired by it when creating some of their institutions, they are still different in that one essential aspect.

Here we shall not go into the "classificative" debate on fascism/authoritarianism, but one of the assumptions will be that there are some important differences which separated the regimes which constituted the fascist model (Italy and Germany) and the ones which were closer to the authoritarian model.[5] By intuition alone, it seems easy to see that whatever the position we adopt with regard to the typologies available on the interpretive market, Salazarism was closer to the authoritarian "ideal-type." The aim of this essay is to marshal some elements of the Portuguese New State with particular emphasis on three of its dimensions: ideological origins and political inspiration, political system, and relationship with society.

1. THE CRISIS OF PORTUGUESE LIBERALISM

Recently a student of fascism suggested a return to the origins and stressed the importance of going back to the study of the crisis which made way for it.[6] The literature on the crisis of the democracies after World War I has never ceased to grow and rejects many monocausal simplifications of the origins of the authoritarian and fascist regimes. The authors are, however, all unanimous on one conclusion: fascism was one of several possible dictatorial options, and it was not insignificant that it was fascism that took power and not some other conservative or radical right coalition.[7]

The crisis of Portuguese liberalism raises the problem of the complex relationships between fascism and the different political families into which conservatism was divided in the first half of the twentieth century. It seems clear today that the rise of fascism was possible only in conjunction with ideologies, factions, and an electorate which up to then had been represented by different conservative parties, but mixing them together does not help us to understand their novelty and singularity. As Martin Blinkhorn has said, "It cannot seriously be denied that as movements, parties and political ideologies, conservatism and fascism occupied very different positions within the early and mid-twentieth century European right, converging at some points and conflicting at other."[8]

Some structural factors in Portugal seem immediately to eliminate some of the classic themes of fascism and go back to specific aspects of Portuguese political and social evolution since the end of the nineteenth century. When Portugal entered the maelstrom whipped up by World War I, it lacked some of the tensions in the relationship between home and foreign policy mentioned by students of fascism. Portugal had already basically solved the "national question": the "state" and the "nation" got on well and shared a significant cultural uniformity; it had no national or ethnic and cultural minorities; it had no territorial claims in Europe; it lay within the British sphere of influence, which guaranteed its vast colonial heritage; the "age of the masses" arrived with none of the mobilizing themes of radicalism normally associated with the fascist movements. Moreover, this "massification of politics" would be moderate in the case of Portugal.

In the second half of the nineteenth century Portugal could be categorized as a nonindustrialized country with a stable oligarchic parliamentarism. The dynamic of its social and economic change did not differ much from other semiperipheral countries that Nicos Mouzelis has defined as having an "early parliamentarism and late industrialization."[9] Undertaking the exploitation of the colonial African patrimony while timidly furthering an industrializing policy based on import substitution, this oligarchic and clientelistic liberalism would begin to come apart at the turn of the century.[10] The emergence of the republican movement, which would mobilize large sections of the urban middle (and popular) classes until then excluded from politics, was expressive of that crisis.[11]

Some of the sources of mobilization of the first fascist movements were in fact represented in Portugal, in a varied combination, by important sectors of the republican movement, especially by its rough Jacobin component, with its nationalist and anticlerical authoritarianism. This has led some authors to consider it a type of "proto-fascism."[12] Whether one agrees with this controversial theory or not, the truth is that the Portuguese case is, as Juan Linz says, a good illustration of the difficulty experienced by the fascist movements in political situations where powerful "competitors" occupied parts of their potential political space.[13]

The republican elites adopted a program of universal suffrage, anticlericalism, and nationalism based on the fight against British dependence and on the defense of Portugal's colonial heritage. As early as 1910, legislation for rapid secularization was passed and there was a strong, urban, anticlerical movement. These measures, mostly inspired by those taken five years earlier by the French Third Republic, had a profound impact on the Catholic hierarchy. But suffrage was not to be extended after all, on the pretext of the first monarchic revolts which broke out in Spain. The Democratic Party, which inherited part of the electoral caciquism of the liberal monarchy, rapidly became the ruling party. Portugal's participation in World War I, defended by the republicans as a way of protecting its colonial heritage, and the crisis which ensued served only to emphasize the crisis of legitimacy of liberal parliamentarism.[14]

The small but pugnacious workers' movement of anarcho-sindicalist hegemony frightened the ruling classes in face of the republican regime's notorious inability to promote its inclusion. However, the role played by the Portuguese *bienio rosso* in the authoritarian wave which overthrew Portuguese liberalism should not be exaggerated. According to A. F. K. Organski, cleavages like those between city and country or traditional and modern elites were typical of a "dual society" like that in Portugal in the 1920s and are of more use when analyzing the fall of Portuguese liberalism than the cleavage between the industrial bourgeoisie and the working class.[15]

When analyzing some of the structural factors affecting the instability of the First Republic, some researchers have proved with solid arguments that the conflict between the agrarian and industrial sectors, which derived from Portugal's semiperipheral position, and the impossibility of parliamentary cooperation were decisive factors and that the situation was made worse by the postwar crisis.[16] On the political level, conservative dominance was evident, from the republican parties to the associations of interest, in the whole process of the fall of the republic.

The military coup of 28 May 1926, which ended the parliamentary republic, was not only a praetorian military intervention in political life.[17] Republican liberalism was overthrown by an army that was divided and politicized mainly by Portugal's participation in World War I and was also receiving calls for a coup from organized factions within its ranks. These ranged from conservative republicans and social Catholics to the integralist extreme right and its respective fascist appendices, which particularly influenced the young officers.[18] Let us not forget that these officers constituted the base of the first modern dictatorship established in Portugal, the brief dictatorship of Sidónio Pais (1917–18), which already showed with its antiplutocratic populism some of the traits of fascism.[19]

The influence of these ideological agents was obviously not equal. The main ones were without doubt the integralists and the

Catholics. The former, traditional monarchists, made integral corporatism their alternative base to liberalism and emphasized rural and anticosmopolitan values.[20] The social Catholics also maintained these values but adopted the corporatism of the papal encyclicals, and although almost all were monarchists, they adopted a pragmatic acceptance of the republican formula.[21] However, they joined the antiliberal intransigence of the integralists to a more concrete program to strengthen the influence of the church and directly voiced the opinions of a religious hierarchy deeply shaken by republican anticlericalism and its program of secularization.

Some researchers have tried to "solve" the absence of a fascist movement in Portugal by drawing attention to its contribution, albeit fragmented and weak, to the movement which led to the overthrow of liberalism. Their rather voluntarist exercise was hasty and showed little sensitivity to scale. They attempted to prove that Portugal, after all, had everything that the classic studies pointed out as the origins of fascism (modernism and futurism, nationalism, traumas from World War I, a workers' offensive, anticommunism, a young military politicized by the extreme right, the *avant la lettre* Fascism of Sidónio Pais, "massification of politics," liberalism's legitimacy crisis, and even fascists). One should, however, note the scale and explain why fascists were not the protagonists in either the overthrow of liberalism or the authoritarian order which followed.

In the Portuguese case, the main factor to emphasize for the purpose of comparison was the absence of a fascist movement in the overthrow of liberalism and in the building of the authoritarian order. The very coalition of political forces which supported the overthrow was characterized from the start by a predominance of conservative and radical right-wing parties. Fascism, now seen as a movement, was the eternal loser in 1925–26, during the military dictatorship, and in the 1930s, when Salazar was already in power.[22]

As soon as the republican regime was overthrown, the military dictatorship immediately found negative solutions for some of the problems dear to the conservative bloc. The Democratic Party was ousted from power and its leaders exiled; the working class lost its right to strike, and its unions saw the room for legal maneuver considerably restricted. Revolutionary attempts against the dictatorship were made almost exclusively by the republicans, with the exception of a failed general strike in 1934, when Salazar established the corporatist system. The Catholic Church, although cautiously in view of the presence of many republican military men and civilians, blessed the coup and immediately offered its secular members for possible ministerial positions.

Salazarism grew out of the military dictatorship established in 1926, a quite unstable regime. The dictatorship imposed by the military was permeated by a succession of conspiracies, palace coups, and even attempts at revolution, which clearly expressed the fight for leadership within the vast conservative coalition on which it was based.

Difficulties in consolidating an authoritarian regime followed, given the political diversity of the conservative bloc and its ability to penetrate the armed forces. Curiously, it was under the military dictatorship that the fascists enjoyed some influence (owing to their presence in the corps of young officers), attempted to create some autonomous organizations, and played a role in driving republicans out of the military.[23] It was this "limited and self-devouring pluralism," with the military as mediators, that Salazar progressively dominated.

In 1930 the National Union was created by law, an "antiparty" to aggregate the civilian forces that supported the new regime.[24] In 1933 a new constitution declared Portugal a "unitarian and corporatist republic." A compromise between liberal and corporatist principles of representation, the former were perverted by subsequent legislation and the latter limited and relegated to the background. The result was a dictatorship of the "Prime Minister" and a National Assembly occupied by the National Union without competitive elections.[25] To avoid any loss of power, even to a House dominated exclusively by the government party, the executive was made almost completely autonomous. General António Carmona remained president to guarantee military interests. The censorship services eliminated any suggestion of political conflict and devoted their attention to both the opposition and (at first) the fascist minority of Rolão Preto, which insisted on challenging the new regime. The political police were also reorganized and used with remarkable rationality. All this was done "from above" without any particular fascist demagogy and relied more on generals and colonels than on lieutenants, more on the Ministry of the Interior than on the streets. By 1934, after a few hitches, liberalism had been eliminated and the old republican institutions replaced.

The more rebellious fascist leaders were exiled, but most of them "got jobs" in minor positions, especially when the Spanish Civil War gave the regime a fright some years later. The great republican figures were forgotten in exile after the brief optimism caused by the Spanish Popular Front. The anarcho-syndicalist leaders went to prison or died in Spain, leaving the leadership of the clandestine opposition to the small and young Communist Party.

The regime institutionalized by Salazar was admired by wide fringes of the European radical right, above all those of Maurrasian and Catholic traditional origins, because the New State expressed a very similar cultural origin. This identity went beyond the mere "order" program but at the same time did not include the "totalitarian," "pagan" aspects that were bringing Nazi Germany and fascist Italy closer and closer.

It is in the ideological spectrum of radical right and antiliberal social Catholicism that the cultural and political origins of Salazar's regime are to be found.

2. THE NEW STATE'S POLITICAL SYSTEM

Although some of the institutional construction of Salazarism was inspired by the fascisms in power, particularly that of Italy, it adopted the elements which tended to unite the right-wing dictatorships of the period and rejected precisely those which characterized only fascism. This differentiation was visible in the leadership, the function of the political system, and its way of relating to society.

Many studies of modern dictatorships, whether because of their theoretical point of view or the pragmatic character of the dictator, ignore the leader. In the case of the New State it would be a mistake to do so. Salazar came from a particular political milieu, but in fact he had a world view and ran the whole institutional design of the regime, and once he had become unchallenged leader, little legislation, from the most important to the most trivial, could be published without his approval until he became decrepit in the 1960s.[26]

Salazar always kept some ideological traits which derived from the cultural milieu from which he came: Catholic integralism of the traditionalist and antiliberal mold in a context of secularization and accelerated modernization which for him symbolized the First Republic. He was ultraconservative in the most literal sense of the term. He steadfastly defended his preliminary rejection of democracy and its ideological heritage based on an "organicist" vision of society of traditionalist and Catholic origins. As he ran the country, he was aware of the inevitability of this modernization but always thought of the patterns and well-being that were threatened by it. Everything else derived from or was added to this ideological basis. The additions, moreover, were not insubstantial as, unlike other dictators, he was a professor of finance and had clear ideas about the management of a state's balance sheet.

Portugal's dictator rejected fascism's model of charismatic leadership from both ideological training and political choice, not for pragmatic reasons or because of the nature of Portuguese society, whose structure was not unlike many societies which experienced a populism closer to fascism. The presence of the single party in Portugal was not an important factor in the formation of Salazarism's political elite, as its functions in this field were limited.[27] Its presence did, however, strengthen Salazar's authority and limited the organization of blocs and pressure groups, allowing the dictator a certain technocratic pluralism of choice.

According to the 1933 constitution, the National Assembly would consist of two houses: Deputies elected by direct suffrage, and the Corporatist Chamber, which would constitute the top of the corporatist system. The House of Deputies was filled by the National Union, and the Corporatist Chamber, due to the delay in creating corporations, was coopted among the *forças vivas*. The first parliamentary elections, held in 1934, had clear legitimizing intentions. In general, these elections reflected the nonmobilizing character of the regime. Held regularly, they were always acts in which there was never any intention of even simulating a 99 percent participation. Civil servants were mobilized, and within an already restricted number of registered voters, the electoral rolls were manipulated to correct any imbalances.[28]

THE SINGLE PARTY

The differences between the National Union and any fascist party are easily recognizable even when, as in Italy, the party became dependent on the state. The nonfascist nature of Salazar's party has always been used as a point of reference when trying to define the Portuguese regime.

The National Union was a creation of Salazar's, established and organized by governmental decree (legislation was passed on the party in the same way as on the administration of the railways) and dominated by the administration, put to sleep and reawakened in accordance with the current situation. In view of the nonfascist nature of the party and its governmental inspiration, its comparison with the fascisms that came to power only emphasized the differences. A prospectively much more fruitful comparison should be made precisely with those parties which had similar origins, like the regimes of the same period which created parties from above, from the dictatorship of Primo de Rivera in Spain (and even that of Franco) to those of Central and Eastern Europe. Indeed, from this point of view, considering the longevity of the Portuguese regime, the National Union makes an extremely interesting case study of the functions of the parties which, unlike the fascists, either did not reach power at all or, once created, did not fulfill functions of control and monopoly of access to power or mobilization of the masses, which in general the fascists did.

Some of the genetic and legitimizing functions of the party in the process of the institutionalization of the New State were obvious. We should not forget that Salazar formed the regime out of the military dictatorship established in 1926, which was based on heterogeneous support, functioning extremely unstably, and was permeated by many political clienteles. The resistance and competition from both the republican opposition and the fascist party (the National Syndicalists) on its creation were indicative of its original function: to support the monopolization of political power by the government, neutralize all forces likely to dispute Salazar's power, legitimize the regime through elections, and unite the different factions and oblige them to solve possible conflicts inside the National Union so as to not destabilize the regime.[29] The National Union seems to have been an empty, undetermined space into which were formally sent (generally by repressive means, as in the case of the fascists, organized autonomously during the military dictatorship) those who wanted to join the regime and which, once full, was closed. The army was kept away from public life. Political activity was prohibited outside public life, which was by no means small, as in addition to the fascists, the Catholics and monarchists, who still had some power over the military, were still legally organized.

Several authors have noted the absence of the role of ideology, propaganda, or mobilization of the masses on the part of the National Union, demonstrated by the fact that the party all but disappeared during the 1930s. The party was reawakened in 1945, when, in an adverse international situation, the regime permitted the appearance of an electoral opposition, always under control, and it was therefore necessary to encourage votes for the government's lists. However, even this action to ensure victory was more administrative than political since electoral motivation, even for propaganda purposes, was always avoided and in fact a lack of commitment was openly encouraged. The National Union also was not the exclusive channel of access to political office; members of the Corporatist Chamber, ministers, and secretaries of state did not pass through the party. It did have some control over access to the lower echelons of the civil service, where it was essential to join the party in order to be admitted. As Braga da Cruz says, however, "its importance grew as one went from central administration to local administration."[30] Finally, the social composition of the party also distinguishes it from fascism. The National Union had none of the petit bourgeois, popular, and much less working class components typical of the fascist parties and their "social" demagogy. Its composition pointed rather to the typical point of confluence of local notables: landowners and businessmen formed most of its local committees in the 1930s.[31]

The provinces with their local influence constitute a wide field for research for a better understanding of the role of the party. This field has, unfortunately, been studied very little. It should not be forgotten that the New State did not succeed a democracy but a clientelistic and oligarchic republic based on restricted electoral participation with some obvious points of continuity inherited from the old constitutional monarchy of the nineteenth century.[32] Although it changed the rules of the game, the National Union was a central instrument in the reconversion of the local notables, as has been shown by one of the rare case studies written.[33] It was in this field that we feel its role was most important.

This characteristic of the Portuguese regime separated it from the typical tension between party and state in fascism.[34] In fact the opposite was the case in that its dependence on the state was characteristic of the life of the National Union right from the beginning, and they often merged. The New State was never a "dual state," and Salazar governed over and with the administrative apparatus while relegating the really "political" institution to second place.[35]

THE CORPORATIST APPARATUS

The same administrative vocation was visible in the regime's corporatist apparatus. As far as "third way" ideologies are concerned, corporatism was the prime candidate of the New State. It was provided for in the 1933 constitution and played a central role in the institutional structure, the ideology, relations with social groups, and the state's economic policy under Salazarism. The declaration of the principles of Portuguese corporatism was influenced by its Italian counterpart but was moderated by the doctrine of social Catholicism. On the other hand, the 1933 constitution offered to the "organic elements" the monopoly of representation that the radical right wanted.

Corporatism was one of the elements of the Italian version of fascism, but Italy was far from having a monopoly, for it covered a wide ideological spectrum of the antidemocratic right since the beginning of the century. As far as authoritarian regimes were concerned, corporatism was not a specific element of fascism, and it is actually doubtful whether it can be applied to German Nazism.[36] It did, however, constitute a central element of legitimation for most of the postwar authoritarianisms like those of Austria, Spain, Romania, or Vichy France.

Corporatism was relegated to second place in the political system of the New State. The Corporatist Chamber had only consultative powers in the National Assembly, which had hardly any power anyway. The corporatist building itself was never completed, contrary to the original plans. However, its functions, whether in the state's economic policy or as a buffer for social conflict, are worthy of more detailed study, as they reflected the regime's economic and social project. Since there were no actual corporations, which should have represented the "organic elements of the nation" in the Corporatist Chamber, neither were there a lot of intermediate organizations (there was a rupture between the bases and the members of the Chamber which the state maintained); the Procurators were chosen by the "Corporatist Council." This council, however, consisted of Salazar and the ministers and secretaries of state for the sectors involved.

ROLE OF THE CATHOLIC CHURCH

It would be difficult to comprehend fully the political system and the ideological foundations of the New State without going over the determinant influence played by the traditionalist Catholicism present in all of the regime's major texts and institutions, from the constitution to the declaration of the principles of corporatism, from the weakness of the party and the paramilitary organizations to the propaganda. Many of the definitions of the type "clerico/..." reflect this essential component of the regime, but some of the fascist features of Salazarism in the 1930s, associated with Portuguese Youth (Mocidade Portuguesa) or the Portuguese Legion (Legião Portuguesa), have received more attention. It is a dimension which should be compared with regimes like that of Franco, Dolfuss, and even Vichy, since they all received important clerical support and also were established after republican secularization programs.[37]

The Portuguese Catholic Church not only contributed to the ideological mold of the regime, but also was "one of its essential instruments always under its political direction."[38] In effect, the postponed concordat (planned in 1933 but signed only in 1940) maintained some of the basic principles of the separation of church and state: it maintained divorce for civil marriages and established relative control of the state over the religious institution. As Hermínio Martins points out, "While in Spain the 1950 Concordat granted the Church virtually everything it could ask for, the 1940 Concordat did not turn Portugal into a confessional state, nor did the Church receive considerable educational or financial privileges."[39]

When in 1936 organizations directly inspired by fascism were created—like Portuguese Youth, a paramilitary organization depending on the Ministry of Instruction, and the Portuguese Legion, a voluntary anticommunist militia which arose from the "red peril" in Spain—they were immediately taken over by the religious services, which could be found everywhere in both institutions. In the case of the organization of youth, which was indeed a sensitive matter in relations between the Church and the State in fascist regimes, care was taken to neither dissolve nor integrate the Catholic organizations (which maintained their autonomy) into Portuguese Youth and to ensure their influence on the official organization.

The close association between the Church and the state in Salazarism went far beyond a mere convergence of interests. One could identify an ideological and political nucleus common to the Church and the regime, from corporatism to antiliberalism and anticommunism.

ECONOMIC POLICY

The economic policy of the New State is perhaps the field which has been studied and debated most by Portuguese research.[40] Its inclusion in an analysis of the relations between fascism and Salazar's regime is not direct, as for many authors fascism never had *one* economic policy which distinguished it clearly from other political regimes. In other words, the problem is to find out if, beyond the political sphere, there "was also a specific set of economic attitudes and policies which may equally aptly be labelled 'Fascist.'"[41]

The debate on whether Salazar's regime had a "developing" or "stagnating" effect in the sphere of Portuguese capitalism goes back to an important theme of the ideological struggle within the different political families of the opposition to the New State in the 1960s, which was later expressed in the academic field. These works, most of which were Marxist interpretations, not only placed the regime within the development of the capitalist mode of production in Portugal, but also considered it a factor in the political "recomposition" of the national ruling classes. They developed a whole series of reflections on the class content of the dictatorship and the role of the different factions of the bourgeoisie (agrarian, commercial, and industrial).[42]

The significance of some of the measures taken by the regime is relatively undebated. These measures are common to all the authoritarian and fascist regimes of the period: the destruction of the trade union movement and its substitution by organizations of a corporatist type strictly controlled by the state; the adoption of an interventionist model substantiated by bureaucratic control through (or not) the same apparatus. In the analysis of the weight of the rural and industrial elites and the accompanying ruralizing resistance versus industrial development of the economic policy throughout the 1930s there is much less agreement.

Albeit with many nuances and lateral variations, two positions have been taken. According to the first, the regime developed a "model of programmed stagnation" during this period as a result of the "historical compromise" on which it was based and owing to the political weight of the agrarian sector. Part of the "mystery" of the long life of the regime lay in this model since "the slower and more controlled the economic and social growth, the more chances there are of the inevitable effects of growth being absorbed without the model being endangered."[43] This position was supported by other authors who stressed the restrictive role of the regime's industrial development, in agreement with the ideology expressed by the regime in the 1930s, and tried to prove that "the Salazar regime, while recognizing the need for industrial development, operated to control the pace of industrialization to prevent the formation of a potentially disruptive urban proletariat."[44] Of a slightly different opinion were the studies which, in the wake of Poulantzas's work, saw in the political economy of the regime a strong, interventionist state bringing about the transition from competitive to monopolistic capitalism and the progressive "submission of the different spheres of production to big industry."[45]

On close examination the two positions tend to lose importance, and most of the authors quoted do not disagree with the synthesis presented by some authors on the political and social significance of the regime's economic strategy arising from 28 May 1926. According to one, Alfredo Marques, the economic policy of the 1930s expressed a "class alliance," which Marques calls an "agrarian-industrial alliance (AIA)." Owing to the diversity of interests represented in this AIA

> and to the incapacity for leadership of all its main components, the State took on the role of guarantor of the compatibility of these different interests and undertook a plan of action to reconcile their differences and alleviate their contradictions which, however, would only be possible through the maintenance of the *status quo*. This plan of action required not only the reinforced

presence of the Administration, but also the State's guardianship over the private economy. For this purpose, State jurisdiction was to achieve an extreme degree of autonomy in relation to the social forces with which it was closely united.[46]

Another economic historian, Fernando Rosas, developed this thesis in a work in which he concentrated on the political aims and the state's instruments of economic intervention (basically through the corporatist apparatus) and in which he explained the interconnection between the economic policy, the political system, and the social groups. For him the New State's mission regarding the divided and crisis-stricken bourgeoisie was to "arbitrate" its contradictory interests, "to interpret them . . . as a whole and bring about the composition and balance of their different social aims and strategies."[47]

Until the 1980s, as we can see, research into the economic policy of the New State adopted the old Marxist debate on the "role of Fascism as a response to the workers' offensive during the capitalist crisis in the imperialist phase" even though it was attenuated by some of the problems inherent in the internal debate of the Portuguese political and intellectual elites during the last years of the regime. Seen outside this context of ideological struggle, the difference in the positions is not always discernible.

Apart from the classical literature on the relationship between fascism and capital, in the field of theoretical references this debate revolved mainly around Organski and Poulantzas. They have, however, been quoted less in recent years, and there have been fewer references to fascism, as either a concept or a historical experience.

Although there are no comparative studies about the economic policy of the New State, some references quoted above contributed to Alan Milward's doubts, and in Portugal's case added the problem of division into periods. According to Alfredo Marques, "If, in the whole period of the Portuguese dictatorship, there is a set of economic measures which reminds us in some way of the interventionism of 'paradigmatic' European dictatorships (Germany and Italy)," it was not that of the 1930s but that of the 1950s, when a strategy for "economic growth" was drawn up.[48] Marques considered this strategy to have been a failure in view of the resistance of the old AIA, which proved its solid implantation in the "Portuguese economic and social structure."[49]

Some studies have also pointed out the singularity of Salazar's industrial policy with its extreme governmental bureaucratic control through the law of *condicionamento industrial*. After a comparative study of the models of intervention of Francoism and Italian fascism, one author concludes that the extreme control and conditioning of Portuguese industrial development represented a "specific national solution."[50] In its first phase at least, the New State, from the point of view of the inclusion of the variable economic policy in the concept of fascism, seems to contribute new problems.

3. AUTHORITARIANISM, STATE, AND SOCIETY

Many students of fascism who use the antithesis authoritarianism/totalitarianism tend to emphasize the fact that regimes like Salazar's were nonmobilizing. If this is understood merely as synonymous with an absence of mobilization and of totalitarian tendencies, this position is certainly correct. Even during the "Fascist Era" the New State was deeply conservative and trusted more in the traditional instruments like the Church and the provincial elites than in mass organizations. It did, however, protect its interests in the field of relations with society by creating a whole cultural and socializing apparatus directly inspired by fascism.

Corporatism was never completed within the political and institutional apparatus but was, at least, the official cultural model of the New State. An eminently "organicist" conception dominated the image that the regime tried to project of itself and of the country. As far as propaganda was concerned, it could be said that it applied the project of the integralist radical right with the blessing of social Catholicism.

The basis of the corporatist system was the Sindicatos Nacionais (National Syndicates), the Casas do Povo (Houses of the People), and for employers the Gremios (Guilds). The liberal professions kept their "orders" with a few alterations which limited their autonomy and would later allow them to be included in the corporatist structure. The political discourse which accompanied the creation of the corporatist organs was a synthesis of fascism and social Catholicism and was moderated by the Catholic values established in the constitution, which held as a principle the limitation of "exaggerated profit on capital which should not be allowed to deviate from its humane and Christian function."

The Sindicatos Nacionais were created by the undersecretary of state for corporations and were strictly controlled. The procedure was highly bureaucratic, and the break with the old unions was almost total. Their statutes and leaders were approved by the state, and to prevent infiltrations the government could dissolve them whenever it wished. Only in certain cases was it compulsory to form a *sindicato*, but everyone was represented, and the state decided on the dues payable. The use of these dues by the unions depended on the state, as did permission to draw up new collective work contracts.

Laws on the Gremios were more moderate and cautious. The old associations were allowed to continue their activities in a transition phase, but this transition dragged on until the end of the regime. The organization of the Gremios could be voluntary or compulsory, and it was the state which decided on the "discipline of competition" and the "interests of the national economy." In fact it was the state's strategies for economic intervention which determined the compulsory nature of some gremios and not the criteria of the coherence of the corporatist system. Corporatization was almost total in agriculture, and the gremios were organized by product (wheat, wine, etc.). In industry some traditional sectors were forced to organize (canned fish, etc.). But above the gremios were the "precorporatist institutions"—i.e., the state, which controlled their activities.[51]

In 1933, the regime created the Secretariat for National Propaganda (SPN), headed by António Ferro. In the cultural field, Ferro had nothing to do with Salazar and was a cosmopolitan journalist with connections in futurist and modernist circles and had been an admirer of fascism since the 1920s. He enjoyed the dictator's confidence and, depending on him directly, Ferro created a machine which greatly exceeded the mere needs of the management of Salazar's image. Although he had little to do with the leader's provincial integrism, or precisely because of this, Ferro gave the regime a "cultural project" which skillfully combined "modern" aesthetic resources with a true "reinvention of tradition." It was the SPN that coordinated and fed the regime's press, ran the censorship services, organized the mass demonstrations that were transported to the capital from time to time, and encouraged the leisure activities directed at the popular classes in close association with the corporatist apparatus. It also organized numerous activities directed toward the elites and motivated cultural relations with foreign countries. For these activities the SPN was skillful in recruiting intellectuals and artists, who without the "modernistic" intervention would hardly have been attracted by the profile of the head of government, and some of whom had been militants in the fascist groups which opposed Salazar. Finally, to provide cultural activities for the working classes the Federação Nacional para a Alegria no Trabalho (National Federation for Joy in Work) was formed.

This cultural combination of the modern and the traditional was openly dominated by the latter. As other similar regimes, Salazarism's cultural project sought the "systematic restoration of traditional values."[52] Particular attention was given to a whole "ethnographic/folkloric" movement which included revitalizing (pure fabrication in most cases) local folk groups, restoring the symbols of Christian reconquest and their social use, holding competitions for "the most Portuguese village in Portugal," and the like. The culmination of this movement, at the beginning of the 1940s, was the Exhibition of the Portuguese World, which reproduced the traditional forms and habits of the populations of the whole "empire." Another important activity was the promotion of Portuguese cinema, which transmitted the healthy values of Christian honesty and of the poor but honorable family.

The selective orientation of the censorship was also a clear indication of the ideal organicist type. In a society where conflict had theoretically been abolished, nothing was published that might testify to its survival. Indeed the regime did not ban or systematically dissolve publications which supported the opposition. These publications survived throughout the 1930s, isolated or reduced to an intellectual readership, and were able to debate the social significance of art or the German-Soviet pact as long as they stayed strictly within the limits of the Lisbon cafes and did not reach the working class, as Salazar had no fears for the rural and provincial bastions and trusted the traditional frameworks. As Salazar said, "Politically speaking, there exists only what the public knows to exist,"[53] and in the field of the compulsory "social peace" the censors were ruthless.

The school system received almost obsessive attention from the regime. Religious instruction was reintroduced in state schools and literally inundated the curricula, particularly in primary schools, which were the symbol and pride of republican secularity, where a detailed set of rules was adopted together with the new programs. Parallel to this, a nationalistic and traditionalistic revision of Portuguese history was introduced. If its attitudes toward the school system are gauges of its strategies against modernization, the New State's reforms expressed an accentuated fear of literacy and were characterized, apart from the radical alteration in the content of the syllabuses, by a veritable "educational stagnation."[54] The state school network continued to exist, however, and no significant financial concessions were made to the Church's private school ventures.

Another central element in the regime's legitimacy was, as has already been mentioned, the Catholic Church. It was not just a question of public political support whenever it was requested or the willing efforts to lend most of its rites and symbols; it was also the Church's blessing of the anticommunist and antiliberal crusade in the 1930s, its support of the regime's *fascisant* institutions like the Portuguese Youth and the Portuguese Legion, its participation in the "electoral" campaigns after World War II, and its defense (at least during the first years) of the colonial war in the 1960s. The Church also provided a model of mobilization, synchronizing the "renewal of religious practice," of popular *piétisme* with the role of savior of the new political power, a point which is sometimes underestimated. The religious cult of Fátima and the parapolitical functions it fulfilled are the most obvious example.[55] The legitimizing functions were numerous not only at a central political level—after each crisis, above all after 1945, there was a corresponding declaration of support which began to be more discreet only in the final phase of the regime—but also mainly in the "provinces" of the rural areas and small towns where a whole logistic apparatus contributed to a considerable "political socialization."[56]

In 1936, however, two organizations inspired by fascism were created and were unexpected if we consider the regime's initial projects. The first was an official youth organization of a paramilitary nature, the Mocidade Portuguesa (MP). To legalize the dissolution of Preto's National Sindicalism in 1933, the SPN had created the Acção Escolar Vanguarda (Vanguard School Association), the first official fascist youth organization, which was for volunteers.[57] After Preto's movement had been dissolved, the regime abandoned this first proj-

ect and created the MP. Membership was compulsory and organization was controlled by the Ministry of Education. Directed at urban
areas where "dissolute vices" corrupted young people at secondary
schools, the MP never achieved the dynamism of its fascist equivalents and, as pointed out above, was immediately taken over by
religious services as the Church showed some concern about this
official venture.

The second organization had different aims, and the fact that its
creation was authorized represented the introduction of a fascist
choreography at the time of the Spanish Civil War. The Legião Portuguesa (LP) was formed in 1936 as an anticommunist militia with
paramilitary functions and police information which sent volunteers
to fight on Franco's side. Under strict state control, it was joined by
part of the fascist minority duly accompanied by army officers. Any
attempt to see in this organization any fascist "tension" or influence
on the regime has no empiric foundation, but its creation certainly
reflected the regime's cringing before the "red threat" in Spain even
though the dictator always relegated it to the background.[58]

Institutions like the SPN and the paramilitary institutions responded to the fascist example, but little or nothing essential passed
through them. Almost all the other dictatorships of the period
showed similar characteristics and inspirations. Basically the New
State did not share the passion for mobilization of its fascist counterparts but encouraged apathy. The regime isolated the small urban
universe, did not even trust the mass mobilization, and counted on
four important agents: police, bureaucracy, local notables, and the
Church.[59] The regime skillfully mingled the administration and the
party, which included the notables, and counted on the traditional
elites and the political police to maintain the social order. The
cooperation of the Church was enough to maintain the provinces in
a desired unchangeable order. It should be noted that the regime
did not even need to create or transform rural unions to the corporatist system since they did not exist in the north or center of the
country. In the south, where there were mainly large estates and
where the agricultural proletariat was active, the police were alert,
while in the rural areas in the rest of the country this was not
necessary.[60]

4. THE LONG SURVIVAL OF THE NEW STATE

After numerous attempts at revolutions on the part of the republicans and the end of anarcho-syndicalism as a dominant force in the Portuguese working class, it was the small Communist Party which rose rapidly to the leadership of the clandestine opposition to the regime. In contrast to the opposition to similar regimes, Portugal did not have an important opposition in exile (it reappeared only in the 1960s).[61] After the dissolution of some of the movements of exiled republicans at the end of the 1920s and the fall of the Spanish Republic, it was inside the country and using all possible legal spheres of action that the opposition gradually reorganized to emerge in the 1940s with a certain strength.[62] Although it is only after 1945 that one can talk of an "electoral opposition" to Salazarism, the clandestine opposition was able to continue in various legal publications which, in spite of tough censorship, survived in the 1930s.

For a few short years after the defeat of fascism in 1945, the Portuguese opposition nourished the illusion that the downfall of the Salazar regime was imminent. However, the regime's surprising longevity well illustrates the conclusion drawn by many studies of the opposition to authoritarian regimes: it is extremely difficult to overthrow them from the inside through an underground opposition. In Portugal's case the long colonial war in the 1960s would be the main reason for the fall of Salazar's successors. Salazar himself died in 1970, convinced that he was still running the country.

INTERNATIONAL FACTORS

International factors were not an important element in the overthrow of republican liberalism and the implantation of Salazarism. If there is anything to emphasize in this respect, it is exactly the opposite—i.e., the relative independence of internal political factors. Unlike the authoritarian experiences of the same period in the East European countries, Portugal's case was a typical example of the establishment of an authoritarian regime in a small country on the periphery of Europe, without any significant intervention from the dominant powers and of a genuinely native character.

The central focus of Portuguese foreign policy and the main concern of the national political elites from the end of the nineteenth century were the defense of the country's vast colonial heritage left by history and by British interests. Britain was the power which had dominated and guaranteed Portuguese independence since the seventeenth century. There was, in fact, no change in this respect between the liberal republican regime and Salazar's New State.

Some research into British attitudes to the dictatorship leads us to conclude that the Foreign Office kept up with events without interfering but that it favored Salazar's rise to power. This was a far cry from the time when it was the British Embassy that gave orders, as in the nineteenth century, and when their permission had to be obtained before beginning any break, as was the case with the revolution of 1910. In the process of transition to authoritarianism, "if anything, the pattern of British attitudes towards the political events in Portugal during that period is one of expectancy,"[63] especially since there were no signs of a change in foreign policy on the part of the Portugal.

The only international event which was decisive and which had a significant impact on Portuguese internal policy was the crisis of the Spanish Republic and the subsequent civil war in Spain, which was felt to be a genuine threat to the consolidation of the regime.[64] The repressive clampdown and the creation of paramilitary organizations which until then had not been planned and were actually viewed as hostile by Salazar are usually associated with this international event. This movement has been characterized by some historians as the driving force of what they called the "Fascistization" of the regime. It was also during this period that, for the first time, there was discursive and street choreography of a fascist nature, but this lost its importance as soon as Franco's victory was assured after 1938.

The situation in Spain dominated Portuguese foreign policy well into World War II. At first, Salazar supported the Francoist insurrection and discreetly opened his territory to the insurrectionists while formally remaining neutral. This was followed later by more open support but without ever endangering the Anglo-Portuguese alliance. After Franco's victory and during the first phase of World War II, the main concern of the Portuguese regime was to avoid Spain's participation on the side of the Axis owing to the fact that Spain belonged to the Anti-Komintern Pact, in an attempt at maintaining the neutrality of the Iberian Peninsula. Students of the period have tended to overlook the mistrust on the part of the New State, both ideological and from the point of view of international relations, of German fascism and, more strangely, of Italian fascism. Even before the convergence of Rome and Berlin, when fascist Italy made some "internationalist" efforts in the name of "Latinity" in competition with Nazism, the regime's reaction was unenthusiastic and distrustful.[65] The invitations to take part in the Comitati d'Azione per la Universalità di Roma were discreetly refused in the name of Portuguese independence, and Mussolini's colonial claims gave rise to a certain distrust on the part of the regime, which trembled at the slightest attempt to change the political balance in Africa.

Another subject on which Portuguese historians have contributed toward clearing up doubts is the attitude of the regime toward World War II. Salazar's neutrality was genuine and not "forced" and used all the "concessions" to Britain to prove the country's progressive autonomy without ever endangering the guarantee of Portugal's colonial heritage.[66] Salazar was, in this respect, different from Franco, who was closer to the Axis at least until the turn in the war.

THE MILITARY

The military were the main participants in the different processes of political disruption in Portugal in the twentieth century, and it was they who were responsible for the beginning and the end of the authoritarian regime.[67] They were the only institution that Salazar feared, and indeed theirs were the most threatening initiatives to overthrow him. The only occasion that the dictatorship hung by a thread—at the beginning of the 1960s, when the colonial war broke out—was brought on by high-ranking military officers. It was also a dissident officer, General Humberto Delgado, who was the unifying force behind the serious electoral shock of 1958 caused by the opposition movements.

We now know considerably more about the republicans' inability to reform the armed forces, the impact of Portugal's participation in World War I, the politicization of the army after the war, and the influence of the radical right within its ranks. On the other hand, the essential facts behind the conspiracy which led to the *coup d'état* of 1926 have long been reconstructed quite accurately, even if the relations between cause and effect were given a deterministic formulation.

Less attention has been given to the withdrawal of the military from the political limelight with the consolidation of the authoritarian order and to the type of relationship the New State had with the military, whereby it successfully "civilized" the dictatorship established in 1926.

The fascists and radical right had considerable influence over the so-called "lieutenants of the 28th of May." Those members of the military hierarchy who occupied political posts, including several prime ministers, like Vicente de Freitas or Ivens Ferraz, were conservative republicans and frowned on Salazar's strategy.[68] General Carmona, President of the Republic after 1928, was sensitive to any attempts to relegate the armed forces to second place and had more power in the 1930s than his feeble image of the postwar period might lead one to believe. In spite of this and of the tensions which existed between the regime and the armed forces, there seems to be no doubt that the New State removed the military from the political limelight, established a new type of relationship between the political powers and the armed forces, and ensured a relatively peaceful domination over them at least until the end of World War II.[69]

The corporatist compensations given to the military institution were substantial, but some of them, such as the immunity of members of the military before civilian courts and police, came from the First Republic.[70] Some of these privileges disappeared in 1945, to be followed by strict police control over the military institution after the attempts to overthrow the regime associated with the "democratic opposition" began. We may conclude that the mere coincidence between the spontaneous ideology of "order" that most of the military adopted and the nature of the regime is not enough to explain their relationship.

TO RESIST: THE POST-1945 PERIOD

Anticipating a new international situation after the defeat of fascism, the regime prepared a cover-up operation in 1944. The single party was resurrected to ensure a "certain victory" in the general and presidential "elections," in which the opposition was allowed to participate.[71]

In the postwar period, the New State came to define itself as an "organic democracy" and endeavored, without too much difficulty, to conceal the outward signs of its association with fascism. The paramilitary organizations, the MP in particular, acquired a more "former student" and "sporting" character. The SPN changed name and leader. It acquired a more anodyne image as a promoter of tourism and information. The LP, downgraded since 1939, when Franco won the Spanish Civil War, vanished from the streets and went into terminal decline.

In the unfavorable international climate of 1945, Salazar was able to secure the survival of his regime. This he owed to his neutrality during the war, to his military concessions to Britain and the United States, and to the rapid onset of the cold war, which gained him the recognition of the new international community. Portugal joined the United Nations (after a first veto of the Soviet Union) and NATO at the end of the decade. However, changes at the level of institutions and decision-making machinery proved very limited. There were no basic changes in 1945 as far as the authoritarian nature of the regime was concerned. It was only when Salazar was replaced by Marcello Caetano in 1968 that a series of reforms took place and that part of the political elite associated with the old dictator was removed.

It was not easy for the regime to adapt itself to the new international scenario—especially with regard to the dominant position of the United States, a country which the dictator had always feared and mistrusted. This feeling was heightened as Africa's decolonization commenced and Portugal's colonial policies suffered their first international condemnations from the UN's Afro-Asian bloc, foreshadowing the beginnings of the pro-independence guerrilla movements. But the regime continued to survive, cultivating an external image of a benign and aging authoritarianism, an "anticommunist bulwark of Western civilization," while efficiently reining in the internal opposition.

After suffering through a period of internal turmoil, when Delgado obtained significant results in the 1958 presidential elections, the regime was to go through an even more serious coup attempt, launched in 1961 by members of the military establishment. Having neutralized the conspiracy, Salazar embarked rapidly and forcefully upon the colonial war which would erode his regime, shattering it thirteen years later.

One of the classic themes in academic work on neighboring Spain's transition to democracy has been the modernizing economic boom in the 1960s. During the same time period, although in more modest proportions, Portugal can be said to have made a qualitative modernizing leap. According to one Portuguese historian—who probably exaggerates—Portugal "stopped being dominated by the primary sector; the tertiary one took over, marking the passage from a peasant society Portugal to another, post-industrial one, that never knew the characteristics of an industrial society."[72] Economic development was marked by the progressive opening of the country's economy, acceptance into the European Free Trade Association, and rising foreign investment. And at the same time that emigration to more developed parts of Europe from the rural interior was on the rise, a new urban middle class was growing whose values had little in common with the official ideology. The tourist boom and the money the emigrants sent home would multiply the effects a few years later. Despite the progressive rise in military spending due to the war, Portuguese society was markedly changed by this trend in the 1960s. The contradiction between the changes going on and the official political ideology is exemplified by the dictator himself, who continued to advise his fellow citizens in the 1960s against the "light which projects itself intensely over the material life, economic development, and the unending rise in the standard of living" which would "leave in darkness all that is spiritual in man."[73]

The facts behind the downfall of the New State are not a subject of this article. Yet the process of change that would lead to the 1974 military coup and transition to democracy should not let us forget the surprising ability to survive shown by Portuguese authoritarianism.[74] For forty-eight years Portugal lived under an authoritarian regime, giving it the top spot in any longevity tournament in twentieth-century Europe.

CONCLUSION

The peculiarity of the processes of the crisis of democracy associated with the rise of fascism did not lie in the structural factors which contributed to the instability of the liberal political system but in the basic components of the antidemocratic coalitions which overthrew them. It lay in the fact that the fascist parties led the process and took power. Fascism, that "new kind of popular coalition, in the specific circumstances of an interwar crisis . . . was not a universal phenomenon," and it does not seem necessary to force it to appear in all the processes of the overthrow of the liberal order of that period.[75]

As a first step it is well to synthesize the nature of the regime overthrown in 1926. Portugal's First Republic was not a young democracy taking its first hesitant steps in the "era of the masses," as were so many others in the Europe of 1918. It was not a product of increased popular suffrage based on mass parties, as were the Weimar Republic and postwar Italy, and later the Spanish Second Republic. The republican movement was the embodiment of the political aspirations of the "excluded" and of "oligarchic liberalism." With a program of modernization steeped in nationalism, anticlericalism, and a certain antiplutocratism, it united under its umbrella various sections of the urban middle classes (which at the turn of the century practically meant Lisbon), on the one hand, and the popular sectors on the other.

Of course, while Portugal shared certain unifying characteristics with the countries that went fascist, such as World War I and the crisis which followed it, the republican parliamentary regime did represent an attempt to go beyond oligarchic liberalism. But taking on the trappings of a state and a parliamentary system based on one-party hegemony, it pushed a program of accelerated secularization and sacrificed almost all the rest of its program to the interventionist strategy for defending the colonial patrimony. Following Sidónio Pais's brief 1917 dictatorship—which would anticipate numerous features that would come to characterize certain peripheral variants of fascist populism—the republic was overthrown by a vast conservative coalition with the military acting as mediators.

In the questionable logic of a certain "sociology of modernization" as to the relationship between economic and social change and the breakdown of political systems, Portugal's case would seem to illustrate the classic example of a reaction by the traditional sectors, unable to brake the modern sector's stride within the bounds of the parliamentary system. Or, to use Organski's terminology, a compromise from above was preferred, which would allow for the recuperation of some of the lost social and political hegemony. From this perspective it appears clear that the New State not only made room for the claims of the traditional sectors in the 1930s, but also tenaciously defended them over time.[76]

Salazar once said to Henry Massis that his aim was to "make Portugal live by habit."[77] Apart from its conscious demagogy, this *maître mot*, which so delighted his French supporter, sums up perfectly the traditionalist permanence of Salazarism. A functional interpretation, however, could argue that Salazar's dictatorship did not undergo the totalitarian tension of fascism because, owing to the nature of Portuguese society at the time, it did not need it. This interpretation, however, does not wash since this tension did exist in societies as industrialized as or less industrialized than the Portuguese. As for more industrialized societies, it is enough to mention France, where, according to this theory, society would "ask for" the totalitarianism that Vichy did not give it. Salazarism was, rather, voluntarily nontotalitarian and allowed most of the population to "live by habit" as long as they did not "get mixed up in politics," which was an activity reserved for the ruling minority.

It is, however, a mistake to confuse Salazar's regime with a "pragmatic" dictatorship, at least in the period with which we are concerned here (1933–45). Salazarism officially instituted an "organic" vision of society and tried with a certain perseverance to use all the ideological and social control instruments within its reach to bring it about: administration, corporatism, school system, state propaganda, local elites, and the Church. On the other hand, it reinforced the presence of the state in the economy, limited the autonomy of the economic elites, and disciplined them with an iron hand.

Like all the other right-wing authoritarian regimes of the same period, Salazarism was inspired by a vast spectrum of "third way" ideologies which had developed in Europe since the beginning of the century and basically include elements of social Catholicism and the Maurrasian radical right.

As far as its institutions and political elites were concerned—i.e., the creation of a single party closely dependent on the government, the hegemony of the administration, the corporatist apparatus, the recruiting and composition of the political elite—Salazarism was close to the dictatorships of the same period which did not experience the more determinative aspects of fascism.[78]

NOTES

A first draft of this chapter was discussed in two research seminars at the European University Institute, Florence. The first was organized by Stuart Woolf, and the second ("National Socialism, Fascism and Dictatorships in Europe, 1920s–1940s: Recent Research and Debates"), by Gisela Bock. An expanded version was discussed in the panel "Nationalism and Fascism" of the Second Conference of the ISSEI, Catholic University of Leuven, Belgium, 3–8 September 1990.

1. For a review of the relevant literature, see António Costa Pinto: "O salazarismo e o fascismo europeu: As primeiras interpretações das ciências sociais," in *Salazar e o salazarismo*, ed. J. Brandão de Brito et al. (Lisbon, 1989), pp. 155–88; "O salazarismo na recente investigação internacional sobre o fascismo europeu: Velhos problemas, velhas respostas?," *Análise social* 25 (1990): 695–713. For an expanded version of these articles, see my book, *O salazarismo e o fascismo europeu: Problemas de interpretação nas ciências sociais* (Lisbon, 1992).

2. They were much more clear in Francoism. Manuel Ramírez defined three phases: totalitarian (1939–45); empirico-conservative (1945–60); and techno-pragmatic (1960–75) (*España, 1939–1975: Régimen político e ideología* [Barcelona, 1978], pp. 23–35).

3. Helgio Trindade, "La Question du fascisme en Amérique Latine" (Florence, November 1982), mimeo.

4. As a summary of the theoretical debate at the end of the 1970s, see Ernst A. Menze, ed., *Totalitarianism Reconsidered* (Port Washington, 1981). Of special interest are the essays of K. D. Bracher and Hans Mommsen ("The Concept of Totalitarian Dictatorship versus the Comparative Theory of Fascism"). See also K. D. Bracher, *Controversias de historia contemporánea sobre fascismo, totalitarismo y democracia* (Barcelona, 1983), and K. D. Bracher and Leo Valani, eds. *Fascismo e nazionalsocialismo* (Bologna, 1986), as an example of the recent historians' insistent use of the concept of totalitarianism. For a more recent review, see Giovanni Sartori, *The Theory of Democracy Revisited* (Chatham, N.J., 1987), pp. 193–203.

5. Juan J. Linz, "An Authoritarian Regime: Spain," in *Mass Politics: Studies in Political Sociology*, ed. Erik Allardt and Stein Rokkan (New York, 1970), pp. 251–83. Linz later developed his typology in "Totalitarian and Authoritarian Regimes," in *Handbook of Political Science*, ed. F. Greenstein and N. Polsby (Reading, Mass., 1975), vol. 3, pp. 175–411.

6. Geoff Eley, "What Produces Fascism: Preindustrial Traditions or a Crisis of the Capitalist State?," in *Radical Perspectives on the Rise of Fascism in Germany, 1919–1945*, ed. Michael N. Dobkowski and Isidor Wallimann (New York, 1989), p. 92.

7. Juan J. Linz and Alfred Stepan, eds., *The Breakdown of Democratic Regimes* (Baltimore, 1978).

8. Martin Blinkhorn, ed., *Fascists and Conservatives* (London, 1990), p. 13.

9. Nicos P. Mouzelis, *Politics in the Semi-Periphery: Early Parliamentarism and Late Industrialization in the Balkans and Latin America* (London, 1986).

10. Manuel Villaverde Cabral, *Portugal na alvorada do século XX: Forças sociais, poder político e desenvolvimento económico* (Lisbon, 1979).

11. Pedro Tavares de Almeida, *Eleições e caciquismo no Portugal oitocentista (1868–1890)* (Lisbon, 1991).

12. Mario Baptista Coelho, "O republicanismo nacionalista e autoritário em Portugal, do radicalismo nacionalista ao proto-fascismo dual (1903–1928): Um ensaio crítico e interpretativo" (Lisbon, 1987), mimeo.

13. Juan J. Linz, "Political Space and Fascism as a Late-Comer," in *Who Were the Fascists: Social Roots of European Fascist Movements*, ed. Stein Ugelvik Larsen et al. (Bergen, 1980), pp. 153–89.

14. Douglas L. Wheeler, *Republican Portugal: A Political History, 1910–1926* (Madison, 1978).

15. A. F. K. Organski: *The Stages of Political Development* (New York, 1965), and "Fascism and Modernization," in *The Nature of Fascism*, ed. S. J. Woolf (New York, 1968), p. 20.

16. Kathleen C. Schwartzman, *The Social Origins of the Democratic Collapse: The First Portuguese Republic in the Global Economy* (Lawrence, 1989).

17. João B. Serra and Luís Salgado de Matos, "Intervenções militares na vida política," *Análise social* 18 (1982): 1165–95.

18. António José Telo, *Decadência e queda da I República Portuguesa*, 2 vols. (Lisbon, 1980–84); Douglas L. Wheeler, *A ditadura militar portuguesa, 1926–1933* (Lisbon, 1988).

19. Manuel Villaverde Cabral, "A Grande Guerra e o sidonismo: Esboço interpretativo," *Análise social* 15 (1979): 327–92.

20. Manuel Braga da Cruz, "O integralismo lusitano nas origens do salazarismo," *Análise social* 18 (1982): 137–82.

21. Richard Robinson, "The Religious Question and the Catholic Revival in Portugal, 1900–30," *Journal of Contemporary History* 12 (1977): 345–62, and Manuel Braga da Cruz, *As origens da democracia cristã e o salazarismo* (Lisbon, 1980).

22. António Costa Pinto, *O fascismo em Portugal nos anos 30* (forthcoming).

23. António Costa Pinto, "The Radical Right and the Military Dictatorship in Portugal: The 28 May League (1928–33)," *Luso-Brazilian Review* 23 (1986): 1–15.

24. Manuel Braga da Cruz, *O partido e o estado no salazarismo* (Lisbon, 1988); also my review in *Annales ESC*, May–June 1988), pp. 691–93.

25. Manuel Lucena, *A evolução do sistema corporativo português*, vol. 1, *O salazarismo* (Lisbon, 1976).

26. We are still waiting for a good biography of Salazar; meanwhile see the one written by one of his ministers, Franco Nogueira, *Salazar*, 6 vols. (Coimbra, 1977–85).

27. In Francoism, the single party was much more important in this field. See Miguel Jerez Mir, *Elites políticas y centros de extracción en España, 1938–1957* (Madrid, 1982).

28. See Philippe C. Schmitter, "The Impact and Meaning of 'Non-Competitive, Non-Free and Insignificant' Elections in Authoritarian Portugal, 1933–74," in *Elections Without Choice*, ed. Guy Hermet, Richard Rose, and Alain Rouquié (London, 1978), pp. 145–68.

29. Arlindo Manuel Caldeira, "O partido de Salazar: Antecedentes, organização e funções da União Nacional (1926–34)," *Análise social* 22 (1986): 975.

30. Braga da Cruz, *O partido*, p. 177.

31. Caldeira, "O partido de Salazar," p. 960, and Braga da Cruz, *O partido*, p. 234.

32. For a summary of the question of political clientelism in Portugal, see Fernando Farelo Lopes, "Panorama de la littérature sur le clientélisme au Portugal," *CEMOTI*, no. 9 (January 1990): 85–90.

33. Rui Ramos, "O Estado Novo perante os poderes periféricos: O governo de Assis Gonçalves em Vila Real (1934–39)," *Análise social* 22 (1986): 109–35.

34. Emilio Gentile, "Le Rôle du parti dans le laboratoire totalitaire italien," and Philippe Burrin, "Politique et société: Les structures du pouvoir dans l'Italie fasciste et l'Allemagne nazie," *Annales ESC*, May–June 1988, pp. 556–91, 615–37.

35. Lawrence S. Graham, *Portugal: The Decline and Collapse of an Authoritarian Order* (Beverly Hills, 1975).

36. Peter J. Williamson, *Corporatism in Perspective: An Introductory Guide to Corporatist Theory* (London, 1989).

37. António Costa Pinto, "'L'État Nouveau' de Salazar," in *Le Régime de Vichy et les Français*, ed. François Bederida et al. (Paris, 1992), pp. 674–88. On Spain see Javier Tusell, *La dictadura de Franco* (Madrid, 1988). On Austria see Gerhard Botz, "Fascismo e autoritarismo in Austria: Heimwehr, nazionalsocialismo e 'austrofascismo,'" in *Il "Caso Austria": Dall' "Anschluss" all'èra Waldheim*, ed. Roberto Cazzola and Gian Enrico Rusconi (Turin, 1988), p. 48. As an introduction to the several interpretations, see John Rath and Carolyn W. Schum, "The Dolfuss-Schuschnigg Regime: Fascist or Authoritarian?," in Larsen et al., eds., *Who Were the Fascists?*, pp. 249–56.

38. Silas Cerqueira, "L'Église Catholique et la dictature corporatiste portugaise," *Revue française de sciences politiques* 23 (1973): 504.

39. Herminio Martins, "Opposition in Portugal," *Government and Opposition* 4, 2 (Spring 1969): 262. See also Thomas C. Bruneau, "Church and State in Portugal: Crises of Cross and Sword," *Journal of Church and State* 18 (1976): 463–90.

40. Eloy Fernandez Clemente, "A história económica de Portugal (séculos XIX e XX)," *Análise social* 24 (1988): 1318–23.

41. Alan S. Milward, "Fascism and the Economy," in *Fascism: A Reader's Guide*, ed. Walter Laqueur (Harmondsworth, 1979), p. 409.

42. For a review of the economic policy in the 1930s, see Fernando Rosas, *O Estado Novo nos anos trinta: Elementos para o estudo da natureza económica e social do salazarismo (1928–1938)* (Lisbon, 1986), pp. 23–53.

43. Manuel Villaverde Cabral, "Sobre o fascismo e o seu advento em Portugal: Ensaio de interpretação a pretexto de alguns livros recentes," *Análise social* 12 (1976): 895.

44. Elizabeth Leeds, "Salazar's 'Modelo Económico': The Consequences of Planned Constraint," in *Portugal in Developoment: Emigration, Industrialization, the European Community,* ed. T. C. Bruneau, Victor M. P. da Rosa, and Alex Macleod (Ottawa, 1984), p. 13.

45. Joel Frederico da Silveira, "Alguns aspectos da política económica do fascismo: 1926–1933," in *Fascismo em Portugal,* ed. António Costa Pinto et al. (Lisbon, 1982), p. 386.

46. Alfredo Marques, *Política económica e desenvolvimento económico em Portugal (1926–1959)* (Lisbon, 1988), p. 24.

47. Rosas, *O Estado Novo,* p. 121.

48. Marques, *Política económica,* p. 25.

49. *Ibid.,* p. 26.

50. José Maria Brandão de Brito, *A industrialização portuguêsa no pós-guerra (1948–1965): O condicionamento industrial* (Lisbon, 1989), p. 141.

51. Lucena, *A evolução;* Philippe C. Schmitter, *Corporatism and Public Policy in Authoritarian Portugal* (London, 1975), Sage Professional Series, Contemporary Political Sociology Series, vol. 1; Howard J. Wiarda, *Corporatism and Development: The Portuguese Experience* (Amherst, 1977).

52. Christian Faure, *Le Projet culturel de Vichy: Folklore et révolution nationale, 1940–1944* (Lyon, 1989), p. 7.

53. Oliveira Salazar, *Discursos, 1928–1934* (Coimbra, 1935), p. 259.

54. Maria Filomena Mónica, *Educação e sociedade no Portugal de Salazar (A escola primária salazarista 1926–1939)* (Lisbon, 1978).

55. Cerqueira, "L'Église Catholique," pp. 481–90.

56. *Ibid.*

57. See António Costa Pinto and Nuno Ribeiro, *A Acção Escolar Vanguarda (1933–1936): A juventude nacionalista nos primórdios do Estado Novo* (Lisbon, 1980).

58. César Oliveira: *Portugal e a Segunda República da Espanha, 1931–1936* (Lisbon, 1987), and *O salazarismo e a Guerra Civil de Espanha* (Lisbon, 1988), and Hipólito de la Torre Gómez, *La relación peninsular en la antecamara de la Guerra Civil de España (1931–36)* (Mérida, 1989).

59. Stanley G. Payne, "Salazarism: 'Fascism' or 'Bureaucratic Authoritarianism?,'" in *Estudos de História de Portugal: Homenagem a A. H. Oliveira Marques,* ed. João Cordeiro Pereira et al. (Lisbon, 1983), vol. 2, pp. 523–31.

60. José Pacheco Pereira, *Conflitos sociais nos campos do sul de Portugal* (Lisbon,

1983). On the impact of the regime in rural society, see José Cutileiro, *A Portuguese Rural Society* (Oxford, 1971), and Joyce Firstenberg Riegelhaupt, "Peasants and Politics in Salazar's Portugal: The Corporate State and Village 'Nonpolitics,'" in *Contemporary Portugal: The Revolution and Its Antecedents*, ed. Lawrence Graham and Harry M. Makler (Austin, 1979), pp. 167–90.

61. See the comparative chapter of Stanley G. Payne, "La oposición a las dictaduras en la Europa occidental: Una perspectiva comparativa," in Javier Tusell et al., eds., *La oposición al régimen de Franco*, 3 vols. (Madrid, 1990), pp. 51–64.

62. A. H. Oliveira Marques, *A Liga de Paris e a ditadura militar, 1927–1928* (Lisbon, 1976), and *A literatura clandestina em Portugal, 1926–1932*, 2 vols. (Lisbon, 1990–91).

63. Manuel Villaverde Cabral, "Dependency and Autonomy in Portuguese Politics: Authoritarianism and Democracy in International Perspective," p. 18. Mimeo.

64. César Oliveira: *Portugal* and *O salazarismo*; de la Torre Gómez, *La relación peninsular*.

65. Simon Kuin, "Fascist Italy and Salazar's Portugal, 1926–1936," *Yearbook of European Studies*, vol. 3, *Italy/Europe* (Amsterdam, 1990), pp. 101–18.

66. António Telo, *Portugal na Segunda Guerra* (Lisbon, 1987); Maria Carrilho et al., *Portugal na Segunda Guerra Mundial: Contributos para uma reavaliação* (Lisbon, 1989); Fernando Rosas, *Portugal entre a paz e a guerra* (Lisbon, 1990).

67. For a general introduction, see Maria Carrilho, *Forças armadas e mudança política em Portugal no séc. XX: Para uma explicação sociológica do papel dos militares* (Lisbon, 1985).

68. César Oliveira, ed., *A ascensão de Salazar: Memórias de seis meses de governo— 1929—de general Ivens Ferraz* (Lisbon, 1988).

69. Douglas L. Wheeler, "The Military and the Portuguese Dictatorship, 1926– 1974: 'The Honor of the Army,'" in Graham and Makler, eds., *Contemporary Portugal*, pp. 191–219.

70. See Tom Gallagher, "Fernando dos Santos Costa: Guardião militar do Estado Novo 1944–1958," in *Estado Novo: Das origens ao fim da autarcia*, ed. Stuart Woolf et al. (Lisbon, 1986), vol. 1, pp. 199–219.

71. On the opposition to Salazarism, see D. L. Raby, *Fascism and Resistance in Portugal: Communists, Liberals and Military Dissidents in the Opposition to Salazar, 1941–74* (Manchester, 1988).

72. António José Telo, "Portugal, 1958–1974: Sociedade em mudança," in *Portugal y España en el cambio político (1958–1978)*, ed. Hipólito de la Torre (Mérida, 1989), p. 88.

73. António de Oliveira Salazar, *Discursos e notas políticas*, vol. 6 (Coimbra, 1965).

74. Philippe C. Schmitter, "Liberation by *Golpe*: Retrospective Thoughts on the Demise of Authoritarian Rule in Portugal," *Armed Forces and Society* 2, 1 (November 1975): 5–33.

75. Eley, "What Produces Fascism," pp. 87 and 91.

76. Leeds, "Salazar's 'Modelo económico,'" p. 13.

77. Quoted in João Medina, *Salazar em França* (Lisbon, 1977), p. 50.

78. Paul H. Lewis, "Salazar's Ministerial Elite, 1932–1968," *Journal of Politics* 40 (1978): 622–47. Lewis focuses attention on the predominance of technicians as opposed to politicians in Salazar's ministerial elite.

A HISTORICAL COMPARISON OF PORTUGAL'S FIRST AND THIRD REPUBLICS

Douglas L. Wheeler

> "Democracia é bonita, mas é difícil."
> –Sr. António, Master Barber, Hotel Palácio, Estoril, 3 October 1979

> "The EC will be sorry!"
> –Sr. Vitor António, PSD officer, Lisbon, observing Portuguese bureaucracy "in action," anticipating its impact on EC, Lisbon, June 1989

The jury is still out on the question of whether or not Portugal's Third Republic (1974–) is a fully consolidated democracy.[1] Political scientists might agree that it is now established, but they appear to hesitate to answer the 64 billion escudo question: has Portugal's new political system completed its transition from a flagging dictatorship to a securely maintained democracy *over the long term*?[2]

Given the essential factor of a dual historical legacy in Western Europe's oldest nation-state—both mental and physical—an assessment of the legacies of the First Republic to the Third Republic is a worthy if perilous exercise. A comparison of the two political experiences and an effort to discover any evidence that there may be recurring patterns of political and social behavior in Portugal will make up the bulk of this chapter. The author is aware of the pitfalls of this form of analysis. A considerable amount of what might be termed "historical hysteria" involving the use of the First Republic in political arguments in the early years of the Third Republic, especially 1974–84, has now diminished. During less stable times before the 1987 general election, there was a rightist literature whose major theme was "history repeats itself in Portugal," the Revolution of 1974–75 has failed, the new system is not working, and this is the

First Republic all over again.[3] George Santayana's commonplace dictum that those who are ignorant of their history will be condemned to repeat it notwithstanding, objective observers will do better to keep in mind as antidotes the more apropos epigrams of Paul Valéry ("History is the science of what never happens twice") and the great English historian Maitland ("The essential matter of history is not what happened, but what people thought or said about it").

For Portugal, too, dictatorship is a poor school for democracy, as well as for learning to be circumspect about a nation's troubled past. One of the worst legacies of the Estado Novo—besides systematic depoliticization, censorship, police terror, and excessive centralization of power and authority—was its relentless mystification of the history of the First Republic. While the dictatorship either discouraged serious scholarly study of any period after the coming of "Liberalism" in the 1820s or favored negative interpretations of the Republic and the "Nightmare Republic" image, old Republican oppositionists gave uncritical analyses along the lines of the "Progressive Portugal" image. Only during the Caetano phase of the regime was it possible for a more balanced treatment of the First Republic to be published: Oliveira Marques provided important social and economic analyses of many complex factors and showed that by 28 May 1926 a majority of Portuguese in the "political nation" were hostile to the continuation of the parliamentary Republic.[4]

After eighteen years of the Third Republic, roughly the length of the life of the First Republic (1910–26), there is a sufficiently long record to make suggestive comparisons of the two phenomena.

1

The First Republic was Western Europe's most unstable parliamentary regime. It was marked by excessive instability in many categories: governmental (cabinet), parliamentary, presidential, and administrative. In fifteen years and eight months, there were forty-five governments; four months was the average life of a cabinet. There were ten parliaments; four were dismissed by military coups and several by the post-1919 power of the president to dissolve parliament. Presidential instability was also typical. Eight presidents held office, but only one completed his term of four years; one was assassinated (Sidónio Pais), two were ejected by military coups, and two resigned "voluntarily" after military coups.

In some respects, the Republic was an interrupted or discontinuous civil war which mobilized for armed street combat thousands of civilians and soldiers. Public violence and civil disorder were characteristic: as many as 4,000–5,000 persons died in civil strife and thousands more were injured; these casualty figures do not take into account the thousands of Portuguese killed in campaigns on the Western Front in World War I (1916–18) or in Portugal's colonies of Angola and Mozambique.* Military rebellions, bombings, and shootings occurred regularly. Beginning with World War I, the economy badly degenerated with a large impact on what was already Western Europe's poorest country. In 1910 the Republic inherited a large debt from the monarchy; by 1926 it was near bankruptcy following a series of disasters: the cost of living index rose 2,600 percent from 1914 to 1924; in 1919 and 1920 there was a catastrophic currency devaluation. Portugal's internal and external debts burgeoned following World War I and colonial commitments.

Intensive personalism and factionalism characterized the First Republic's political and governmental processes. While more than a few parties entered the numerous elections, only one, the Portuguese Republican Party, nicknamed the Democrats, resembled an effective, functioning mass party with regional and local roots. Except for one election (1921), it won every general election and had the only effective vote-getting apparatus. The First Republic never developed a true two-party or multi-party system, and no party, except by military force, ever developed a viable alternative to the Democrats.

Military intervention in politics and government was a key feature, and military conspiracy was a substitute for legal, political ways of changing governments. The Republic was established by a Republican-inspired conspiracy to gain control of the military, followed by the failure of the bulk of the armed forces to defend the monarchy; in what was a "negative *pronunciamento*" as much as a military insurrection, 5 October 1910 witnessed the conspiracy of a

---

*Nor do they take into account several hundred thousand Portuguese who were deported for political reasons to Spain and the colonies, political exiles, and emigrants fleeing Portugal for a better life abroad—especially during the more turbulent phases of the Republic, 1911–21. In 1912 more than 80,000 emigrated legally.

minority of officers and sergeants and the neutralization of the majority of forces. Thus began a cycle of military politics that reached a new stage on 28 May 1926, when the bulk of the army officer corps organized the overthrow of the parliamentary system.

Like the First Republic, the Third Republic was founded after the disintegration of a previous system that was rather easily overthrown during a coup. In 1974 as in 1910, public opinion initially was highly favorable to the revolution and change of regimes, and waves of euphoria and optimism followed both events. There were important differences, too: the 25 April 1974 *golpe* was much less costly in human life than 5 October 1910, when nearly three days of fighting left at least 65 dead and 700 wounded. Another important difference was in the manner of the military conspiracy and in the context of the political pressures: 5 October 1910 was preceded by severe labor unrest and strikes in the Lisbon region and the Alentejo, and the assassination of a prominent Republican leader triggered the final civilian-dominated conspiracy, which at first won few army career officer participants. While in 1910 no organization in the officer corps led the coup planning—most of the armed forces except for sections of the navy were "neutral," not Republican[5]—in 1974 the military coup was the work of several hundred career officers in the Armed Forces Movement.[6]

The first Republican revolutionaries of 1910 discovered that the timing of their challenging experiment was poor. It was the tragedy of these "Young Turks" and their civilian supporters that the First Republic coincided with a set of unprecedented crises: the ravages of Portuguese participation in World War I in Europe and Africa; renewed alarm among the ruling groups over the future of Portuguese Africa and fear of the loss of the overseas empire to the larger powers of Britain and Germany; and the worst financial and economic crisis Portugal had experienced in living memory (though the Portuguese probably were worse off in relative terms during two other times of economic, social, and political disaster: 1578–1640 and 1807–22). Economically, Portugal in 1926 was worse off in many respects than in 1974–75, even taking into account the costs in the latter years of receiving the more than 700,000 *retornados* from Africa.[7] In terms of the psychology and the strength of nationalist sentiment, too, the First Republic confronted heavy odds: in the 1920s Portugal witnessed both a Catholic revival and a wave of hypernationalist feelings of despair about threats to the nation at home and to the colonies abroad.[8]

The Third Republic's leadership was challenged by the timing of its revolution. The aftermath of 25 April 1974 coincided with the consequences of a distant, bloody, controversial war in Africa; a hasty, forced decolonization, which led to civil war in one former colony (Angola) and civil strife and a brutal foreign invasion in another (East Timor); a world recession and oil shortage; the worst local economic crisis in memory (but *not* in history); and the clash of classes and groups which took the form of protests of a long-repressed working class and the fears of the more advantaged classes that were associated with an oppressive past and a more closed society. The 1974 revolution's timing was ironic: the very economic and colonial crises that had alienated the middle classes and the military and enabled the "Captains" to prevail with little cost in human life on 25 April later had long-range repercussions that tested Portugal's capacity to retain liberty and an open society.

Both the First and the Third Republics produced controversial constitutions and early political phases that were too "advanced" for the majority of Portuguese. In 1910–11, the sweeping acts of the Provisional Government, as well as the 1911 constitution, which embodied radical anticlericalism and statist action against the Church, estranged large sectors of public opinion. There followed an exhausting, long, and costly struggle to amend or eliminate these laws. In 1975–76 "advanced" acts of the Provisional Government and the 1976 constitution met stiff internal opposition that became more open after 1977. Debate in 1976 and beyond, however, was not about the Church but about the disparity in philosophy and methods between the forces captivated by the Marxist-Leninist spirit of a "classless society" and "transition to socialism" ensconced in the 1976 constitution and more conservative elements outside the government. In both political experiences, then, an advanced, fashionable, but soon discredited, doctrine in law was first challenged by the country and then amended or abolished.

2

If there are similarities between the First and Third Republics, there are more differences. Take the cases of governmental (cabinet), parliamentary, and presidential stability. The First Republic's record was one of world-class instability in all categories. The Third Republic, despite the uncertainties of the early provisional governments and unstable coalitions, enjoyed greater stability from 1977 to 1985 in all three categories, and presidential stability was the most impressive. The figure of about one year for the average life of a government—seventeen governments in eighteen years—is deceptive. During their twenty-five months, the average life of the provisional governments was a little over four months. For constitutional governments, however (eleven during fifteen years as of April 1991) the figure is about 1.35 years—longer than the average life of governments in postwar Italy. It should be noted, too, that two governments lasted from two to four years (Balsemão and Soares), and the Cavaco Silva government was reelected after completing a four-year term. This will be an important milestone for the Third Republic.

Another major difference in favor of the post-1974 system is in the role of the military in politics and government. Except for the early phases in 1974–75, the military did not openly intervene in politics and government. Several other developments since then suggest that at least formally the military has returned to the barracks and plays little or no role in the legislature. The civilianized authority system is being consolidated at least on paper. The 1977 Military Discipline Regulations provide that soldiers on active service cannot participate in partisan politics, join parties, or attend meetings or rallies.[9] The 1982 revision of the constitution abolished the military-dominated Council of the Revolution; and following two terms of President (formerly General) Eanes, Mário Soares became the first civilian president. Whether or not there are still credible coup plots among the military is difficult to know or to verify.[10]

Other differences should be noted in the Third Republic's brief but full history. A functioning multi-party system has emerged, and despite some parliamentary and governmental instability which marked the years 1974–85, there appears to be a possibility that a two-party system will evolve, dominated by the Socialists (PS) and Social Democrats (PSD).[11] Both parties appear potentially strong enough to win and keep for a period a majority of seats in the Assembly, but if they cannot, coalitions with other weaker parties such as the Portuguese Communist Party (PCP) and Christian Democratic Party are problematical if not impossible, and another phase of changing governments may follow. If the history of 1977–85 proves anything, it is that coalitions are inherently unstable in Portuguese politics. With voter patience and what is still a respectable voter turnout at general elections*—a percentage that puts American voter turnouts to shame—the PS and PSD may be able to alternate in power for some time to come.

Unlike the First Republic, the Third Republic has been marked by a relatively low level of public violence and civil disorder, especially since 1976. In the "hot year" of 1975, for example, the loss of life in scattered civil strife and terrorism was estimated at only 24–28 persons. What terrorism has occurred, based on small fringe groups on the left and the right, has not had a destabilizing effect on the political system. Terrorism from the left appears to have little support within Portugal, while terrorism from the right might have greater support in the future. The effectiveness of Portugal's novice counterterrorist system is doubtful. Portugal has experienced a certain amount of international terrorism in the 1980s, related to ongoing tensions in the Middle East. Potential contact with outside terrorists remains a problem for the Third Republic in part because of the location of Portugal (and particularly Lisbon) as a crossroads and transfer point between the West and the Atlantic and the Mediterranean, the Middle East and North Africa, and Europe and tropical Africa.

As for crime, it is difficult to make a strong distinction between the records of the First and Third Republics. A significant increase in organized crime, random crime including crimes of violence, corruption, graft, and larceny was characteristic of the First Republic after 1914. Public response to burgeoning crime in the 1920s was but one part of the political and social disillusionment and alienation of the ruling groups and middle classes as well as the professional military which prepared public opinion for the May 1926 military takeover. We lack a study of crime in the Third Republic and how the state, districts, and municipalities deal with it. As an urban problem alone, crime in the 1970s, 1980s, and 1990s has been encouraged by economic crises, the collapse of the overseas empire and return of

*At the July 1987 general election the voter turnout was over 60 percent.

the retornados, an increase in the possession of firearms from the colonial wars and the military activities of 1974–75, the drug trade, and other international criminal activity which uses Lisbon as an entrepot. In July 1990, the Commandante General of the Polícia da Seguridade Pública (PSP),* General Ámilcar Morgado, was quoted in the press as saying:

> Portugal runs the risk of being able to become the paradise of criminals and the waste bin of drug addicts, vagabonds and the marginal types of the EEC, following the [post-1992] opening of frontiers among member states.[12]

International assistance in fighting crime and terrorism is an important advantage for the Third Republic and represents yet another difference with the First Republic.

Other important differences to note are the following: 1) the higher level of voter participation since 1974; 2) the less prominent place in partisan politics of an overseas colonial question since Portugal, with the slight exception of Macao until 1999, no longer possesses an overseas empire; nevertheless, this must be qualified by a study of the politics of Portuguese claims, protests, and politicking concerning expropriated funds and property in Angola and Mozambique, etc., and there is a vigorous historical debate about "Who is responsible for the loss of the empire?";[13] 3) the greater powers of the president of the Third Republic than those possessed by the presidents of the First Republic, even after the controversial 1919 revision granting presidents the power to dissolve congress (the Third Republic's system is still, to some extent, semipresidential, although the 1982 revision restricted the president's powers of dissolution, naming and dismissing a premier, and vetoing legislation); 4) much wider civil and political rights of citizens in the Third Republic, including the key freedoms of speech, association, and press, and full political rights for women and better representation than American women have in their legislatures; 5) greater independence of the judiciary in the Third Republic, on balance, than that of the judiciary during 1910–26, when the governments relentlessly manipulated the judiciary to suit their purposes; 6) the more educated and literate electorate of today, despite flaws in the educational sys-

*The PSP is an urban national police force of the Third Republic inherited from the Second Republic of Salazar.

tem, than the restricted number of voters of 1911–26. This difference
in the electorate is reflected not only in the higher level of education
and sophistication of the political elite (see Tables 1 and 2), but also
in the remarkably large and growing readership of an improving
periodical press and of books, about one-third of which are translations into Portuguese from foreign languages. For a small country
with a small population, the size of readership of daily papers and
books is remarkable.[14]

3

Next to the difference in the extent to which the citizenry and
the electorates were educated, perhaps the outstanding factor which
distinguishes the First and Third Republican experiences is international economic and financial assistance. The First Republic was the
beneficiary of foreign loans and credits during and after World War
I,[15] but this effort was very limited and had adverse consequences.
Portugal fell more deeply in debt, and the League of Nations pressed
Lisbon on repayment and demanded conditions which offended nationalist feelings. Since 1974, Portugal has been the beneficiary of
significant amounts of economic and development aid by means of
grants, loans, and credits, including support from the oldest secular
ally (United Kingdom) and a new ally (United States), as well as
Common Market assistance, which began in the 1980s and will continue well past 1992, when the trade barriers fall. Although no one
source states the total amount of the economic aid Portugal is due to
receive by the end of 1992 and is planned for after that date, it is this
observer's impression that the sum may amount to as much as, or
more than, Portugal has received in foreign aid since before the
Luso-American agreements started in 1951. Not to be forgotten, too,
are the funds democratic parties and groups received during the
difficult days of 1974, 1975, and 1976 to bolster Portuguese democracy.

International economic assistance, which includes a good dose
of technological expertise, training, and education, will have a major
impact on Portugal's society and its fledgling democracy. It is easier
to estimate patterns of likely development, beyond merely annual
economic growth rates, than it is to assess the politics of the EC

impact on the country and whether the EC impact will make a difference in the long-term consolidation of democracy. There will be a
period of adjustment even if the political system remains stable and
there is no severe economic downturn. To be sure, Portuguese public
opinion is divided over the virtues and vices of the EC-dominated
future. A rising chorus of nationalist voices, who include quite a
range of political ideologies, is critical of the EC impact on Portugal
and raises alarms about loss of national identity, sovereignty, and
independence.[16] Opposing this view are pro-EC groups who see the
Eurocrats as saviors. They hold a semimessianic belief which I
would describe as "Euro-Sebastianism": never mind the potential
loss of many small and medium-size Portuguese companies now
and after 1992; the EC will rejuvenate our economy and save our
democracy.

4

Portugal's still very serious economic and social problems as
well as the international assistance and integration issues aside, it is
instructive to analyze the biographies and backgrounds of the respective ruling groups of the First and Third Republics. As shown in
Tables 1 and 2 the differences outnumber the similarities.

Among the curious similarities to note in both groups are:

1. The average age of deputies and others is 35–50 years.
2. They contain few or no clergy and few workers.
3. Top leadership is no longer young (mainly in the fifties, some
   sixties); Afonso Costa was the youngest cabinet officer at thirty-
   nine; Cunhal is in the seventies; Soares, sixties; Cavaco Silva,
   Lucas Pires, Freitas do Amaral, fifties.
4. Student political experience in high school, but especially at
   universities (Coimbra, Lisbon, mainly) was a major experiential
   and formative factor in political careers both in 1911 and in the
   1950s, 1960s, and 1970s. The Coimbra student strike of 1907 was
   as important to its generation as were the Delgado campaign
   (1958) and student agitation during 1961–74.
5. Rank and file of the elected are relative newcomers with little
   administrative or office-holding experience. In the latter group

Table 1

Occupational Composition of Parliaments and Political Leadership of First Republic and Third Republic

Deputies of 1911 Constituent Assembly (which drew up and approved the 1911 constitution and became the first Republican Congress [1911–15])

Deputies of the Assembly of the Republic elected in 1987 and other politicians and members of municipal, district, and national governments

Occupation	Number	Occupation	Number
Medical doctor	48	Lawyer	75
Armed forces officer	47	Businessman (merchant?)	73
Civil servant	25	Teacher	58
Lawyer	24	Engineer	48
Landowner	18	University professor	32
Teacher	12	Civil servant	29
University professor	11	Accountant/economist	21
Merchant	8	Medical doctor	17
Journalist	8	Politician/party functionary	17
Pharmacist	6	Worker	8
Judge	5	Journalist/publicist	8
Solicitor	3	Student	6
Salesman	2	Architect	6
Student	2	Armed forces officer (reserve)	5
Priest	2	Landowner/farmer	5
Farm foreman	1	Office secretary/worker	3
Engineer	1	Judge	2
Veterinarian	1	Writer/intellectual	2
Barber	1	Chauffeur/taxi driver	1
Worker	1	Interior decorator	1
	226	Pharmacist/nurse	1
		Priest	0
		Pres. Câmara Municipal or undetermined occupation	42
			460

Sources: For 1911—Marcello Caetano, *História breve das constituições portuguesas*, 3d. ed. (Lisbon, 1971), p. 101 (Caetano's main source must have been *As constituentes de 1911 e os seus deputados* [Lisbon, 1911]). For 1987— Candido de Azevedo, ed., *Classe política portuguesa: Estes políticos que nos governam* (Lisbon, 1989).

NOTE: Availability of biographical data for legislators in 1911 and 1987 determined the format of Tables 1 and 2, as well as the decision of the writer to compare the First Republic's Constituent Assembly with the Third Republic's 1987 Assembly of the Republic. To my knowledge no comparable biographical data have been published on a later legislature of the First Republic or on an earlier legislature of the Third Republic.

Table 2

Educational Background of Legislative Deputies of First and Third Republics

First Republic (226 Deputies of Constituent Assembly)		Third Republic (461 Political Leaders, 1987 [See Table 1])	
Level of Education or Background	Number	Level of Education or Background	Number
Attended or graduated from Coimbra University	88	Attended or graduated from Coimbra University	71
Attended or graduated from university or equivalent institution (other than Coimbra)	c. 92	Attended or graduated from university or equivalent institution (other than Coimbra)[a]	216
Participated in 1907 Coimbra University student strike	(most of) 88	Participated in anti-dictatorship student activity	c. 72
Armed forces officers	47	Armed forces officers (reserve)	5
Educated with more than one year abroad	2	Educated with more than one year abroad, or in exile[b]	43
Participated in conspiracy, 5 October 1910 coup	c. 50	Colonial war service (Africa or Asia)	40
High school education or less	c. 45	*Cooperante* in former colony	3
Born abroad (Brazil only)	2	Born abroad or in colonies	17
Women	0	Clandestine PCP work	7
		In MFA 25 April 1974 coup and movement	4
		High school education or less	68
		Arrested by PVDE/PIDE/DGS before 25 April	23
		Women who are Pres., Câmaras Municipais	6
		Women in AR (1987–91)	24

Sources: For 1911—Wheeler, *Republican Portugal*, p. 73. For 1987—Candido de Azevedo, ed., *Classe política portuguesa.*

[a]Most of those who attended or graduated from university level institutions in the 1987 Assembly of the Republic went to the University of Lisbon, the New University of Lisbon, the University of Porto, and other institutions.

[b]Including those with higher degrees earned abroad, like Premier Cavaco Silva.

the 1974 revolution was a major catalyst of political awakening for many; the thirty-five-year olds of 1987 were only twenty-two in 1974 and the fifty-year olds were thirty-seven.

6. Except for members of one established party (PRP in 1911 and PCP in 1974) few of both groups were members of parties before the revolution, an effect of the depoliticization of the Estado Novo; except for the clandestine PCP, no parties to speak of existed before 25 April 1974.

7. Only three of the 1911 Assembly and three of the 1987 Assembly were cabinet ministers in the previous regime.

Nevertheless, the differences in background between the "class of 1911" and the "class of 1987" (July 1987 general election of Republican Assembly and political figures who were not members of that legislative body) are numerous and striking:

1. A superior level and extent of education and training of the 1987 group, in general, with some exceptions; a higher percentage of university graduates and persons with advanced degrees in a much larger variety of fields.

2. Administrative and political experience in office is relatively greater in the class of 1987; while one-fourth of the class of 1911 had some administrative experience or office-holding, the class of 1987 some thirteen years after the revolution has accumulated wider experience in politics and government.

3. Foreign contact, residence, experience, and education is considerably wider in 1987 (see Table 2), including education abroad (the premier has a doctorate in economics from a British university, for example) and service in the armed forces in the former colonies.

4. A much richer variety of professions and occupations in 1987 than in 1911. The two largest occupations represented in 1911 were medical doctors and armed forces officers, while in 1987 doctors were not a large category and only 5 officers (in the reserves, not on active duty, as required by law) were included. Much the largest categories in 1987 were lawyers (the largest category), businessmen (second), teachers (third), engineers (fourth), and university professors (fifth). When one counts up the academic contingent in all categories, including those who

are classified as "economists" and consultants, the figure is 159, an important portion of 460.

5. Landowners (18) in 1911 contrast with a less representative number in 1987 (5 only).

6. The role of women in the class of 1987 is still small, at 24 out of 250 deputies in the AR and only 6 Presidentes da Câmara Municipal, but contrasts with no women in 1911 or any legislature of the First Republic.

7. While an education at Coimbra University still has a significant place in the background of some of the elite, education at other universities has assumed a much greater prominence.

5

Our comparison between the First and Third Republics suggests that there are more differences than similarities between the two experiences. Particularly striking in the Third Republic is presidential and increasing governmental and parliamentary stability; a functioning multi-party system; international economic and technical assistance; and an international environment conducive to the keeping of a democratic, pluralist system. The main elements of a democratic system are in place despite Portugal's staggering social and economic problems of rural underdevelopment; poverty; a bloated, ineffective bureaucracy;* a large external debt; increased crime and drug abuse; an agrarian problem that continues to be troublesome; and difficulties in adjusting to integration into the EC.

There are indications, however, that a purely political or economic analysis of "indicators" such as the party system, bureaucracy, inflation, growth figures, performance of the legislature, and education statistics do *not* take into account the extent to which traditional problems and tensions in Portuguese society may work against the consolidation of the novice democracy. Analysts who can be described as more pessimist than optimist on how the system is operating include scholars like Walter Opello and Joaquim Aguiar,

*A sign of one aspect of the public's growing contempt for too much of Lisbon's bureaucracy is the hybrid word now in common usage among some entrepreneurs: *burrocracia* (author's interview with member of Lisbon business community, July 1990).

who suggest that local studies of how political influence functions will provide a more realistic picture of another side of the Third Republic.[17] Ken Gladdish's analysis of how the political parties functioned in the transition to democracy calls for suspended judgment or "an open verdict."[18] Gladdish quotes a telling sentence from Aguiar:

> In fact, the traditional features of Portuguese society were internalised by the parties themselves, which are now one more specific element of the clientelistic network, enclosing a circle of self-sustaining interlocked interests . . . typical of a patrimonialistic society.[19]

While the Third Republic has distinct advantages over the First Republic and it is hard to document any precise connections either through persons or institutions which link the two experiences, the future health of democracy will depend on too many different variables of current and future conditions, events, new generations, and emerging patterns of behavior to predict any definite outcome now.* It is difficult to spot any destabilizing forces in the system in 1990, except perhaps rightist and hypernationalist sentiment. Economic disaster if it were to come, in whatever form, would provide ammunition for political extremists. Would a crisis which combined an energy shortage (we recall 1973 only too well now), the sudden exodus to Portugal of 700,000 retornados from the Portuguese communities in strife-torn south Africa, and a return to the uncertainties of coalition governments in Lisbon be enough to cause more than talk in the barracks? When discussing possible military intervention, it is appropriate to recall that it is difficult to phase out a traditional activity, however much of the public may oppose it, which has 150 or more years of history behind it.

In conclusion, the First and Third Republics should be placed in comparative historical perspective. The First Republic was Portugal's *first* sustained attempt to establish and keep a parliamentary democracy. Republican good intentions, ideals, and energy failed to create a stable, fully progressive and enduring system. It inherited a

---

*It is not insignificant, in this regard, that the person of President Mário Soares embodies a direct link with the First Republic: his father was a minister in several of the fugitive governments of the First Republic and devoted his later life to private education.

tragically heavy burden of debt and staggering problems from the failing monarchy, and it saw the awakening of aspirations of various classes and interest groups which its system could not constructively satisfy or reconcile. The First Republic tried to accomplish what no other Portuguese system of governance yet had tried in the establishment of civil freedoms, political and military mobilization, social action, social justice, and cultural freedom and to "build a modern people" among Western Europe's poorest and least educated populace. At the same time, it tried to begin the economic development of its extensive overseas empire.

The Third Republic is Portugal's *second* sustained attempt to set up and maintain a democracy. After eighteen years, it has a record of improving political and economic stability, a more educated citizenry, and limited public violence, and has been the beneficiary of an unprecedented aid program. Like the First, the Third Republic has tried to do what no other regime in the country's history attempted: to establish and maintain a *truly pluralist* democracy; to bring a more complete economic and social development to a country which is still very poor in many sectors and which still has not eliminated the classic tensions of modern Portuguese history (personalism, factionalism, agrarian development patterns, and a geographic and administrative cleavage between "the State" [Lisbon] and the provinces); and finally, to bring the colonial wars to an end and to decolonize the empire as quickly and as expediently as possible. As General De Gaulle mused about his answer to the Algerian question: "For every solution, there is a problem." It will be a long time before the country recovers completely from the effects of the decolonization process of 1974–75. Until the outstanding policy questions regarding East Timor, Macao's future, relations with the governments of the former colonies, economic claims, and emigration are resolved, the Third Republic's foreign policy agenda will be problematical.[20]

The Third Republic confronts a heavy historical legacy which, as memories fade and new generations appear, bears an interesting paradox: economic momentum, growth, and some development along with the dictatorship's gold reserves ironically assisted the survival of the democratic Third Republic during troubled times on the brink of civil war, 1974–75. While the memories of the First Republic recede, those of the dictatorship grow larger. The dictatorship's legacy in all its complexity to the Third Republic, then, will continue to exercise public opinion and will constitute a major topic of study for future historians. Similarly, the First Republic will continue to be studied as part of the origin of the Estado Novo and not simply as the final phase of the liberalism which began in the 1820s.

History seldom allows revolutionaries or reformers the freedom to choose their moments of power. Like the doers, the dreamers must take their *aberturas* (openings) when they appear. So it was in 1910 (and in 1926!), and so it was again in 1974. It was the challenge and the tragedy of the First Republicans that their opportunity coincided with World War I, renewed hysteria over the African colonies, the worst financial and economic crisis the country had witnessed in modern times, and the awakening of aspirations of various classes and groups which could not be constructively satisfied within "the bullring of the Republic."

The Third Republic's leadership and its citizenry need not be reminded that the timing of their opportunity for changing Portugal after 1974 through the exercise of a new power and authority, their opening to become a respected partner in a new Europe, coincided with an economic recession, an energy shortage, increasingly unmanageable pressures for decolonization, and the stirring aspirations of large groups of Portuguese for a better life and for more liberty. While the successors of the "Captains" of 25 April 1974 cannot choose their timing for power either, at least they can help demystify and clarify the history of the first parliamentary republic, the ill-fated regime which gave birth to Western Europe's longest-surviving authoritarian system. It is vital that every Portuguese understand what the First Republic was and what it was not and to place in perspective with renewed hope the brief but eventful life of Portugal's novice democracy, the Third Republic.

124 *Douglas L. Wheeler*

NOTES

1. Regarding the question of the consolidation of Portugal's new democracy, there has been a great deal published which is theory and uninformed speculation. Analyses which attempt to look beneath the surface of structures and processes are rare. One of the more circumspect expert recent studies of the Portuguese party system within a wider framework is Ken Gladdish, "Portugal: An Open Verdict," in *Securing Democracy: Political Parties and Democratic Consolidation in Southern Europe*, ed. Geoffrey Pridham (London and New York, 1990), pp. 104–25.

2. A number of recent studies by foreign political scientists and historians reserve final judgment about the long-term prospects of Portuguese democracy but acknowledge that it is well established: Philippe C. Schmitter, "An Introduction to Southern European Transitions from Authoritarian Rule: Italy, Greece, Portugal, Spain and Turkey," and Kenneth Maxwell, "Regime Overthrown and the Prospects for Democratic Transition," in *Transitions from Authoritarian Rule: Southern Europe*, ed. G. O'Donnell, P. C. Schmitter, and L. Whitehead (Baltimore, 1986), pp. 3–10 and 109–37 respectively; Thomas C. Bruneau and Alex Macleod, *Politics in Contemporary Portugal: Parties and the Consolidation of Democracy* (Boulder, 1986). For the multiple views of a variety of Portuguese scholars on political, constitutional, and governmental processes, see Mário Baptista Coelho, ed. *Portugal: O sistema político e constitucional 1974/1987* (Lisbon, 1989).

3. For soundings and gentle speculations by this observer, see Douglas L. Wheeler: "Will Portuguese Democracy Learn from History?" *Christian Science Monitor* (international weekly edition, London), 2 October 1978, p. 31; and "Why Second Republic [*sic*] Is Not Like First," International Herald Tribune (Paris), 3 October 1983.

4. See the seminal work by A. H. de Oliveira Marques, *A Primeira República Portuguesa: Alguns aspectos estruturais* (Lisbon, 1971 [1st ed.], 1975 [2d ed.]). An edited version of this material is found in other works by Oliveira Marques, including his *História de Portugal* (various eds., 1972–present). For a foreign historian's analysis, see Douglas L. Wheeler, *Republican Portugal: A Political History 1910–1926* (Madison, 1978); Portuguese edition of same work: *História política de Portugal, 1910–1926* (Mem Martins, 1985).

5. Douglas L. Wheeler, "The Portuguese Revolution of 1910," *Journal of Modern History* 44 (1972): 172–94.

6. Avelino Rodrigues, Cesário Borga, and Mário Cardoso, *O Movimento dos captães e o 25 de Abril: 229 dias para derrubar o fascismo* (Lisbon, 1974).

7. I do not subscribe to the judgment that the 1974–75 period was the most catastrophic int he country's history; this view is found, for example, in Harold V. Livermore, *A New History of Portugal* (Cambridge, 1976).

8. See Wheeler, *Republican Portugal*, pp. 214–33; and Richard Robinson, *Contemporary Portugal: A History* (London, 1979).

9. See *Regulamento militar da disciplina* (Lisbon, 1977).

10. See Gladdish, "Portugal," pp. 115–24; Bruneau and Macleod, *Politics in Contemporary Portugal*, pp. 16–17, 22.

11. Thomas C. Bruneau, "Portugal's Unexpected Transition," in *Portugal: Ancient Country, Young Democracy*, ed. Kenneth Maxwell and Michael H. Haltzel (Washington, D.C., 1990), pp. 9–20.

12. "Disseram . . . Portugal," *The Portuguese American* (Providence, R.I.), 18 July 1990, p. 10.

13. This debate is carried on in various venues including the print and electronic media, in some scholarly circles, and in books, memoirs, etc. Historian Jorge Borges de Macedo suggests that since the 1974–75 revolution the Portuguese sense of national identity has been weakened; see "Não temos o direito de desistir," *Prelo* (Lisbon), no. 1 (October/December 1983): 7–10.

14. On general election voting figures in Lisbon, 1911 to November 1925, the last general election of the First Republic, see Wheeler, *Republican Portugal*, p. 229.

15. A. H. de Oliveira Marques, *História de 1ª República Portuguesa: As estruturas de base* (Lisbon, 1978), pp. 463–514.

16. See *Entre duas revoluções. Salazar, 100 anos/25 de Abril, 15 anos*, in Lisbon weekly paper *Expresso*, 22 April 1989—articles by a variety of scholars and writers, left to right in political views, which demonstrate the growing conviction among some circles that Portugal cannot maintain its independence in the EC-dominated Europe without its overseas empire—especially the article by António José Saraiva, "O Salazarismo."

17. Walter C. Opello, Jr., *Portugal's Political Development: A Comparative Approach* (Boulder, 1985); see also his article, "Local Government and Political Culture in a Portuguese Rural County," *Comparative Politics* 13 (1981): 271–89.

18. See Gladdish, "Portugal."

19. *Ibid.*, pp. 104–5, citing Joaquim Aguiar's paper, "Hidden Fluidity in an Ultra-Stable Party System," Conference on Modern Portugal III, International Conference Group on Portugal, University of New Hampshire, June 1984; and Aguiar's important book, *A ilusão do poder: Análise do sistema partidário, 1976–82* (Lisbon, 1983).

20. For useful information on the problems, prospects, and activities of the Chinese and Portuguese communities in Macao, due to be transferred to Chinese sovereignty in 1999, see the monthly magazine *Macau*, produced by the information arm of the Macao government, an excellent example of a Luso-Chinese magazine which sets a high standard of *reportage*.

THE HISTORICAL ROOTS OF THE MODERN PORTU-GUESE ECONOMY: THE FIRST CENTURY OF GROWTH, 1850s TO 1950s

Jaime Reis

1

Between the 1850s and the 1950s, Portugal experienced a long period of sustained growth, probably the longest and fastest it had ever experienced until that time. In comparative terms, however, this growth and the accompanying structural change were slow. As Portugal had started off in the middle of the nineteenth century as one of the poorest nations in Europe, the net result was that it continued to enjoy this status one century later. In spite of a somewhat more dynamic performance during the first half of the present century, both in relative and in absolute terms, this did not enable the economy to recoup the relative decline which marked the 1850–1913 period, when the rest of Western Europe experienced far more rapid growth.

Around 1950, there was a dramatic change in this situation. As in general in the West the economy surged, and for the next quarter of a century, rates of growth were extremely high. What was particularly remarkable about the Portuguese case, however, was not just that this performance was so much better than it had ever been before, but that for the first time Portugal expanded appreciably faster than most of the developed economies. Its "poverty gap" relative to the advanced world was finally beginning to close, after one century of widening or at best of simply standing still. Indeed if we include the period up to the 1974 revolution, it becomes clear that, in a broad perspective, it was the nineteenth century rather than the twentieth, and in particular the period prior to the Estado Novo and not the fifty years of the Estado Novo itself, which accounts for the country's position at the foot of the tables of European income per capita.

The impressive performance of the Portuguese economy from the 1950s to the 1970s (which may be continuing at present after a hiatus in the late 1970s and early 1980s) was the result of a number of favorable circumstances which materialized during these years. Probably chief among these was the external climate of economic dynamism which once again enveloped the country and became a still more powerful force with Portugal's formal integration into a broader international trade framework after 1959. This brought not only access to markets, but also a tide of foreign investment and technical know-how that contributed significantly to the modernization of the economy. At the same time, economic liberalization policies and a considerable rise in domestic savings helped to fuel a substantial rise in capital formation, without which the diversification and technological progress which are prerequisite to increases in output and productivity are hard to achieve.

From an historical point of view, this is not the first time that favorable conditions such as these have been present in Portugal. Yet in earlier periods, particularly the nineteenth century, the results were far less positive. The difference, I would argue, must be found in certain factors of a long-run nature which eventually ceased to be the barriers to economic growth they had once been, either because they evolved over time or because gradually they became less relevant to the growth process.

The purpose of this essay is to try to identify these factors and the role they have played in Portugal's economic history since the middle of the last century, with a view to drawing a clearer picture of what has rendered possible the experience of "catching up" with which the last generation or two have lived. I shall begin by outlining the course of growth of the economy from the mid-nineteenth to the mid-twentieth centuries, as well as pointing out the emergence and consolidation of some of the more salient features of its structure and some of the ways in which this period contrasts with recent decades. The following section will set out the principal causes of Portugal's apparent long-run inability to either sustain rates of growth similar to those of other Western countries or, better still, catch up with them. This focuses on the period 1850–1913, when the country most clearly fell behind the "European norm" (Crafts). The third and final part will examine the changes which have occurred, particularly during the first half of the twentieth century, and which have helped to attenuate or even eliminate these long-term barriers to growth. We shall focus on resource endowment, access to markets, government intervention, and the integration of the domestic economy.

2

The century with which we are concerned here is important for contemporary Portuguese history for several reasons. In spite of what was said above, inevitably for a small country immersed in a rapidly changing environment, it was a time of economic change and pronounced structural shifts. And yet very early on, some of the features that defined the character of this period and gave it a certain homogeneity were already becoming evident. The locational shift in population, wealth, and economic activity, from the interior to the coast and from the north to the south, is one of them. As recent research has shown, another is the consistently faster performance of industry relative to agriculture, even when (according to some authors) economic expansion was led by an export-induced agricultural expansion (A. R. Pereira). In fact, the latest evidence points to a persistent difference in growth rates, over the long run, of one or two percentage points between these two sectors, even at the time when Portugal was still an agriculturally based country.

With the study of Portuguese historical statistics still in its infancy, it is not surprising that considerable disagreement should exist concerning the evolution of these and other economic aggregates. It is generally recognized, however, that not only was there growth of national income at constant prices between 1850 and 1913, but also that this was faster than population growth. Although it is hard to reach a consensus regarding how much poorer than other countries Portugal was at any time, it is also accepted that while the dozen or so more advanced countries of Europe were growing at a little more than 1 percent a year in per capita terms (constant prices) during these years, Portugal's performance was at best somewhere in the region of 0.7 percent a year. Over a period of sixty years, this meant a relative "loss" of some 30 percent, which, added to a likely difference of some 30 percent less in terms of per capita income at mid-century, would imply that early in the 1900s the Portuguese must have had a standard of living roughly half that enjoyed on average in these countries—a fact that is corroborated by the qualitative evidence available.

Paradoxically, less is known about these matters for the period from 1913 to 1950. Although open to some methodological doubts, the latest results reasonably suggest that Portugal was now able to keep up with the advanced economies, with overall growth rates for real income per capita growth in both cases at around 1.1 percent (Maddison; Nunes, Valério, and Mata). Indeed if we consider only the interwar years, there is evidence to suggest that Portugal may already have started to catch up then, given that agriculture was expanding at 2.4 percent per year and industry apparently at a good deal more than this. Most advanced economies in the aggregate did not exceed the 2 percent mark.

While it is not surprising that throughout these hundred years and even beyond, the product mix in agriculture should have remained fairly unchanging—cereals, wine, and olives, with animal products in a subordinate role—it is interesting to note how soon after its emergence in its modern form industry too took on the productive structure which was to endure until the 1960s. Not only had today's main industrial centers already emerged as such by the 1880s—Lisbon, Oporto, Braga, Setubal, and Aveiro—but also by then the prevalent sectors were already the food and beverages; the textile, clothing, and shoes; the wood and cork; the metal-working and the construction industries which were to dominate the scene until the structural changes that began in the late 1950s.

As for the international aspects of this economy, again very little changed in the course of these hundred years, except of course in times of war or international crisis. An impressive flow of labor steadily left the country, whose economy never seemed capable of absorbing its own population surpluses. In contrast, capital inflows played only a minor role in building up productive capacity, with the exception of certain very special activities. This was undoubtedly related to the essentially closed nature of the economy, as reflected by the low propensities to both import and export (relative to gross national product) in comparison with other equally small states. It has been suggested in fact that this may have been the principal cause of the sluggish overall growth performance that was the hallmark of this period (Lains 1986).

Without constituting a complete break with these characteristics, there can be little doubt that the 1950s were a watershed in the long-run evolution of the Portuguese economy. The outstanding feature in this was the sharp acceleration in the growth of national output which, at roughly 6 percent a year for almost a quarter of a century thereafter, made it possible for Portugal to overcome some of its secular backwardness, in spite of this being a time of rapid growth elsewhere. (On average the sixteen most advanced countries had a yearly growth rate of 4 percent.) Most of the increase in output arose in manufacturing, which overtook the primary sector as far back as 1947, even though the latter still continued to be a larger employer of labor for many years. The gap between them widened dramatically, with a difference of some 7 percent developing between their respective growth rates as a result of agriculture's near stagnation while the manufacturing sector was reaching rates in the range of 9 percent a year.

Unlike what had been common until then, industrial growth ceased to be stimulated only by internal demand and import substitution, and was increasingly determined by the performance of its exports. The main actors in this vigorous opening to foreign markets were some of the "traditional" sectors—textiles, clothing, and shoes—and it was not long before, for the first time, Portugal ceased to be foremost a producer and exporter of primary products, to become essentially a manufacturing nation (Baer and Leite). The appearance in the meantime of a whole range of "new industries"— steel, chemicals and petroleum, electrical equipment, and ship-repairing—which were based on high technology and a high capital-intensity and benefited from substantial economies of scale, led to a profound reshaping of the country's industrial structure. By 1973, the "traditional" sectors accounted for only one-half of manufacturing output.

3

Traditional explanations for the poor economic performance prior to 1913 have relied on either one or a combination of the following three factors. First, excessive dependence on Britain prevented industrialization from taking place and compelled an unfavorable specialization in primary production for export. Second, a social structure which was too strongly rooted in the *ancien régime* left the country with a weak bourgeoisie which was unable or unwilling to bring about a sufficient degree of social and economic modernization. Last, an agrarian system that had evolved over centuries and was consolidated by the post-1834 liberal reforms prevented long-term productivity gains in either the minifundiary or the latifundiary components on which it was based.

In the last few years, however, different views on this problem have come to prevail. It has been argued that these negative factors were far from decisive and that if Portugal is looked at in a comparative perspective, what was lacking was not less but more external dependence, even of the kind that has been hitherto considered so harmful to growth (Reis 1984). Besides this, while not denying entirely the validity of some of these explanations, other unfavorable circumstances appear to have been more important. Some of these would not have been inimical to growth at other times and under different economic and technological conditions. In some cases, as we shall see, their effect could have been attenuated or even removed. In other times, though immutable, they might cease to matter as conditions changed. What made for Portugal's exceptionally poor economic performance comparatively speaking was not that all these factors were not present in other countries as well, but that they were present in Portugal all at once and to a particularly strong degree.

Natural resource endowment is one of the most obvious of these other negative factors. Given the type of economic modernization that was taking place in Europe during the second half of the nineteenth century, Portugal was clearly at a considerable disadvantage in this respect. Not only did it lack the strategic minerals of the Industrial Revolution (coal and iron), but also it did not have practically any of the other mineral or forest products which helped to fuel growth and industrialization (initially through the export of raw materials) in other similarly small and poor countries. In this connection, it is suggestive that the two sectors which exhibited the most dynamic performance in terms of both growth and exports—cork and sardines—were very much resource-based activities, making use of natural assets that were abundant in Portugal but not commonly found elsewhere.

Conditions for agriculture were not more favorable. On the one hand, both soil and climate were unsuited to the application of the kind of advances in agricultural techniques of which the better-off north European countries were able to take advantage and which came to be known as the Agricultural Revolution. At the same time, good or even reasonable land was not abundant. According to recent surveys, only one-fourth of the national territory—i.e., 2.5 million hectares—is suitable for cultivation (Medeiros). Yet by 1867, this much was in use, which means that the considerable physical expansion of agriculture which went on thereafter and into the early 1900s was carried out on marginal lands, something which was hardly conducive to great improvement in productivity. Finally, it must be pointed out that natural conditions imposed on Portugal a specialization in the sorts of agricultural products—essentially of the Mediterranean variety—for which the demand at this time, both at home and abroad, was least dynamic. What Europeans wanted to consume more and more were meat, eggs, and dairy products, not wine and olive oil, and, as Pedro Lains (1986) has shown, if Portugal's exports did not fare well during the second half of the nineteenth century, it was not only that they were not competitive in their own markets, but also that they consisted of goods for which international markets were the slowest of all to grow.

When it comes to human resources, matters cannot be said to have been much better. In this case, however, it was not simply a problem of endowment since a good deal could have been done to remedy the situation. Not only did Portugal rank among the countries of Europe with the lowest literacy achievement at mid-century (approximately 15 percent of the population), but also it failed to make the effort and investment in basic education which, during the following fifty years, enabled most low-income countries on the continent to begin to close their literacy gap vis-à-vis the advanced countries of northern Europe. In 1911, still only 25 percent of the population was able to read and write, and the picture was no less bleak with respect to the higher forms of educational attainment.

The exact nature of the connection between human capital formation and economic development has baffled social scientists for quite some time. Nevertheless, few would disagree that in the nineteenth century, the quality of the work force was an important ingredient for raising productivity. In general terms, it would seem that a paucity of human capital could not but have been a strongly negative influence on the process of Portugal's economic growth. It certainly seems to have contributed to the low productivity of industrial labor which, it was often remarked at the time, operated with the same machines as its English or French counterparts (since they were often imported from these countries) but got a considerably poorer result from them. In cotton textiles, for example, where output per worker was less than half that of the British or French equivalents, Portuguese workers could operate only two looms each, whereas abroad three or four was the norm, something which was attributed to a lack of training and education (Reis 1986).

Low educational standards acted no less as a brake on agricultural productivity. In part, they were responsible for the slow and diffident penetration of new techniques—particularly (though not only) those that were more science-based, such as machines and chemical fertilizers. But the fact that the vast majority of Portuguese farmers were illiterate peasants probably also accounts for the even more serious problem represented by the lack of competitiveness in foreign markets of Portuguese primary products. The consequence of this was the failure to achieve significant export-led growth. Of the two reasons why during this time Portugal tended to lose its market share abroad, one was the inferior quality of its farm produce, and this was clearly related to the lack of general and technical sophistication on the part of producers. This could have been overcome to some extent by farming cooperatives to process and package goods for sale and export, but again, in the late nineteenth century, it was among the more highly educated peasants of Scandinavia, Germany, and France that this movement took root, not in Portugal, where it was a signal failure.

An excessively rigid supply response to changes in market conditions, especially abroad, was the second of these reasons and can also be linked in part to the inadequacy of human capital. Producers showed considerable difficulty in adjusting to variation in consumer preferences—as, for example, in the case of Portuguese table wines, which failed to evolve in harmony with the change of taste in Europe in the direction of beverages with a lower alcoholic content. The result was that they were unable to penetrate markets to the extent that others did, and this was a major cause of the unimpressive export growth during the late 1800s.

Although a trifle later than in many other countries, Portugal had its transportation revolution during this period too, in the shape of a railway network (3,000 kilometers) and a modern road system (8,500 kilometers). There can be no doubt that this constituted an impulse for growth, particularly as the situation prior to the 1850s had been very deficient in this respect. Until then there had been hardly any satisfactory roads built, even for military purposes, and, compared to other countries, Portugal suffered from a dearth of natural and improved waterways—for instance (after allowances for differences in size), it had one-tenth as many kilometers of rivers and canals as Belgium in 1850.

Transport modernization was not, however, the unmixed blessing it seemed initially to its champions and promoters. In spite of lower labor costs, the railways were not cheaper to build per kilometer and had none of the spinoffs for local industry which they had in the more advanced economies since nearly all the material used had to be imported. At the same time, their use was a good deal less efficient, whether this is measured in terms of revenue or tonnage of goods transported. There are several reasons for this, but two should be singled out. One was the lack of complementarily with the road network, which in turn did not cover the country adequately. The other was the low level of income of the population, which generated a comparatively low demand for efficient transport services and therefore assured a below optimal load for the railway network.

The upshot of all this was that this major investment represented a very heavy relative burden on the resources of this impoverished country, while the benefits it generated were far fewer than they might have been. Thus Portugal gained less than most other countries from one of the principal technological advances of the nineteenth century and lost thereby yet another fraction of the potential for growth then available. Indeed as Oliveira Martins put it, "When applied to a healthy body that is capable of bearing it, the railway is an instrument that increases its vigor; when applied to an enfeebled organism, it simply exhausts it" (cited in Justino).

Whether in agricultural or industrial activity, very low productivity was one of the distinguishing features of the nineteenth-century Portuguese economy. This meant that export markets were either closed or hard to penetrate for most sectors, which therefore had to rely on selling in the home market, where they enjoyed the protection afforded by one of the highest tariff barriers in Europe. They suffered, however, from the reduced size of this market, the result of the small size of the population, its low income per capita, and the poor integration of the national market caused by the deficiencies in the transport system. In particular, this placed Portuguese industry at a disadvantage and was a major reason for its less than brilliant performance prior to World War I.

One consequence of these limitations of scale was that certain important lines of manufacturing, particularly in metallurgy, could find no place in Portugal. In the case of steel production, for example, besides the debated question of the lack of raw materials, the home market simply did not consume enough to justify the existence of even a single Bessemer converter. In other already fairly significant sectors, like textiles and engineering, there were potential economies of scale to be reaped which eluded Portuguese firms because the limited market precluded either specialization in a few products, the mechanization of certain tasks, or even just the learning by experience which arises only with sufficiently long runs of production. A classic example is that of the Lisbon cotton mill which in 1891 was compelled to diversify to the extent of producing seventy-two different types of cloth and sixty-seven different varieties of thread because of the limitations of the market (Reis 1986).

The last of the circumstances which conspired to keep Portugal's growth below the European norm was the role of the state. We do not argue, of course, that everything under this heading was prejudicial. On the contrary, as a provider of a framework in which expanding economic activity could take place, the Portuguese state could hardly be faulted. Institutional and administrative development and modernization followed the normal course for nineteenth-century European countries, and the record here overall was positive. Legislation on land, labor, mining rights, patents, weights and measures, company formation, and the fiscal system did not lag behind other countries and was of a satisfactory standard. At the same time, the political and constitutional arrangements, which emerged after the 1830s civil war and were consolidated in the 1840s and 1850s, ensured an enviable degree of social tranquility and a polity remarkably free from the tensions which bedeviled many other European nations at this time.

While as a supplier of public goods such as order and justice the state's role can be deemed positive, the same can hardly be said of it as an agent which intervened directly in the economy and allocated resources among competing ends. The first weakness in this role was a product of the unusually high share of the national income that was collected as fiscal revenue and disbursed as public expenditure. That the Portuguese state should have been one of the largest spenders in Europe both in per capita terms and as a proportion of the country's output need not necessarily be viewed with disfavor. In fact, in Alexander Gerschenkron's view, given that this was a backward country with some catching up to do, public expenditure would constitute a highly desirable ingredient for a spurt of rapid growth. The trouble lay, however, in how these resources were administered. A recent and exhaustive survey of public finance (Mata) has shown that only 10 percent of public expenditure during the period 1852–1914 could be classed as investment, the remainder going to defense, administration, the service of the public debt, and so on. This means that the state "sterilized" a massive proportion of the funds at its disposal and indeed a considerable share of national resources, rather than channeling them toward reproductive ends and thus contributing to development.

A second problem was that throughout this period government finances were chronically in deficit. The persistent inability to raise sufficient revenue for its needs led in turn to a constant recourse by the state to public borrowing, both at home and abroad, something which made it a dominant client in the market for credit. Given its size as an economic agent and its less than impeccable creditworthiness, not only did the price it had to pay for these loans have to be high, but it drove up the cost of loans for private borrowers as well. In this "crowding out" effect by the state lies one of the chief reasons for Portugal being one of the countries of nineteenth-century Europe where capital costs were highest—the rate in Lisbon was always two or three points above Paris or London—and one of the more serious handicaps faced by the Portuguese economy and Portuguese entrepreneurs.

4

If it is true that Portuguese economic backwardness during the 1850–1913 period can be ascribed to the adverse factors outlined in the previous section, the question which naturally arises next is to what extent they changed or were even removed in the succeeding period to make possible the discernible improvement in economic performance that followed. The answer will not only shed light on the four or five decades leading up to the 1960s, but will also serve to check the validity of the interpretation given thus far for the difficulties experienced before World War I.

Although usually thought of as a given, the natural resource endowment of a country can change, as a result of either technological change or through the agency of human effort. In Portugal, both these sources now provided improvements to the earlier situation. One instance of this was the advent and rapid growth of hydroelectric power, which gave a significant value to much of the hitherto little used water resources of the country. In turn, this spelled the development of the electrical equipment industry between the 1930s and 1950s. A second case, already at the close of the period we are considering, is the emergence on the Portuguese coast of a new sector—ship-repairing—which took advantage of the country's location (also a part of its natural endowment) in connection with the development of long-distance maritime bulk haulage after World War II. Likewise, a long and sustained effort at tree planting, starting already in the late nineteenth century, eventually made Portugal into one of the most forested countries on the continent and provided the resource base for two important and rapidly growing export-oriented industries—paper pulp and resinous products.

In spite of this more favorable outlook, the changes just mentioned can hardly be held responsible for more than a small part of the acceleration in economic activity that took place in the first half of the twentieth century. The industries they favored, despite having high rates of growth and a high technological content, were still small and their contribution to gross national product was much less important than that of the traditional manufacturing sectors.

A similar conclusion can be drawn when we examine the colonial supply of raw materials, which came to play a significant role in provisioning certain branches of Portuguese industry between the advent of the Estado Novo and the 1960s and might seem also to deserve consideration as a windfall gain of the sort we have been looking at. Given that the commodities in question—chiefly cotton, cocoa, sugar, and hides—were freely available on the world market, except for short periods in times of war, this could be considered an advantage for metropolitan industry only if the latter were able to purchase them at below international prices. In fact, the years of the Estado Novo appear to have had mixed results from this point of view (Clarence-Smith). At times, colonial prices were favorable; at other times they were not. All in all, it is far from clear that Portugal gained much directly from the intensification in the use of natural and human resources in the colonies during the twentieth century.

One of the greatest barriers, from a natural resource point of view, was the lack of strategic minerals. Another was the poor quality of soil and climate which to a considerable extent blocked serious progress in agriculture (Pintado; Gomes et al.). Neither of these was surmountable by dint of either human effort or the passage of time, but this is not the case with the formation of human capital, in which much could and was done during the first half of the present century.

Although Portugal continued to be one of the least endowed countries of Europe in this respect, in fact down to the present, enormous strides were made in both elementary and more advanced forms of education. As a result, the literacy rate rose from about 25 percent of the population in 1900 to 60 percent in 1950. What is more important, however, is that it was fairly early on in the century—between 1910 and 1930—that the 30 percent mark was passed, the level above which, it has been argued by development economists, increases of this sort in human capital begin to make a significant contribution to the process of economic growth. A higher level of technology and capital per worker had an important influence too; it is difficult to think that this change was not instrumental in the productivity increases achieved by industrial labor after World War II (Neves and Confraria).

The diversification and expansion in the higher reaches of education was perhaps even more striking owing to the advances made in a field that had previously had an almost trivial quantitative expression. The Harrison and Myers index of human capital formation, which is a composite expression of the levels of secondary, technical, and university education, shows a sharp improvement, with the index rising from 0.4 to 1.3 points between 1900 and 1940 and increasing by another 300 percent in the following twenty years.*

For a country where nature has not been generous, human capital formation, if carried out to any serious extent, is one of the most cost-effective ways of improving economic performance. Even though Xavier Pintado still worried in the mid-1960s that the poor quality of labor was one of the greatest handicaps faced by Portuguese industry, in spite of its low wages, it is interesting to note that during the following decade, it was the labor-intensive industries that proved to be by far the most competitive internationally (Lains 1988). Likewise, it seems probable that the inordinate concentration of illiterates in the primary sector, as a result of rural-to-urban migration and the expansion of industrial employment, was one of the reasons for the abysmal performance of agriculture after 1945, a time when a good deal of technical improvement became available to this sector.

Until the international integration of the Portuguese economy in the 1960s, the problems of market scale and the weakness of this integration continued to be a drag on growth and development. Even as late as this, the country's 8 million inhabitants were rated as equivalent to only 2 million consumers from the European Free Trade Association (EFTA), which the country was now entering. One of the great difficulties for Portugal's development continued to be that the market was too small to sustain by itself the capital and intermediate goods industries which should complement its consumer goods industries in order to derive the maximum benefit from industrialization (Pintado).

Nevertheless, some changes for the good occurred during the decades prior to 1960. One of these was the very considerable roadbuilding effort undertaken by the Estado Novo, which raised the total number of kilometers from 14,000 in 1931 to 29,000 in 1952 (Medeiros). It is not yet clear whether until the 1950s this had much of an impact. Motor haulage by road did not develop much before

*The Harrison and Myers index, a very much used indicator in evaluating the impact of nonprimary education, is calculated as $I = Rs + Rt + Ru$, where Rs, Rt, and Ru are the enrollment figures relative to the appropriate age cohort for secondary, technical, and university education respectively.

the war, although the highway system made a difference in the carriage of passengers (Vieira). What could be argued, however, is that it made the rail network much more accessible to all agricultural producers, an economic benefit which needs to be quantified but which seems to have been considerable since by 1945 lack of integration in the market no longer appears to have been a problem (Gomes et al.). In fact, it is likely that this was one of the variables which accounts for the healthy performance of the agricultural sector during the interwar period, when it grew at something like 2.4 percent per year in real terms (calculation based on data in the *Anuario estatístico* for several years).

A second market improvement came via the strengthening of the "colonial pact," which under Salazarism gained a new lease on life. By means of quotas, tariff protection, and exchange regulation, metropolitan exports to the colonies rose to 25 percent of the country's total in the 1940s and 1950s, compared with 10 percent in 1926. The main beneficiary in this was the cotton textile industry, which was allowed to conquer the colonial markets completely. The importance of this trade, however, did not lie only in the fact that "the imperial market was the stepping stone to foreign markets" (Clarence-Smith). It was also one of the main sources for the high profits through which the industry subsequently financed its modernization in the 1940s and 1950s, thereby creating the competitive conditions which rendered possible the entry into the European and American markets later.

Other industries expanded their sales to the colonies, their only external outlet, particularly after the war, but for none of them did this have the importance it had for cotton textiles. This was not the only sector, however, to benefit from "captive markets" or politically induced demand. State programs for hydroelectric development and for railway modernization constituted a powerful stimulus for the growth of the cement, electrical equipment, and transport equipment industries. The significance of this resides in the fact that, if left to themselves, very likely these "modern" branches of manufacturing would not have achieved either the level of performance or the share of industrial output which they were able to attain by 1960. And without this, Portuguese industry would have been quite different—much more heavily weighted toward the "traditional industries" and with a probably slower long-run growth. Between the

1950s and 1970s, the sectors in question accounted for over a third of manufacturing growth.

The final but also the most complex of the analytical categories we are using here is the role of the state in the economic development of Portugal in the twentieth century. In part, this complexity has to do with the much expanded scope of this role in the economy. It also has to do with the controversy which still surrounds both the politics of the period and the intentions of the public figures and interest groups which were involved in the decisions taken.

The first point is that as a mechanism for allocating scarce resources, the state appears to have been a more positive influence in the first half of the present century than in the second half of the last century. Between the late 1920s and late 1950s public expenditure as a percentage of gross national product remained fairly stable and was not significantly greater than it was under the monarchy. However, the share of this that went into investment, including education, rose appreciably, from about 18 percent for the years 1891–1919 to 25 percent in the succeeding decades (Valério). The increase is obviously associated with the successive public investment plans which started in the mid-1930s and went on until the end of the Estado Novo, the full evaluation of which is yet to be made. Although criticized on various scores, it should be noted that by the early 1960s this effort had contributed to economic development by generating valuable externalities in three crucial areas in which private action would otherwise hardly be forthcoming: electricity, education, and communications (Pintado).

Thanks to fiscal orthodoxy and a strict monetary policy, the decades of the Estado Novo were not bedeviled by high interest rates and an excessive presence of the state in the capital market. Thus a second aspect of the state's role in the economy is whether the benefits accruing from such a policy outweighed the disadvantages caused by the restrictive stance that often became necessary. This is open to discussion, but the absence of a severe recession during the 1930s (Rosas 1986), when economic policies of this kind were perhaps tightest, suggests that at least for this period the harm done may not have eclipsed the favorable influence on private investment and overall growth.

Even without absorbing more resources than before, from World War I on, the state's impact on economic activity was also felt more as a result of the wide extension of its regulatory efforts, as indeed happened in all Western countries. With the advent of the Estado Novo and as a matter of both principle and policy, this interference increased and ended up being one of the hallmarks of this regime. Even during peacetime, prices for many products were set administratively, and the government determined how and by whom they were to be traded, both domestically and internationally. Industrial activity was subjected to strict licensing arrangements (Brito). In the labor market there was also a high degree of rigidity, particularly with respect to wage levels, since the government took control of the unions and employers organizations and exerted strong influence over collective bargaining.

In our present state of knowledge, it is extremely difficult to make a useful assessment of what these various influences can have meant for the long-run evolution of the economy. Prima facie, though, one would expect the overall impact to have been negative, if only because of the many distortions that the system introduced in the functioning of both factor and product markets, something which has been convincingly argued for the not dissimilar Spanish case (González). In the case of industry, it is evident that the *condicionamento industrial* policy reinforced oligopolistic structures and encouraged price distortions. In particular, it held back innovation and the introduction of new processes by favoring licenses for the extension of existing activities, rather than opening the field to newcomers.

Pricing policy enables us to touch on one of the most controversial and still far from settled issues of this period—namely, that of the Salazar regime's attitude toward agriculture. Contrary to what has been claimed until recently (Moura) and as far as the available evidence shows, the terms of trade between agriculture and industry were consistently favorable to the former (Mendes). If one is to evaluate this in purely economic terms, the conclusion is that this was not the best way to encourage efficiency in the economy since it held back the shift of resources from the primary to the secondary sectors and therefore slowed down the progress of productivity. Probably due to a misguided fear that a speedier exist of labor out of agriculture would cause unemployment because of the inability of industry to soak up the surplus manpower, the Estado Novo permitted agriculture to act as a brake on the economy.

By the late 1940s, it was becoming clear that the potential for growth in agriculture was practically exhausted. Yet, curiously, in the following two decades, the position was made worse by creating price incentives in favor of "traditional" crops instead of contributing toward the emergence of a better product mix with more emphasis on fruit, vegetables, and animal products.

In the view of authors such as Francisco Pereira de Moura and Miriam Halpern Pereira, when the model of industrialization under Salazar emerged after World War II, it involved "sacrificing" agriculture by imposing low prices on it, with a view to helping industrialists with cheap raw materials and cheap food. The latter would enable them to keep salaries low. As we have just noted, however, it was precisely the contrary that happened. What should be argued is that the protection of agriculture, particularly traditional agriculture, prevented industry from growing faster and from becoming internationally competitive sooner. During the 1930s, the artificial protection of primary production could have been justified by the need to reduce the balance-of-trade deficit, something which was indeed achieved as regards food products (Gomes). In the 1950s this was no longer a sufficient justification, and the problem was not that industry had to export because internal demand was so weak, but rather that it needed to penetrate foreign markets increasingly in order to raise its output and efficiency. If domestic demand for manufactures was weak, it may have been because agricultural prices were artificially high, not because they were kept low by government fiat.

Regulatory intervention may nevertheless have had some points in its favor. During the 1930s, for example, it might be said that the impact of the Depression on Portugal was attenuated by policies that boosted agricultural production and employment and that imposed collusion and market-sharing on industrial producers in order to prevent what was then known as "ruinous competition," thereby averting the collapse of large numbers of industrial firms. Later, protectionism for manufacturing, through tariffs and quotas, may have helped to create a favorable impetus for the development of "infant" sectors. The creation of highly protected markets—the state, the colonies, or simply the controlled domestic market—was intended to, and probably did, stimulate some capital formation. On the other hand, since this was an encouragement to productive inefficiency, it is necessary to know more—particularly about how the transition in the 1950s and 1960s of some of these industries from the home to the export market took place—before passing judgment on the matter.

It would be inappropriate to end this section without a word on what has been one of the great bones of contention with respect to the Estado Novo's economic policies: its failure to reform the agrarian structure of Portugal, held by so many to be not only socially unjust, but also economically pernicious. Leaving aside the first of these aspects (which belongs to another kind of speculation), on the second, two points can usefully be made. To begin with, if it is assumed that by carrying out this reform, agricultural performance would have been raised to the level of what was achieved in similarly endowed countries, such as Greece and Spain, where structural problems are not claimed to have required a major reform, this would have added no more than 0.4 percent to the rate of growth of GNP during the 1950s and 1960s. In other words, the available gain was an improvement of less than one-tenth of the achieved rate of growth.

The second point is to consider that any meaningful reform would have required a substantial allocation of resources for investment in agriculture; otherwise relatively little would be gained in productive terms. This would have had to be diverted from some other use, and the doubt this raises is whether, from the point of view of efficiency, this would have been the best course of action. Writing in the 1960s, Xavier Pintado expressed concern repeatedly about the low capitalization of manufacturing compared to other countries and the inappropriateness of channeling resources into slowly maturing investments—in irrigation, for example, where the capital/output ratio was high relative to industry.

A third question would have been the population movements that would have been associated with any far-reaching agrarian reform. In a capital-scarce country such as Portugal, this would have entailed a considerable allocation of capital—first to constitute, on a viable basis, the medium-sized farms that were the ideal outcome of the reform, and second to invest in the creation of urban infrastructure and housing, which would become necessary as part of the population of the minifundiary regions left the land for good. Admittedly, some people would have gone to northwest Europe to join the swarm of their countrymen already emigrating to those parts in search of a better life, but it is doubtful whether the capacity of those economies to absorb unskilled Portuguese labor could match all of the population surplus that these changes would have released. In a country which was also struggling to build up a much needed capital stock in manufacturing, it is debatable whether in economic terms agricultural reform would have been the best decision.

5

The first century of growth for the Portuguese economy, from the 1850s to the 1950s, left the country very much where it was initially relative to its neighbors—that is, as one of the poorest in Western Europe. During the first sixty years or so, real income per capita showed an upward trend, but the rate of growth was often lower than for most other countries. The following forty years made up for this relative decline and saw the latecomer begin to catch up, thanks to rates of economic growth during the interwar period and after World War II which were among the highest in this part of the world.

In the last few years, the study of Portugal's economic past has singled out a number of factors to explain the sluggish performance of 1850–1913. These include the poor resource endowment, the paucity of human capital, the inadequacy of the transport grid, the small size of the market, and (limited though this was) the negative impact of state intervention. The question we have sought to address here is what, in the course of the first half of the twentieth century, were the changes in this rather bleak picture that made the difference and rendered possible not only a higher rate of growth, but also one that was higher than those enjoyed by most countries surrounding Portugal.

Regarding natural resources, the position does not appear to have changed radically, although new technologies and certain political decisions helped to diminish the disadvantages on this score, particularly in the areas of forestry, energy, and naval engineering. More significant is the fact that by this time, Portugal was compensating for this shortcoming by vastly increasing its investment in human capital. This laid the basis for an industrialization process which accounted for sharp rises in output and productivity, even though the economy did not yet enjoy the benefit of easy access to large and rich foreign markets, something which was to come only around 1960.

In this light, the fostering of an internal market which was capable of absorbing the best part of this increased manufacturing production was of crucial importance, and the policies adopted by the state were a very positive contribution. A determined protection of the domestic market was one feature of this. Another was the program of infrastructural development, which converted an incomplete and therefore inadequate transport grid into a much more integrated system. The fact that much state investment was now in areas of fairly high technology and that procurement was firmly aimed at Portuguese producers also became a stimulus to the modernization of Portuguese industry and its preparation for the internationally oriented expansion which took place in the 1960s and early 1970s.

If state intervention had beneficial sides to it, there was a negative side too. Excessive regulation of markets for both products and productive factors must have been a serious source of inefficiency. Nowhere is this more evident than in the behavior of the terms of trade between agriculture and industry, which, owing to the choices made in the field of agricultural policy, helped to hold down resources in the low productivity primary sector instead of helping to funnel them into more promising areas. Direct intervention throughout the structure of manufacturing, in the shape of the condicionamento industrial policies, is another dramatic instance of the harmful consequences of the strongly regulatory propensity of the Salazar regime.

The twentieth century is unfortunately one of the least studied periods of Portugal's economic history. It is also one of those most pervaded by myths. Many of the ideas advanced here are consequently more in the nature of informed guesses than of conclusions built on a basis of solid historical facts. The main themes which concern those who seek to understand this reality, however, have not and are not likely to change much over time. As the country moves into the fourth decade of its second century of economic growth, the central problem is and will continue to be how to explain the persistently low level of income per capita and how to account for the chronic difficulty in catching up with the more advanced rest of

Western Europe. The answer to whether in the course of the next generation or so the Portuguese economy will successfully converge toward the standards of its neighbors is no doubt to be found in the analysis of present-day performance but, we would claim, not entirely. Without a firm grasp of the country's recent economic history and understanding of what has propelled and hindered long-run growth, the picture will never be complete.

REFERENCES

Baer, Werner, and Leite, António Nogueria. 1989. "The Peripheral Economy, Its Performance in Isolation and with Integration: The Case of Portugal." Mimeo.

Baklanoff, Eric. 1990. "Portugal's Political Economy, Old and New." In *Portugal: Ancient Country, New Democracy,* ed. K. Maxwell and M. Haltzel. Washington, D.C.

Bowman, M. J., and Anderson, C. A. 1963. "Concerning the Role of Education in Economic Development." In *Old Societies and New States,* ed. Clifford Geertz. Glencoe, Ill.

Brito, José Maria Brandão de. 1989. *A industrialização portuguesa no pos-guerra (1948–1965): O condicionamento industrial.* Lisbon.

Clarence-Smith, Gervase. 1985. *The Third Portuguese Empire, 1825–1975: A Study in Economic Imperialism.* Manchester.

Confraria, João, and Monteiro, Manuel Leite. N.d. "Industrialização e desindustrialização em Portugal." *Estudo,* no. 17. Departamento de Economia, FCH, Universidade Católica Portuguesa.

Crafts, N. R. 1984. "Patterns of Development in 19th-Century Europe." *Oxford Economic Papers* 36: 438–58.

O Estado Novo das origens ao fim da autarquia, 1926–1959. 1987. Lisbon.

Girão, José António. 1980. *Natureza do problema agrícola em Portugal (1950–1973): Uma perspectiva.* Oeiras.

Gomes, Mário de Azevedo, et al. 1944. "Traços principais da evolução da agricultura portuguesa entre as duas Guerras Mundiais." *Revista do Centro de Estudos Econômicos,* no. 1: 23–203.

González, Manuel-Jesús. 1979. *La economía política del franquismo (1940–1970): Dirigismo, mercado y planificación.* Madrid.

Justino, David. 1989. *A formação do espaço econômico nacional, 1810–1910.* Lisbon.

Lains, Pedro. 1986. "Exportações portuguesas, 1850–1913: A tese da dependência revisitada." *Análise social* 22: 381–419.

————. 1988. "Breve síntese sobre a industrialização recente de Portugal (1950–1985)." Mimeo.

————. 1990. *A evolução da agricultura e da indústria em Portugal (1850–1913): Uma interpretação quantitativa.* Lisbon.

Maddison, Angus. 1982. *Phases of Capitalist Development.* Oxford.

Mata, Maria Eugênia. 1986. "As finanças públicas portuguesas, da Regeneração a Primeira Guerra Mundial." Ph.D. dissertation, Lisbon Technical University.

Medeiros, Carlos Alberto. 1987. *Introdução à geografia de Portugal.* Lisbon.

Mendes, Fernando Ribeiro. 1983. "O sector agrícola, a economia nacional e as relações de troca intersectoriais (1950–1980)." *Análise social* 19: 421–38.

Moura, Francisco Pereira de, et al. 1954. "Estrutura da economia portuguesa." *Revista do Centro de Estudos do INE*, no. 14: 7–219.

————. 1973. *Por onde vai a economia portuguesa?* Lisbon.

Neves, João César das, and Confraria, João. 1988. "The Portuguese Economy 1948–1985: A Brief Survey." Mimeo.

Nunes, Anabela, and Valério, Nuno. 1983. "A Lei da Reconstituição Econômica e a sua execução: Um exemplo dos projectos e realizações da política econômica do Estado Novo." *Estudos de economia* 3: 331–59.

Nunes, Anabela; Valério, Nuno; and Mata, Maria Eugênia. 1990. "Portuguese Economic Growth, 1833–1985." *Journal of European Economic History* 18: 291–330.

Pereira, A. Ramos. 1956. "O mercado monetário em Portugal no período de 1931–1955." *Estudos de economia* 9: 5–34.

Pereira, Miriam Halpern. 1979. *Política e economia, Portugal nos séculos XIX e XX.* Lisbon.

Pintado, V. Xavier. 1964. *Structure and Growth of the Portuguese Economy.* Geneva.

Reis, Jaime. 1984. "O atraso econômico português em perspectiva histórica (1860–1913)." *Análise social* 20: 7–28.

————. 1986. "Industrial Development in a Late and Slow Developer: Portugal, 1870–1913." *Rivista di storia economica* 3: 67–90.

Rosas, Fernando. 1986. *O Estado Novo nos anos trinta (1928–1938).* Lisbon.

————. 1990. *Portugal entre a paz e a guerra (1939–1945).* Lisbon.

Schwartzman, Kathleen. 1989. *The Social Origins of Democratic Collapse: The First Portuguese Republic in the Global Economy.* Lawrence, Kansas.

Valério, Nuno. 1986. "The Role of the Government in Portuguese Economic Growth, 1851–1939." *Estudos de economia* 7: 63–70.

Vieira, António Lopes. 1980. "Os transportes rodoviários em Portugal, 1900–1940." *Revista de historia econômica e social*, no. 5: 57–94.

III

The Culture

NATIONAL IDENTITY IN TRANSITION

Manuel Braga da Cruz

Portugal is a country without any obvious or serious problems of national identity or unity. With the oldest borders in Europe, if not indeed in the world, and with its centuries-long combination of state and nation, Portugal is one of the few real nation-states.[1] With no inter-ethnic problems, no linguistic pluralisms, and no cultural conflicts, Portugal's national unity is undergoing no visible, or even apparent, crisis. However, several questions have recently been put to the Portuguese with regard to their identity. This is not so much because of any "collective personality" crisis or of any doubt about their origins or nature, but mainly due to questions about Portugal's place in the world, arising from the profound changes which took place during the recent political transition. The question that the Portuguese have been asking themselves more and more insistently is not *what they are* but *where they are* and *why they are* or, in other words, what their position and role are in the international order.

1. THE DEMOCRATIC TRANSITION AS A EUROPEAN AND REGIONAL TRANSITION

The transition to democracy in Portugal meant not only the transition from an authoritarian to a democratic regime, but also, and perhaps above all, the transition from overseas integration to European integration and with it the transition from a nationalism which claimed to be multiracial and pluri-continental to a regionalizing Europeanism. Portugal, in fact, passed not only from one form of state to another—from an authoritarian, centralized state to a democratic, decentralized one—but also from one system of external references to another—from the overseas system to the European one.

This was, without doubt, the most decisive aspect of the changes that took place in Portugal because while democracy had already been tried before, what had never been either tried or sought was complete and definitive decolonization.

In Portuguese contemporary political history the problem of the nation has been traditionally a response to the progressive decolonization which began at the beginning of the nineteenth century with the independence of Brazil. The more modern Portuguese nationalism of the nineteenth and twentieth centuries has been a nationalism with deep colonial roots.

Liberal nationalism—the first excitement and the first rising of the nation—was a product of the loss of Brazil and the crisis which accompanied it.[2] Republican nationalism arose from the loss of the "Mapa-Cor-de-Rosa" and the British ultimatum of 1891 and was inspired by the theories of decadence of the peninsular peoples.[3] It was reinforced in the theaters of the 1914–18 war, in which Portugal's participation was justified by the republican government precisely in the name of the defense of Portugal's colonies threatened by the German imperial appetite.

The nationalism of the New State was, in the same way, a nationalism deeply determined by the colonial situation. The overseas colonies were the be-all and end-all of Salazarism.[4] It was the need for stability in colonial government, particularly felt by the military in the African campaigns at the turn of the century, that contributed greatly to the formulation of the demand for greater authority in metropolitan government. As proof of this, we have the fact that the first constitutional act of the new regime which emerged after 28 May 1926 was the passing in 1930 of the Colonial Act even before the "plebiscitization" of the constitution itself in 1933. The empire's chronological priority, in fact, became a political priority, almost the *raison d'être* of the regime itself, which did not survive decolonization.

It would have been reasonable to anticipate that after the completion of decolonization, which this time was so violent and irreversible, the question of the nation would have arisen again—not as a trauma, since the decolonization was no longer considered an amputation but was now viewed almost as a fatality, but as a new question of position in the external system.

There were two basic, conflicting types of decolonization: decolonization by integration, tried in the 1950s but thwarted in the 1960s mainly by the outbreak of a state of war, and decolonization by independence, which would eventually prevail. Contrary to the colonial imperial concept introduced in 1930 which revered the figure of the native population, depriving the natives of citizenship until they were assimilated culturally and politically, the integrationalist concept abolished the distinction between citizens and subjects and supported the idea of a pluri-continental, multiracial nation, eliminating administrative and legislative barriers between races and politically and economically integrating the territories, with respect for each one's autonomy. In Salazar's words, it was a question of creating a "composite Nation" or "certainly a strange, complex Nation scattered over the seven parts of the world."[5]

This idea of civilizational integration was accompanied by the aim of economic integration that took the form of the Portuguese Single Market (PSM), created in 1961 with a view not only to the free circulation of goods, people, and capital, but also a new system of inter-regional payments within the Portuguese area. The creation of the PSM and Portugal's entry into the European Free Trade Association (EFTA) at the same time constituted an alternative to the invitation received, and refused, to join the European Economic Community (EC). This refusal was based, on one hand, on the constitutional impossibility of accepting supranational authority and jurisdiction and, on the other hand, on the incompatibility between a policy of overseas integration and a policy of European integration. It was the desire to maintain the overseas territories under Portuguese sovereignty that led both to the creation of the PSM and to the choice of EFTA rather than the EC in terms of economic relations with Europe. EFTA was an intermediate solution between these two organizations, a compromise between them.

The problem of external integration, however, arose more and more, and the dilemma was: Africa or Europe? Portugal's integration with Africa (because this is basically what overseas integration meant) turned out to be infeasible in the face of the growing pressure and strength of European integration. Emigration and trade began to define, independently, in a disorganized but categorical manner, a tendency toward favoring integration in Europe. With the increase in the migratory flow toward Europe there was a corresponding decrease in migratory movement overseas, which was also affected by the growing militarization of the white population caused by the state of war. The collapse of overseas integration meant the undeniable confirmation of European integration.

The transition, however, was not just from an overseas to a European vision of national integration; it was also to a new conception of the state—that is, from an authoritarian concentration to a democratic decentralization. The new constitution of 1976 brought in political regionalization and administrative decentralization with the figure of the "Unitary State," which respected the autonomy of the local authorities and decentralized public administration.[6]

An important innovation in this decentralizing concept was the introduction of the regionalistic point of view with the figure of the region—both the autonomous region and the administrative region. The idea of autonomous regions had, in fact, already been accepted but not put into practice in the 1971 revision of the 1933 constitution for the "overseas provinces," which could even "be designated States . . . when the progress of their social milieu and the complexity of their administration justify this honorary title."[7] This was the recognition of what Marcelo Caetano classified as a "decentralized unitary state," which was an intermediate term between the unitary state and the federal state.[8] This regionalism involved its own autonomy of government, administration, and economic life for each regional state. Thus progress was being made toward political decentralization, and not only from the administrative point of view, with the creation of their own governmental and legislative organs, while federalism was rejected. Federalism was exactly what General Spínola defended in the book that would spark off the operations which led to the events of 25 April.[9] The collapse of the regime, however, did not allow this regionalism to come into force, and it happened only with the new democratic order.

In the constitution of 1976, the figure of the autonomous region was reserved for the Azores and Madeira. It implied the existence of political and administrative statutes that established the regions' own government organs (parliament and government) with their respective legislative, executive, and fiscal capacity. As far as the autonomy of the administrative regions was concerned, they were attributed only the management of public services and the coordination and support of municipal activities, as well as regional planning, for which they have a Regional Assembly and Council with administrative but no legislative or executive powers.

Autonomy and regionalization first satisfied the old ambitions of the island populations and, second, the increasing demand for administrative decentralization. However, if autonomy was attained rapidly, as was done in order to forestall an incipient separatism, regionalization has not gone beyond a mere constitutional intention. It was promised by successive electoral and governmental programs but turned out to be complex and difficult to put into practice. All parties are in favor of it, but none of those which have so far been in government have put it into practice or even shown any intention of doing so.

There have been countless forms of resistance to regionalization, and not the least of them is that arising from the contradictory political reaffirmation of an old, centralizing administrative category—the district. This reinforcement of the district arises above all from the acceptance of the old district electoral constituency, inherited from the old regime, for the mainland electoral circles. With the organization of the electoral circles based on the districts, and in spite of the fact that the members of parliament represent not the circles by which they are elected but the whole country, party organization itself was based on the districts.[10] Thus resistance to the substitution of the district by the region arises from the actual geographical organizational structure of the parties, based on the district.

2. EUROPEAN INTEGRATION AND THE NATION-STATE CRISIS

European integration, with its new federalistic and regionalistic conceptions of the state, has been threatening the traditional system of European states. The sovereignty of the nation-state has been undergoing progressive erosion from above and from below by "Europeanism" and "regionalization," which have given rise to what could be called limited sovereignty on the one hand and shared sovereignty on the other. The nation-state, as Daniel Bell has observed, is becoming too small for the big problems and too big for the small problems of postindustrial society.[11]

European integration has been causing a progressive crisis in the European system of nation-states because it has increasingly questioned the notion of sovereignty on which it is based. The European union, which many upheld as simply a Europe of motherlands or nations, is today seen more and more as a Europe of citizens. The nation is surrendering its place to the citizen as the basic unit for the political construction of Europe and is thus heading for the constitution of a new European sovereignty and not merely of a Europe of sovereignties.

As Ernest Gellner has pointed out, the identification of the state with the nation—that is, of the state with a homogeneous culture (or homogenized by education of the masses) brought about by the beginning of the industrialization of society and the expansion of the systems of representative government—did not arise for merely political reasons, but was also caused by economic demands, particularly the need to create national markets.[12] The nation-state, from this point of view, was also a political requirement of the markets of the industrial societies. Cultural unification, of which linguistic unification was one of the most visible expressions, was a requirement of market expansion and the social division of work.

Similarly the creation of the European common market has established a need for European common political unity. The national framework, more and more outmoded in terms of the European market, is also growing out of date in political terms. Economic internationalization has been accompanied by the internationalization of the problems of military defense and the protection of the environment and also by the growing internationalization of public opinion and the law.

On a par with the demands of internationalization, we also have those of regionalization—i.e., political decentralization. The traditional sectoral logic of government organization is combining with the new regional logic. We are also passing more and more from sectoral policies, structured vertically, to regional, horizontally integrated policies. Government used, above all, to be a question of keeping sectors under control and placing them in their correct order of priority in economic and social terms. Nowadays it also implies a capability to homogenize regions internally and to eradicate disparities between them, for both market purposes and political and cultural reasons.

Regionalization is required not only for *reasons of economic and social efficiency*, but also for reasons of strategy of social mobilization and political participation—i.e., for *reasons of legitimacy*. A centralized Europe would obviously be a weakened Europe. Only a regional Europe, mentioned more and more nowadays, can guarantee not only the degree of efficiency but also the degree of participation that national competition and cooperation imply. Therefore, uniting, in European terms, also means regionalizing.

Regionalizing means not only recognizing the diversity of nation-states, in some cases even the national diversity of the states, but also agreeing to go beyond the limits of the European nation-states' borders. The regions are sometimes not confined to the limits of the state but go beyond them. The existence of the so-called *trans-frontier regions* goes to show that national frontiers do not always coincide with geoclimatic, social, or cultural limits of the nation-state.

Regionalism is beginning to be viewed as a new "patriotism." Thus there is a certain rivalry between the nation and the region with the growing transfer of the concept of motherland nation to the region. This "regional patriotism" arises as a logical consequence of growing cosmopolitanization. The more open to the world, the more cosmopolitan, the greater the need for the feeling of regional belonging, of local roots. The solidity of the "great space" seems to be rooted in the intensity of belonging to the "small space." From this point of view, regionalism is no longer considered a symptom of social and cultural underdevelopment and is now thought of as a postmodern sentiment, a requirement of participation, a counterpoise and reaction to world standardization brought about by the development of scientific civilization.[13]

3. NATIONAL IDENTITY IN THE TRANSITION

A recent opinion poll showed, on one hand, that the Portuguese in relation to other Europeans have considerably greater feelings of national pride and, on the other hand, show a national self-esteem above that of a number of other nations in the world.[14] (See Tables 1 and 2.) This seems to prove the general impression, already noted by qualified observers, that Portugal is not undergoing a national identity crisis in either cognitive or affective terms.[15]

Strangely, the degree of national pride varies in inverse proportion to social position: the lower the position, the greater the pride in being Portuguese; the higher the position, the less the pride. The

Table 1

National Pride
(Percent)

Level of Pride	Portugal	Spain	Italy	Europe
Considerable	68.6%	49.0%	41.0%	38.0%
Some	21.3	34.0	39.0	38.0
Little	8.1	8.0	- -	- -
None	1.4	4.0	- -	- -
Other	- -	- -	20.0	24.0
No answer	0.6	5.0	- -	- -

Sources: For Portugal—M. Braga da Cruz, "Nacionalismo e patriotismo"; for Spain, Italy, and Europe—Francisco Andrés Orizo, *España, entre la apatía y el cambio social. Una encuesta sobre el sistema europeo de valores: El caso español* (Madrid, 1983), pp. 249–50.

Table 2

Self-Esteem
(Percentage of Those Saying the Nation They Most Respect Is Their Own)

Country	Percent
Portugal	64.8%
United States	59.0
Canada	35.0
Great Britain	33.0
France	26.0
Italy	15.0
West Germany	12.0

Sources: For Portugal—M. Braga da Cruz, "Nacionalismo e patriotismo"; for other countries—Morris Janowitz, *The Reconstruction of Patriotism: Education for Civic Consciousness* (Chicago, 1984), p. 193.

lack of national pride is greatest in young people, increases with the degree of education, and is greatest in the most urbanized regions of Oporto and Lisbon and also in the Atlantic regions of the Azores and Madeira. In contrast, pride increases in elderly people and is greatest in rural areas and inland in the north of the country.

This "national feeling" seems to vary with political and religious influence: being a Catholic and right wing favors the existence of national pride, while it decreases among non-Catholics and the left wing. (See Tables 3 and 4.) However, this strong nationalistic feeling coexists with considerable regionalistic feeling as well. Unlike other Europeans, the Portuguese are more regionalistic than nationalistic or, in particular, cosmopolitan. On being questioned about their geopolitical identity—i.e., when asked about the unit to which they felt they belonged "first and foremost"—most Portuguese (53.7 percent) preferred the region as opposed to their place of birth, country, Europe, or the world. (See Table 5.) This regionalistic feeling, like the nationalistic feeling, seems to vary with certain social factors: it increases with age and rurality and decreases with a higher level of education and social position. In the same way, cosmopolitanism seems to be strengthened by education, upward social mobility, secularization, and a left-wing position.

In this light, while cosmopolitanism seems more a result of modernizing factors (such as social mobility, urbanization, secularization, education, and youth), nationalism and regionalism are

Table 3

National Pride and Political Position
(Percent)

	Right	Center Right	Center Left	Left
Pride	94.2%	92.0%	87.4%	84.7%
No pride	5.4	8.0	12.4	15.3

Source: M. Braga da Cruz, "Nacionalismo e patriotismo."

Table 4

National Pride and Religious Position
(Percent)

	Practicing Catholics	Nonpracticing Catholics	Others
Pride	94.3%	87.8%	77.2%
No pride	4.7	12.0	20.0

Source: M. Braga da Cruz, "Nacionalismo e patriotismo."

Table 5

Feelings of Geopolitical Identity
(Percent)

Unit of First and Foremost Belonging	Portugal	Spain	Italy	Europe
Place or city	21.8%	40.0%	44.0%	42.0%
Region	53.7	17.0	9.0	15.0
Country in general	18.0	34.0	24.0	27.0
Europe	1.7	2.0	4.0	4.0
Whole world	3.9	6.0	16.0	9.0
Don't know	0.3	0.2	5.0	4.0
No answer	0.6	--	--	--

Sources: For Portugal—M. Braga da Cruz, "Nacionalismo e patriotismo"; for Italy, Spain, and Europe—Francisco Andrés Orizo, *España, entre la apatía y el cambio social.*

more dependent on factors which reflect traditional social milieux (like rurality, living inland, religiosity, and old age). This seems to confirm Ronald Inglehart's theory that the emergence of a cosmopolitan political identity is facilitated by a change in values toward postmaterialism since the raison d'être of nationalism and the nation-state was profoundly materialistic—namely, the maintenance of order and the safety of people and goods.[16] Everything points to a subnational regionalism—i.e., a regionalism that, in a continuum between parochialism and cosmopolitanism, is situated in the middle between parochialism and nationalism—as opposed to a regionalism arising from intense internationalization.

The same study also showed that apart from a strong feeling of national and regional identity, the Portuguese show a great attachment to their sovereignty and national unity. In effect, most Portuguese accept European integration (65.8 percent), but a great majority (81.8 percent) also believe that it is the Portuguese, not a European, government that should have the last word. Thus for the majority (70.1 percent) European integration should not threaten national independence.

In the same way, the majority of Portuguese (56.6 percent) believe that regionalization will not constitute a significant threat to national unity. The regional autonomy of the Azores and Madeira is considered adequate and positive by most Portuguese (51.8 percent), while 21.2 percent think that it is still not enough and is a step toward greater autonomy of the islands in the future.

Support for European integration grows with the level of education and social position and also with youth. In the same way, the fear that regionalization will affect national unity seems to decrease with the level of education and social position. This shows that both European integration and regionalization seem to be favored by modernizing factors. These factors, however, do not seem to give rise to any weakening in the attachment to national sovereignty. The defense of both European integration and regionalization coexists with the reinforcement of capacities traditionally attributed to national government. When asked who should have power of decision in a number of matters which are traditionally ascribed to national sovereignty (questions of defense, policy on energy and finance, judicial and maritime matters), most Portuguese felt that the power of decision should continue to belong to national governments. However, the opinions of people from the Azores and Madeira differ significantly on this point. While most Madeirans tend to attribute these capacities to the regional government, the Azoreans, although in smaller percentages than people from the mainland, favor the capacity of the central government, except when it comes to the exploitation of territorial waters and seabeds, which they attribute to the regional government. The higher degree of autonomism of the Madeirans is also confirmed by the higher percentage in the Azores (10.9 percent) than in Madeira (3.4 percent) of those who feel that their present autonomy is excessive, and by the higher percentage in Madeira (38.3 percent) than in the Azores (10.9 percent) of those who feel that their present autonomy is insufficient.

4. CONCLUSION

We can conclude that today the Portuguese view European integration and the prospect of regionalization with a strong sense of national identity, a consistent national unity, and a deep sense of national sovereignty. The strength of these feelings and opinions has deep roots and social and historic reasons. Neither of the new prospects, internationalization or regionalization, seems to have weakened these national feelings, which in Portugal arise from strong traditional factors and which, for this reason, may later undergo changes with the growing modernization of Portuguese society.

NOTES

1. Orlando Ribeiro, *A formação de Portugal* (Lisbon, 1987), p. 21; Juan Linz, "The Portuguese Constitution in Comparative Perspective," *Camões Centre Quarterly* 2, 1 and 2, 2 (Spring and Summer 1990): 9.

2. Valentim Alexandre, "Os sentidos do império: Questão nacional e questão colonial na crise do antigo regime português" (Lisbon, 1988); mimeo.

3. Teófilo de Braga, *História das ideias republicanas em Portugal* (Lisbon, 1880); Baptista Teles, *Do ultimatum ao 31 de Janeiro, Esboço da história política* (Oporto, 1905).

4. Manuel Braga da Cruz, *O partido e o estado no salazarismo* (Lisbon, 1988).

5. António de Oliveira Salazar, *Discursos* (Coimbra, 1966), vol. 6, p. 94.

6. *Constituição da República Portuguesa*, Art. 6.

7. *Revisão Constitucional 1971: Textos e documentos* (Lisbon, 1971), Art. 133.

8. Marcelo Caetano, *Manual da ciência política e direito constitucional* (Coimbra, 1963).

9. António de Spínola, *Portugal e o futuro* (Lisbon, 1974).

10. *Constituição da República Portuguesa*, Art. 152, 3.

11. Daniel Bell, "Estão as nações preparadas para enfrentar problemas globais?" *AIP Informação*, no. 2 (February 1989).

12. Ernest Gellner, *Nations and Nationalism* (Oxford, 1983).

13. On the relationship between the parochial-cosmopolitan continuum and development, see Gabriel Almond and Sydney Verba, *The Civic Culture* (Princeton, 1963).

14. Manuel Braga da Cruz, "Nacionalismo e patriotismo na sociedade portuguesa actual: Alguns resultados de um inquérito," *Nação e defesa*, no. 59 (1989).

15. Eduardo Lourenço: *O labirinto da saudade. Psicanálise mítica do destino português* (Lisbon, 1978); *Nós e a Europa ou as duas razões* (Lisbon, 1988).

16. Ronald Inglehart, *The Silent Revolution* (Princeton, 1977).

BELLES LETTRES, REVOLUTIONARY PROMISE, AND REALITY

João Camilo dos Santos

1

One of the forms of expression that man's dissatisfaction with his existence and with the world takes is literature. Discontented, aspiring to some other destiny, men write, leaving the signs of their discontent engraved on paper. All important literary works speak of a maladjustment, minimal in some cases, fundamental or tragic in others, between man's condition and the destiny of which he judges himself worthy or capable.

Discontentment and the aspiration to another form of existence, as they are expressed in literature, are simultaneously the symptom of ontological unease and a form of criticism and protest in relation to social structures. In certain time periods and in certain writers the former of the two aspects predominates; in other periods and other authors, the latter takes precedence.

The poetry from the romantic age and the literary movements into which it rapidly metamorphosed, although they are at the same time a form of revolt against the established bourgeois social order and the recovery of individual liberty in the face of the corrupted ideals of the French Revolution, seem to express, above all, an individual ontological unease that announces the moral solitude that we find later in the works of Kafka and the French existentialists, such as in *La Nausée* (1938), by Jean-Paul Sartre, or in *L'Etranger* (1942), by Albert Camus. The nineteenth-century realist and naturalist novel, with its predominantly social preoccupations, shows us on the other hand that the individual can put the blame for his ontological unease (now transformed into "social unease") and his dissatisfaction on the socioeconomic structures and the political powers. Realism and naturalism principally insist on the social reasons of our discontent and lack of happiness, in the same way that romanticism predominantly insisted on the individual reasons and manifestations of that existential unease. In the first case we have a literature concerned with "we"; in the second case, a literature focused on "I."

It is difficult, and somewhat artificial, to separate an individual's ill-being from the historical and social reasons which in one way or another have provoked his condition. However, it is an undeniable fact that certain literary currents and certain authors give greater weight to the individual and purely ontological aspect of their discontentment with life and themselves, while other literary currents and authors pay much more attention to sociohistorical conditions.

2

Twentieth-century Portuguese literature has been marked by two important literary movements. The first, called Orpheu, after the name of a literary magazine, occurred around 1915. The second movement, Neo-realism, began near the end of the 1930s. Orpheu, a movement linked to such literary names as Fernando Pessoa, Mário de Sá-Carneiro, and Almada Negreiros, has been considered above all as an "aesthetic revolution." Nevertheless, that revolution (apparently just aesthetic), which had its most visible consequences and results in the area of poetry, in reality even today continues to be the most important revolution that, from many points of view, came about in Portuguese society since the generation of Eça de Queirós and Antero de Quental in the nineteenth century. The generation of Eça and Antero de Quental found its truest voice and finest achievements in the novel; Antero de Quental's poetry, for example, aged hopelessly, while Eça's novels still seem modern to us, demanding new and ever deeper interpretations.

Our idea of modernity, in the most interesting and broadest sense—that is, not only aesthetic, but also ideological—is an idea whose roots must be sought in the generation of Orpheu. Why? Certainly because beneath the guise of a simple aesthetic revolution, Orpheu accomplished an approximation of literature to real life, already considered indispensable, but which was felt to be revolutionary. By the same token, Orpheu led to a provocative rediscovery of everyday, common, normal forms of language, thought, and feeling. Orpheu took the expression of Every Man and yet dressed it in literary dignity. On the other hand, Orpheu's poets, Fernando Pessoa and Mário de Sá-Carneiro in particular, are the ones who herald the essential philosophical questions that confront today's man. They are also the writers who most clearly and tragically formulated the problem of the disintegration of the self. Literature was not, for Orpheu, a futile exercise in gratuitous provocation or aesthetic virtuosity; nor was it reduced to the adoption of a superficially showy behavior. Rather, it was a way to seriously and profoundly question self and existence.

Neo-realism, in the closing years of the 1930s, is oriented, in practice, and contrary to Orpheu, not so much by aesthetics as by an ideology: Marxism. Neo-realism aspired deeply and with conviction to socialist revolution, and it was only out of fear of censorship that the movement adopted in Portugal the euphemistic name by which it is known.

I hope that I do not shock anyone by affirming, after what I have just expounded, that Orpheu and Neo-realism seem to me today to be the two most important forms and manifestations of revolt against the social structures and power that twentieth-century Portuguese literature has taken.

3

What would Fernando Pessoa have thought about the 1974 April "revolution"? What did the neo-realists think about that revolution? If I ask these questions, it is to emphasize that in the twentieth century it was these two organized movements and their followers who aspired most openly and systematically, and with the greatest persistence, to a true and profound transformation in lifestyle, in ways of thinking and feeling, and consequently in ways of speaking and writing within Portugal. At first glance, Orpheu does not seem to have preoccupied itself directly with class struggle, preferring to situate its fight predominantly in the ontological field, and acting in the name of intelligence and good sense (although not in the name of bourgeois good sense, which appeared exactly like the lack of good sense) and in the name of modernity also. Neo-realism, however, never was, in general terms, aesthetically on the same level as the ideological ambitions of the movement. On the contrary, Neo-realism, especially in its polemical and more doctrinaire initial phase, represented an evident step backward, not only in relation to Orpheu, but even in relation to the nineteenth-century novel, as well as to some twentieth-century novelists. Nevertheless, I do not think that this invalidates the perspective that I have adopted. Orpheu, in its predominantly aesthetic tendencies, and Neo-realism in its principally ideological tendencies, are the movements in which Portugal's "revolutionary" aspirations have been most clearly delineated in the twentieth century.

In order to respond to the first question that I posed above, I would say that I do not know if Fernando Pessoa would have allowed himself to be misled by hope in April 1974. Revolutions, the very word revolution, are mythical entities. We hear the word or the news, and we imagine that everything is going to change immediately, abruptly. We imagine that everything that is wrong will be righted; finally we are all going to be happy, with the money, the home, the car we want; perhaps we will even find the maturity or the romantic fulfillment that until now we have been denied. Revolution announces, as Mircea Eliade, the Romanian historian, would say, a new beginning of the world. And we can easily imagine that, everything being new, pure, virginal, nothing will remain outside of our grasp. Why wouldn't our wants and needs be fulfilled? If it were not to satisfy our desire, why did the revolution take place?

The misunderstanding and disillusionment begin immediately. Revolutions not only do not make good on their promises right away; they never bring about the changes that it seems they promised. This is because what revolutions seem to promise is the satisfaction of what each individual holds in his or her imagination. But, as we all know, each person's real life and imagination have different needs and hopes, which are impossible to fulfill completely. The revolution that Major Otelo Saraiva de Carvalho was trying to carry out was not, as was verified later, the same one that Mario Soares or Álvaro Cunhal desired. By the same token, the revolution sought by the neo-realists had nothing to do with the revolution conceived by the poet Sofia de Mello Breyner. Thus what happened was that the "revolution" of 25 April 1974 that had been lived in a mythic and poetic fashion by so many (Portuguese as well as foreigners who went to Portugal to contemplate the "great and unexpected spectacle") in reality soon showed its true colors. Portugal's revolution, apparently an event so full of promise, very soon showed itself to be what all revolutions are: a power struggle. Some important changes occurred in the country, particularly with respect to the functioning of political institutions, social security, and land reform—although many gains were later lost. But in the last analysis, postrevolution Portugal was limited to reclaiming its place among the other European countries, and the principal gain of the April 1974 revolution was institutional democracy. Consenting to democracy was a way for the Portuguese to be reminded of something they had perhaps forgotten during the festive days of the "revolution": that our daily existence is at the mercy of political will and decisions, which in turn are slaves to social and economic conditions, not only on a national and European level, but also on a global level.

As we have already understood, there will never be a revolution that completely satisfies us. The Portuguese revolution, with its touch of obviously irrational Sebastianist messianism, certainly forced the Portuguese to understand that everything has human limits (historical, economic, social limits) which are difficult to overcome. Even the so-called revolutions.

4

What can the neo-realists have been thinking, what did they think, with regard to the remains of their transformed ideals, or with regard to the 1974 revolution? As I already mentioned, the neo-realists had, during more than thirty years, stoically aspired to a true political revolution in Portugal. The history of Neo-realism is partially confused with the history of the antifascist resistence and the history of the movement against the Salazar dictatorship. The social criticism of novelists such as Almeida Garrett, Alexandre Herculano, Camilo Castelo Branco, and Eça de Queirós in the nineteenth century, and then of Aquilino Ribeiro and Ferreira de Castro in the twentieth, was the ideal and the general orientation that the neo-realists picked up and continued. Consequently, the neo-realists should have been satisfied with the revolution, which in a certain sense confirmed the hopes that had encouraged them and which could be seen as a reward for their persistence and their efforts.

What actually happened is that with the novel *Finisterra* (1978), by Carlos de Oliveira, didactic Neo-realism, with its mythic and naive hope in the idea that a popular revolution would miraculously happen and transform Portuguese society, seemed definitively to end. And it is as if with this difficult work, Carlos de Oliveira (who in his youth had published a rather inflammatory novel entitled *Alcateia* [1944], calling for popular revolt) had finally attained a possible synthesis between the aesthetic ideals of Orpheu and the political ideals of Neo-realism. However, another young Portuguese writer, Almeida Faria, had already begun to attain this same synthesis with the publication in 1965 of the novel *A paixão*. In Almeida Faria's work, as in the works of William Faulkner, the treatment of social problems, and even the longing for revolution, did not hinder the in-depth examination of the complexity of the characters' personal life, nor did it impede the attainment of a surprising aesthetic perfection and solid construction.

In 1979 Vergílio Ferreira published *Signo sinal* and Augusto Abelaira published *Sem tecto entre ruínas*. Vergílio Ferreira had started out belonging to the neo-realist movement, but rather early on he had stopped believing that history and economics can satisfactorily explain existential problems, and he had opted for the existentialist novel with the publication of his *Mudança* in 1949. Augusto Abelaira, more attracted in the beginning by the intimist literature that Presença (a movement that arose around 1927 in Coimbra) was championing, soon turned to Neo-realism and remained faithful to the ideals of this movement. His urban novels had, however, always distinguished him from the other neo-realist writers, essentially because these works depicted a middle class of unsatisfied intellectuals whose notoriously bad social conscience did not preclude their interest in artistic problems, nor did it preclude their giving great importance to interpersonal relationships and love. For Abelaira, individual accomplishment never boiled down to the simple resolution of political and economic problems; nevertheless, he always accorded these factors the enormous importance that they merited.

The two novels published in 1979 by Vergílio Ferreira and Augusto Abelaira, two of the principal names in contemporary Portuguese fiction, denounce the "damaging effects" of ideology and make up, along with Carlos de Oliveira's *Finisterra*, what can be considered a kind of officially marked end to Neo-realism as a dominant literary movement. Even the rather anachronistic publication in 1980 of José Saramago's neo-realist novel *Levantado do chão*, cannot negate this affirmation.

In his novel, which according to the author was planned before April 1974, Vergílio Ferreira cynically and harshly calls into question the revolutionary ideal. In the eyes of Vergílio Ferreira's narrator-character, versed not only in history, but also in the reality he is living and contemplating, ideology is viewed as demagogic and harmful, and so the disappointed protagonist prefers to distance himself from the collective projects which he considers to be hysterical forms of struggle for power. In his eyes the revolutionary ideal was limited to substituting for the Christian ideal of salvation, an ideal which had disappeared after the death of God. Men always envision their happiness in the future, and this is revolting to the protagonist of *Signo sinal*. These are the reasons why he isolates himself at a beach, seeking contact with the sea and the sun, becoming aware of his body. In his contact with nature, far from men and their struggles and intrigues, he at times finds pagan happiness and fulfillment.

Abelaira's novel, which according to the author was written between 1968 and 1974, reveals the same disbelief in ideologies and in the revolution. The ideal of collective happiness seems like an outdated myth to Abelaira's characters. For the author, individual salvation is revealed more than ever to be possible only through love. Yet the characters of Abelaira's novels still do not lose the guilty social conscience that always defined them, and they continue to debate national and global political issues.

Vergílio Ferreira's novel, as well as that of Augusto Abelaira, adopts a very harsh position in relation to the political class, which is represented as ambitious but incapable. But the lack of belief in the revolution has deeper roots and arises as a manifestation in Portugal of certain European tendencies of the time, of a more universal disillusionment with the models that had nourished the idealism of several generations. The 1974 Portuguese revolution merely ended up confirming in practice what a good number of intellectuals and writers already knew or had sensed some time before: that revolution was a myth created and nourished by the illusion of absurd hopes. It is as if the ideals of Eça de Queirós's generation had only now been called into question in a seemingly radical way. The solutions for improving society's functioning and for improving individual living conditions were no longer inspired by the simplistic parameters of the past, and writers seem to have become aware of the limits and fallability of ideology.

5

Thus the ideals of Neo-realism were already being questioned even before the Portuguese "revolution" of 1974 took place. The ideological crisis, or what could in any case have been understood as a change in the comprehension of ideology, of socialism, and of revolution, was already a reality evident to a certain number of European writers and intellectuals before the so-called "revolution of the carnations" broke out.

Neither Carlos de Oliveira in his last work, nor Vergílio Ferreira or Augusto Abelaira in their 1979 novels, believe any longer that revolution, any revolution, can miraculously solve the myriad problems that social life poses nowadays. Revolution, perceived in this manner, as a kind of wondrous or legendary solution for social and individual ills, was above all a neo-realist myth, in turn inspired by the myth of the Communist revolution. Nevertheless, it is interesting to note the vision of Portuguese reality, as well as the vision of the revolution itself, that is transmitted to us in other literary works. By going through a few works of other representative and important authors, we should be able to get a more precise idea about this subject.

One of the consequences of the revolution which certainly must be mentioned was the ending of censorship and the creation of a climate of freedom of the press and expression. Another consequence, even more important, was the end of the colonial war and the subsequent independence of the colonies. These circumstances explain why a number of works were published after 1974 that have to do with the colonial war in its various aspects or with political events that had occurred prior to 25 April: these themes could not have been dealt with before the lifting of censorship. I am referring essentially to two novels of neo-realist writer José Cardoso Pires: *Balada da Praia dos Cães* (1982) and *Alexandra Alpha* (1988). I am also including in this list two novels of Nuno Bragança: *Directa* (1977) and *Square Tolstoi* (1981), in addition to some of the novels by António Lobo Antunes, João de Melo, Lídia Jorge, the novels of Almeida Faria, and other authors.

José Cardoso Pires himself evokes in *Alexandra Alpha* the censors who, while the revolution is building in the streets,

> remained seated at their desks, scissors in hand, awaiting the news that they would draw and quarter before it could come out in the newspapers, though it had already been a while that the paperboys had been wandering the streets, yelling, right under the censors' noses. But the censors—no response, they were deaf up until the very last syllable. Fear had made them deaf and had bound them to their chairs (p. 345).

The end of the colonial war and the colonies' subsequent independence forced the Portuguese to wake up to their new reduced borders and to question themselves about their national identity, which was now almost exclusively European. In *Alexandra Alpha*, José Cardoso Pires, like so many other authors, refers to this reality. He evokes the moment when the prime minister, Marcelo Caetano, was preparing to go into exile as he waited in the headquarters of the Guarda Nacional Republicana, located on the Largo do Carmo:

> Thus was ended an empire of Indias, Africas and shipwrecks, and the final act was to take place as we watched, in the small square that even yesterday was not much more than a plaza full of mounted guards, but that now was like an ocean of people, people on the balconies, people on the roofs and on top of the military transports with loudspeakers announcing the surrender (p. 343).

In *Auto dos danados* (1985), one of António Lobo Antunes's characters declares that it was "in Brazil, one or two years after the revolution," that he realized that Portugal

> did not exist. It was a hoax perpetrated by Geography and History professors, who had created rivers and mountain ranges and cities governed by successive dynasties of card-deck jacks of

diamonds, who were in turn (after a half dozen insignificant gunshot bangs) succeeded by a bunch of scraggly-bearded guys with glasses, faces framed in oval portraits (p. 146).

This last phrase is an allusion to the end of the monarchy and the beginning of the republic. Lobo Antunes himself had already initiated an irreverent and bitter, caustic and sarcastic criticism of pre-revolutionary Portuguese reality and values in the novel *Os cus de Judas* (1979), where the recollections of colonial war occupy a central position. But he does not omit pointing out that the revolution was a total failure. Feeling himself to be a decadent European, and not just Portuguese, Lobo Antunes's narrator-character expresses the worn-out values of our Western civilization, and evokes the nostalgia of an uncorrupted Africa and "good black people" that to his eyes utopically represent what we ought to take as the model for a future society:

> I melancholically felt that I was the heir to an old, unhappy, and agonizing country; that I was heir to a Europe complete with tumor-palaces and bladderstone-cathedrals, faced with a people whose inexhaustible vitality I had already glimpsed, years before, in Louis Armstrong's solar trumpet, casting out melancholy and sourness by virtue of the muscular happiness of his music (p. 58).

As one can see, Portugal's historical past interferes with the present at the exact moment when the age-old expansionist dream evaporates, no longer worthy of belief, in spite of the official empire-centered propaganda.

Certain early feminist tendencies in Portuguese literature, which had manifested themselves principally with the scandalous 1972 publication of *Novas cartas portuguesas*, by Maria Isabel Barreno, Maria Teresa Horta, and Maria Velho da Costa, began to develop more vigorously after the revolution, with greater freedom and imagination as well as enormous creative power. This could be thought of as a type of awakening on the part of Portuguese women with respect to their specific condition, while at the same time these feminist tendencies could also be considered part of an undebatable evolution of mentality and behavior, not only in regard to the feminine condition itself, but also in regard to the relation between the two sexes, to the social structures, and to political life.

We should also note the appearance of a series of magazines which expressed a certain irreverence, anticonformism, desire for liberty, an invitation to create and provoke—all elements that confirmed a new sense of hope and the emergence of an intellectual youth, rebellious and dissatisfied with middle-class values and lifestyle. The group A Fenda, created and led in Coimbra by Vasco Santos, who has since continued with his activities as editor in Lisbon, deserves particular mention from this point of view, given the number and quality of the writings that the group published in magazine form or in several collections of books, often by unknown or practically unknown young Portuguese authors, although the group also published some translations of works by provocative, marginal, or "damned" foreign writers.

With respect to the themes and to the language, it seems indisputable that a breath of fresh air blew through Portuguese literature after the revolution, motivated by the illusory hopes that 25 April brought into play. The image that literature gives us of the revolution, nevertheless, is for the most part a negative one. Poets such as José Carlos Ary dos Santos, the revolution's visionary herald José Afonso, Sérgio Godinho, and others all continued to sing of the people in their verses and songs and to criticize the bourgeois and the politician, in the style of the neo-realist and Marxist ideals. Manuel Alegre, the well-known author of lyrically epic and revolutionary poetry, in 1981 was to sing of the revolution's frustration, even though he had taken on important responsibilities in socialist politics:

> April clothed in April (April so green)
> April undressed in April (April that hurts)
> April already done. And still undone
>
> ("April Yes and No," *Atlântico*, p. 99).

But the paths of Portuguese poetry only occasionally intersected with revolutionary preoccupations and themes. The most important names in present-day Portuguese poetry—Eugénio de Andrade, António Ramos Rosa, Sophia de Mello Breyner, Herberto Helder, Pedro Támen, Alexandre O'Neill, Nuno Júdice, for example (and also Ruy Belo and Jorge de Sena, but they died shortly after the revolution)—continued on their own course. Poetry, in the noblest sense of the word, is not overly concerned with present-day political and historical events. These political and historical events to which I am referring were but a point of passage for the best poets, and not even obligatory. A good number of talented young poets, however, seem to have found in the revolution, or in postrevolutionary society, an incentive toward a greater creative freedom, which led them to express even more clearly the difficulty of self-fulfillment in today's society and the desire to attain truer forms of existence.

6

It is in the novel, however, that we are going to find expressed in a more direct and more detailed way a vision of the Portuguese reality in the time of the revolution, in the years that preceeded the revolution (a depiction which could not be presented without fear of censorship before 1974), and in the years that succeeded 25 April. In *Alexandra Alpha*, José Cardoso Pires harkens back to the revolutionary events of 1974, yet does so without fanatical, conventional heroism or patriotism, thus demystifying, with a sense of humor and irony—all the while retaining a touch of tolerance and poetry—the turns taken by the military revolution.

Nevertheless, it is Almeida Faria, in successive novels that form a "Lusitanian tetralogy," who best allows us to understand the course of deception that leads from youthful hope in the revolution to the painful final disillusion that arises with the so-called April revolution (the last novel of the series describes happenings that occurred in 1975). The author's point of view (or the points of view of his characters) does not differ much from that expressed by other writers. But Almeida Faria, who was born in 1943, simultaneously expresses the frustration of the generation that was most directly linked to the April revolution, the generation that probably expected more of it, and consequently felt the lack of fulfillment most sharply.

In 1965, when he published his second novel, *A paixão*, Almeida Faria was twenty-two years old. In this novel, which, like the majority of fiction published until the 1970s, was still linked to the lengthy tradition of the social novel and would be difficult to understand without the existence of a strong background of neo-realist ideals, Almeida Faria was expressing, through different characters belonging to different social classes, a sincere and youthful hope in the revolution. The influence of William Faulkner's *As I Lay Dying* (1930) on the young Portuguese writer seemed evident, above all in the compositional form of the narrative, and this influence has been pointed out several times. By allowing access to his characters' consciousnesses, Almeida Faria demonstrated that the humiliated and the humble, the common folk, also have an interior life and anxieties that are worthy of respect and interest. The common people are not as coarse as Neo-realism at times must have assumed, in spite of the movement's good intentions. *A paixão* deals with a middle-class family from Alentejo, including their daughter, Arminda. Chapter 48 of the novel evokes the "tradition of an opposition of classes that was only visible in social situations long since gone" (p. 173) in referring to Arminda's desire to marry Samuel, a working-class youth. And in Chapter 45 we find expressed in very clear words the reference to the revolution that needs to be carried out. This hope was perhaps couched with a certain touch of naiveté. But this naiveté formed part of Almeida Faria's time and cannot be justified merely as a product of the author's youthfulness or idealism. We can return to the novel and mention another important member of the same family, João Carlos (a young politicized and militant student), who, in a lengthy interior monologue which takes place after a scene of family dispute and misunderstanding, ends up thinking that he is going to

> free himself and assume a new attitude, an attitude that for him was the only acceptable one, given the new life, of entering into another mentality, completely and without reserve; of entering into another class to dedicate himself once and for all to a plan, an idea, to court danger, accept risk and tragedy, anonymity and secretiveness, to suffer if necessary, to immolate himself—but in any case, to help with his own hands to build the world, the new world that he'd dreamed about with the certainty that transcends reality. And he knew that this world would be infallible, urgent and necessary; to succeed would not be easy and would certainly cost some blood; but it was blood, yes, that would save him; blood brought ressurrection; it hurt, burned, cost; but in the end it would destroy the past like a flame and a magnificent future would rise from the destruction, from nothingness (p.159).

But the years passed, and this story was continued, with the same characters and the narration of their attempts to modify Portuguese society and personal destiny, in the novels *Cortes* (1978), *Lusitânia* (1980), and *Cavaleiro andante* (1983). In *Cortes*, finished 13 April 1974, the morass of Portuguese society and the difficulty of change-producing action became quite evident, and the criticism of colonial war and the Portuguese sociopolitical situation continued in a less hopeful tone. In *Lusitânia*, finished 16 March 1975, we witness the actual revolution seen from the perspective of the characters (in the novels of this tetralogy, Almeida Faria usually prefers to eliminate the narrator, availing himself instead of the characters' voices and points of view). João Carlos writes a letter to André, his oldest brother, that gives us an idea of how he has become ever more disillusioned:

> I don't want to live in the Alentejo, I don't want to be a witness or accomplice to a struggle without solution, and the only solution would be land reform. Today I can see that life there is impossible for me; I can't always be in the opposition, it's tiring; but it would be obscene to be in favor. What role do I deserve, what else is there for me? Perhaps the revolutionary individualism that some guys talk about? Should I do what Samuel recommends and profess the Communist party line? I don't have the faith to defend any sect, no matter how anarchistic it may be. And he who doesn't even have the good fortune to take himself seriously can't even be an enfant terrible. I'm just an unlucky guy, gloomy, never there when it's important, the one who is unable to do what is important, if there is something important (p. 64).

Frustration and the inability to act begin to be more evident. The most direct criticism of the revolution emerges in other passages, such as in this exerpt from one of André's letters, dated the "1st of red May":

> It certainly was the greatest [mass movement] that had ever occurred in the capital of tranquility, the capital of sleepy boredom brought about by two centuries of middle-class sterility, and by a few more centuries of static nobility, effortlessly receiving the fruits of the so-called "overseas dominions" (p. 71).

Yet after becoming vaguely enthused by the crowd's parade, André cannot resist the insight of characterizing that mass of people as a "fictitious unity, brought to an end as soon as each group's interests started to undermine the social organization." And he adds that he left before the conclusion of the demonstration because he detests stadiums, which remind him of "football and Hitler" (p. 73). João Carlos is the one who still criticizes the demagoguery of the revolution and of those who took charge of it:

> One is present at the theatrical presentation of a lousy bunch of shameless, rotten parasites, dreadful in every sense of the word, cheap political trash, so sure of themselves, low quality actors (p. 103).

In the same letter, João Carlos refers to the "half-embarrassed, isolated, closed circuit where the same opportunists always function, with periodic changes of masks in order to deceive everyone else, or in order to give the illusion of being someone special" (p. 105). Later on, it is Marta who will write to João Carlos from Venice saying that the revolution is no longer enough for her, she can no longer use it as an alibi "to sacrifice an entire lifetime on behalf of certainly just ideals," nor can she live a second-hand existence, or "postpone her heart" (pp. 167–68). The conflict between revolutionary idealism and the necessity for personal fulfillment becomes evident, as well as the desperation that provokes this conflict. Marta laments that the left has turned into a victim "of its childish sense of triumph," ending up knelt down before the moneylenders, crying for lost opportunities; she criticizes "the nouveau riche consumerism that eats up reserves and currency" (p. 168). João Carlos answers that he understands that she may not want to return to Portugal, "a very sad land," since she is no longer able to allow herself to be deceived by "any type of instant Nescafé decaffeinated revolution" (p. 170). The idea of the revolution is thus becoming progressively more notorious as a myth, leaving itself open to bitter criticism of Portuguese opportunism and mediocrity, two inescapable national defects that impede any kind of real change and progress in the country, according to Almeida Faria.

In *Cavaleiro andante*, the chronicle of the revolution continues, along with the narration of the social situation that grew out of the revolution itself. Close to the end of the novel, João Carlos writes:

"What misery awaits us, for which there is no cure?" (p. 227). In this same letter, João Carlos designates the revolution as "a revolution of the mass-media" more than a revolution of the masses (p. 229). Pessimism makes itself felt throughout the entire novel, it characterizes all of the people, and it is not just pessimism in relation to Portugal's future, but rather a lament for a Europe which is "decimated, plundered by successive waves of barbarians, disfigured, sold, betrayed by her own children, destroyed, oppressed" (p. 184). And it is outside Portugal (in artistic Italy, in adventuresome Brazil, in youthful Africa, places where a different future seems possible and where personal action and effort can still have some effect on reality) that Almeida Faria's characters spread out, in order for us to better understand the fatality of our destiny as an emigrant people because there are no longer solutions in Portugal. There is no revolution that can bring dignity and sense to existence, that can bring justice, that can reestablish the values of intelligence and sensitivity. Confusion reigns in our spirits, and it is simultaneously perceived as collective and individual, all of which underlines, even in light of Marxism, to what extent individual destinies appear to Almeida Faria as inseparable from the social, political, and economic conditions. "During my periods of creaking insomnia I think that I don't belong to myself, that I am not myself, but rather an entire nation lost within itself, confusedly seeking who knows what escape" (p. 131), writes André before he dies. André's death will emerge later as a proof of a personal inability to deal with life and as a symbol of the hopeless dead end in which a generation had permitted itself to be enclosed. This was the generation that had naively believed that when the revolution came to pass, it would bring important changes to Portuguese society with regard to social justice and respect for essential human values. As readers of Almeida Faria's Lusitanian tetralogy, we are present at the birth, growth, and death of a generation's dream.

In *Alexandra Alpha*, José Cardoso Pires once again refers to the excessive hopes that a certain segment of the leftist movement had placed in the revolution, alluding to the errors that it committed as a result of too much utopian idealism. At the same time, the author portrays the return from exile in Madrid or Brazil of various characters belonging to the "golden minorities" (p. 442). In what he calls the Crocodile Bar in Lisbon, we are witness to the return of the "old order," making its appearance after a two-year dormancy. To make us understand better that the revolution was an illusory and failed historical parenthesis, without long-lasting consequences for Portuguese reality, Cardoso Pires describes the ambience that rules in that bar:

> The Crocodile had woken up from its lethargy and had once again taken up its old habits. Servants, lighting, everything was the same. A lovely soda dispenser in full view on top of the counter, the posters on the walls announcing ballets and film presentations prior to the 25th of April. Everything was as if, after two years of sudden paralysis, the world had started up again from the same point in time where it had been interrupted (p. 441).

The memory of the revolution is disappearing, swallowed up by present-day reality. One of the novel's characters strolls along the streets of Lisbon, and what does he see?

> Up and down the streets he saw tattered posters, a penis crudely covering the word Liberty, could it be that the people were as forgetful as everyone said? As the days passed, Miguel felt with ever greater clarity that their forgetfulness was the death-blow for revolutions (p. 442).

In the last analysis, the revolution was a myth, an achievement that toppled. April 25 was a kind of innocent though disorganized popular party that brought about excessive hopes for the transformation of Portuguese society. It is that image, above all, that literature, from Vergílio Ferreira and Augusto Abelaira to Almeida Faria and José Cardoso Pires (to mention just a few names and some of the most important works) gives to us in its presentation of the April revolution and its consequences. It is a portrayal that tends to forget that in reality some victories were attained, preferring to dwell instead on what was *not* achieved. Reality progressively and painfully imposed itself on the imaginary, reducing its ambitions and foolish hopes to unsubstantiated fantasies. Revolution, as people conceive and imagine it, is definitively not of this world.

REFERENCES

Abelaira, Augusto. 1979. *Sem tecto entre ruínas*. Lisbon.

Alegre, Manuel. 1981. *Atlântico*. Lisbon.

Barreno, Maria Isabel; Maria Teresa Horta; and Maria Velho da Costa. 1972. *Novas cartas portuguesas*. Lisbon.

Bragança, Nuno. 1977. *Directa*. Lisbon.

————. 1981. *Square Tolstoi*. Lisbon.

Camus, Albert. 1942. *L'Etranger*. Paris.

Faria, Almeida. 1965. *A paixão*. Lisbon.

————. 1978. *Cortes*. Lisbon.

————. 1980. *Lusitânia*. Lisbon.

————. 1983. *Cavaleiro andante*. Lisbon.

Faulkner, William. 1930. *As I Lay Dying*. New York.

Ferreira, Vergílio. 1969 [1949]. *Mudança*, 3d ed. Lisbon.

————. 1979. *Signo sinal*. Lisbon.

Lobo Antunes, António. 1979. *Os cus de Judas*. Lisbon.

————. 1985. *Auto dos danados*. Lisbon.

de Oliveira, Carlos. 1944. *Alcateia*. Coimbra.

————. 1978. *Finisterra, paisagem e povoamento*. Lisbon.

Pires, José Cardoso. 1982. *Balada da Praia dos Cães*. Lisbon.

————. 1987. *Alexandra Alpha*. Lisbon.

Saramago, José. 1980. *Levantado do chão*. Lisbon.

Sartre, Jean-Paul. 1938. *La Nausée*. Paris.

FAMILY AND NEIGHBORHOOD IN PORTUGAL TODAY

João de Pina-Cabral

In the Iberian ethnographic literature, we often encounter studies of the relationship between familial links and the social appropriation of space at the level of the *casa*, but we rarely encounter discussions of how the familial relations within the casa interrelate with neighborhood relations. This is, in many ways, surprising, for it has long been recognized that a relationship does exist between family types and community types.

As the notion of family has had many meanings and uses, I should specify from the outset that when I talk of *family* or of *family relations*, I am not referring to some notion of an "elementary family," such as was used by functionalist and structural-functionalist thinkers. As an analytical category, the family is not a unit. Rather, it is the realm of social behavior which is delineated by those primary solidarities which the child acquires in the process of his or her integration into society as a social person. Within this realm, all societies

identify one level of social identity which has the greatest structural implications in the integration of the social person and in the social appropriation of the world—namely, through the establishment of the primary level of formally recognized authority. This is also the level at which participants recognize the primary integration between social reproduction and human reproduction.

I call this the primary social unit (Pina-Cabral 1989a, 1990).

One of the interesting characteristics of the primary social unit in Mediterranean and Atlantic Europe is that it tends to assume a typically monadic aspect. Whether it is one of the versions of the Iberian casa, the French *ménage*, the Italian *famiglia*, the English *house-*

hold, or the German *Haus*, the primary social unit in these regions is always presented as a clearly identifiable unit, a microcosm. The reason for this is that "the principles of recruitment used for the primary social unit are not typically extended for the recruitment of more wide-ranging social units" (Pina-Cabral 1989a). In other words, European society does not possess what ethnographers in other areas of the world have called the lineage principle.

As a result, Europeanist ethnographers have tended to study family patterns and patterns of community relations as if they were independent variables. My argument in this essay is that they are not independent of each other. It should be stressed, however, that I am not claiming that one is causally dependent on the other. Rather, I believe that the two areas are closely interrelated, at the level of both the practices which guide the lifestyle of particular communities and the creation and reproduction of sociocultural traditions which identify larger regions.

1. THE HOUSE VERSUS THE COUPLE

If we consider Portuguese ethnography from the perspective of the diversity of systems of reproduction of the primary social unit, we will most certainly alight on two examples which can be seen as polar opposites in the way the process of reproduction is carried out. Interestingly, they are extremes not only from a logical point of view, but also from a geographical point of view. If Portugal is seen as a rectangle oriented in a north/south axis, one of our examples—Rio de Onor (Dias 1981 [1953]; Pais de Brito 1989)—is situated in the extreme northeastern corner, while the other—the *montes* of Martin-longo (Bastos 1987, 1988)—is in the extreme southeast corner.

The reason the first example has become one of the major classics of Iberian ethnography while the other is hardly known at all is not unrelated to the processes we want to single out here. Since 1953, when Jorge Dias first published his study, Rio de Onor has been the prototypical example of the idealized rural community, where the interests of the community are supposed to tower above those of individuals.* For these more ideological purposes, the southern ex-

---

*Here I must give some indication as to how I am using the word "community": "Community is not only a variable in the sense that it may be stronger

ample was not at all appealing: in the mountains of eastern Algarve, individualism appears to reign, there is no distinct communal identity, no communal property, no apparent limitations to the individual's freedom of movement. This, at least, is how the differences between the two ways of life were read.

Rio de Onor is a small rural community on the border between the Portuguese province of Trás-os-Montes and the Spanish province of Orense. On the other side of the riverlet which marks the border there is a sister community with the same name. The primary social unit is the casa, a unit consisting of persons, houses, cattle, and—most important here—communal rights in the use of the agricultural and pastoral lands and other resources which the community controls. Each house is ideally headed by a married couple, and there are never in the same house two couples of the same generation living together. However, it is common for the child who has been chosen to succeed the parents in the headship of the casa to marry and bring his or her spouse to live in the parental home (sometimes after a period of natolocality; see Pais de Brito 1989: 455–56). This means that strenuous efforts are made to prevent the division of the property through inheritance, diminishing the strength of the casa. Many people, men and women, remain single, living their lives out in a house headed by a sibling. As Jorge Dias puts it,

> This tendency for celibacy is born of a respect for the rural household which is almost religious, for it takes the aspect of an extra-terrestrial entity which is indivisible (1981 [1948]: 292–93).

In Rio de Onor, therefore, the primary social unit is reproduced in what I call a *linear* fashion—that is, from generation to generation, it maintains its specific identity independently of the people who inhabit it. The process of alliance, which is indispensable for reproduction due to the incest prohibition, is effected by the simple integration of a spouse for the new head, and this integration does not involve a considerable alteration in the patrimony of the house (for further elaboration, see Pina-Cabral 1990). It can thus be said that in Rio de Onor the dominant principle of familial solidarity is centered on the house; I call this *the principle of the house.*

---

or weaker; there may also be communities within communities, and communities being created at the expense of other communities" (Pina-Cabral 1986: 126).

The situation in the montes of Martinlongo, in the eastern mountains of Algarve, could hardly be more different. These small mountain villages are very different from the montes of Alentejo, which are associated to the system of latifundia. Here the peasants are owners of their land, which is extremely subdivided and not very productive. Each of these montes is comprised of 10–100 people who very often are closely related. The primary social unit is not the casa, as in Rio de Onor, but rather what they call *casas*. This pluralization is significant, as it carries implications about the spatial setup of the village. In fact, the concern with establishing a realm of privacy for the casa, which is so marked in the north of the country, is here totally absent. People's family life is carried out in different places across the village. As everything is distributed equally among the heirs, strategies of manipulation of the inhabited space have developed which give it great plasticity. The walls of the houses are made with loose slate stones, which means that people can open and close doors and windows at their convenience—whenever a new distribution of property occurs. Each couple occupies the spaces that it inherits in the course of its life in different parts of the little village, without feeling the need to unify them spatially.

The principle of the house is so diluted that the moment of marriage does not assume the importance it has in northern Portugal, where it is the marker of the reproduction of the casa and a major public event. Here, on the contrary, the primary social unit creates itself progressively around a couple. As Cristiana Bastos explains, "The first conjugal bed was often the barn [since] the transfer of property is not a question at the time of marriage" (1987: 110). The dedramatization of marriage which the ethnographer observes does not imply a demeaning of conjugality. Quite the contrary. Because the principle of the house is so understated in this society, the primary social unit forms itself progressively around this couple and its fertility, not suddenly, but in the course of their lives, as they gather around them people (their children) and property (their respective inheritances and their earnings). Moreover, it disappears with the death of the couple.

Thus the process of reproduction of the primary social unit does occur, but not in a lineal fashion, for the identity of each specific unit does not survive from generation to generation. Rather it occurs in a *syncopated* fashion, as if by fissiparity. In the mountains of Algarve, then, it is not the principle of the house which rules the process of reproduction but *the principle of conjugality.*

I started this section by stating that these examples are extreme cases, as indeed they are. We will now attempt to show that between these two extremes there is a whole gamut of variations.

2. REGIONAL VARIATION: THE NORTH/SOUTH DIVIDE

I will start this section with a warning. Jorge Dias once said:

Differences of detail between neighboring villagers are enormous, as each settlement [*povo*] is a live whole that behaves according to the particular conditions of its environment. We must never forget this, for those who are not familiar with real life, working only with bibliography, are often tempted to produce schematic generalizations that lead, at times, to wrong conclusions (1981 [1948]: 84).

This comment applies to family patterns as well as to many other aspects of community life. I myself observed that in the Alto Minho there was a significant variation from parish to parish in funeral practices (Pina-Cabral 1986: 214). Yet at the same time, the existence of regional differentiation and regional tendencies was also beyond question (Pina-Cabral and Feijó 1983: 17ff.). This explains why even Jorge Dias in his day was willing to undertake broad generalizations concerning the regional nature of Portuguese familial behavior (e.g., 1963).

If we then put into a regional perspective the two extreme cases which we cited above, we find that the clear differences are somewhat reduced, but that they fit into the well-known division of the country into two broadly defined demographic regimes: in the south (Alentejo and Algarve), a *high-pressure regime* with high rates of birth and mortality and female nuptiality characterized by relatively early and almost universal marriage; in the north (Minho and Trás-os-Montes), a *low-pressure regime* with lower rates of birth and mortality and female nuptiality characterized by relatively late marriage and high rates of definitive celibacy (Rowland 1986: 40–41).

These demographic regimes are deeply associated with regional tendencies in the processes of reproduction of the primary social unit. Thus in areas where the principle of the house has a strong influence, we are more likely to find a low-pressure regime (as Dias had already noted in 1948—see 1981 [1948]: 292–93); in areas where the principle of the house is dormant and the principle of conjugality is dominant, we will most likely find a high-pressure regime.

It has been common for authors who have studied the northwest of the Peninsula (and that applies to coastal and inland Galicia, Minho, Trás-os-Montes, and parts of Beira) to identify the importance of the principle of the house in this region with its importance in the Pyrenean region of the Peninsula (Dias 1981 [1948]: 292; Lisón Tolosana 1971). I follow Dolors Comas D'Argemir (1987) in believing that the two regional systems must be clearly distinguished, for while the Pyrenean systems have impartibility of inheritance as their basic feature, the northwestern systems always presume egalitarian inheritance, but then qualify it depending on how strongly manifested is the principle of the house. This difference in emphasis is demonstrated by a series of factors such as, for example, the existence in the Pyrenean region of kinship terminologies which presume the functioning of an impartible system (Iszaevich 1980, 1981), while in the northwest such terminologies are not encountered. Another symptom of this difference is the occurrence of natolocality during the early years of marriage in northwestern Iberia—a practice which is not reported for the Pyrenean region, where marriage is directly related to the linear reproduction of a household.

Thus I argue that southern regional systems in Portugal are marked by the absolute dominance of the principle of conjugality over the principle of the house, while in the northern regional systems the principle of the house can be more or less dominant by relation to the principle of conjugality. Therefore, in Minho, Trás-os-Montes, and most of Beira, we encounter a range of possibilities which go from instances where the principle of the house is absolutely dominant, to instances where it is clearly secondary, to the principle of conjugality.*

---

*It is worthwhile pointing out here that a third principle of solidarity is encountered in Mediterranean and Atlantic Europe—the principle of the solidarity of siblings. However, in most ethnographic instances studied in the Iberian Peninsula, this principle does not play a dominant role in the reproduction of the primary social unit (Pina-Cabral 1990).

In order to clarify what I mean when I say that northern regional systems are characterized by a variation between greater or lesser stress on the principle of the house in the reproduction of the primary social unit, I will give some examples. We will start with those where the principle of the house is strongest.

The ethnography of the past hundred years has provided us with a number of cases, such as the one studied by Brian Juan O'Neill (1984), where the heir who is going to stay with the house is allowed to marry while the others are encouraged to remain single. These, however, may have illegitimate children, which means that they too may create primary social units; only these primary social units are in both moral and economic terms disadvantaged by relation to the main line—often there are even doubts as to whether they should be called casas.* Therefore, in such a community, we encounter two types of reproduction functioning simultaneously, depending on the access to landed property. Only the wealthy ones manage to maximize the principle of the house in the process of social reproduction. Usually, as O'Neill has shown, this also gives them access to a series of privileges at community level—an issue to which we will return later.

There are other ethnographic instances where the existence of two simultaneous modes of reproduction of the primary social unit, operating at the same time in the same community, is even more marked. In the village of Salto, in the area of Barroso (between Minho and Trás-os-Montes), this separation is radical. The ethnographer who studied this village found that he could trace the existence of six casas as having been reproduced in an unbroken linear fashion at least since the seventeenth century (Castanheira 1988: 943). These six houses control most of the landed property of the parish and dominate communal affairs (both in ritual and political terms). It is interesting to note that the system of inheritance they follow is not that of full impartibility. As is the case throughout northwest Iberia, the main heir has the legal right only to what the Galicians call the

---

*The phenomenon of illegitimacy, which has interested so many of us who have studied northern Portugal (Pina-Cabral 1986; Brettell 1986) is a function of the importance of the principle of the house. In southern Portugal, where universal marriage is the ideal and where the principle of conjugality is so important that formal marriage is no longer a central communal event, bastardy assumes a totally different light (Cutileiro 1977: 179–95; Brettell 1986).

mellora—that is, a percentage of the patrimony. However, the parents attempt to endow the other heirs with cash and other mobile goods. This means that the main identifying features of the casa (the houses and the ploughed land) tend to remain intact in the hands of the favored heir. The remaining people of Salto, whose properties are small, follow a mode of reproduction of the primary social unit where the principle of the house is far less important.

In the majority of situations in Minho, however, the coexistence of two clearly separate modes of reproduction working simultaneously is less distinctively marked. In most rural areas the process of reproduction of the casa depends on some sort of compromise between the principle of the house and the principle of conjugality. In the parishes I myself studied in the Alto Minho, the wealthier families had a greater margin of maneuver in order to reproduce their casa identity from generation to generation, while the poorer people found it difficult to do so. On the whole, one heir—often the youngest daughter—stayed with the parental home and received a slightly larger part of the inheritance. A concerted effort was made to prevent the splitting of the main house and the fields which surrounded it and give it its name (as houses are named after fields) (Pina-Cabral 1986: 37–81).

The important thing to remember, however, is that in Minho and Trás-os-Montes, whenever the two modes of reproduction of the primary social unit coexist, those who manage to maximize the principle of the house are more valued than those who do not—thus in Salto, the people who do not belong to one of the six casas are called the *pobres* (poor people), independently of whether they control other forms of wealth (Castanheira 1988: 942).

One would think that the sort of processes I am describing here apply only to rural contexts. Indeed it is true that in urban contexts the principle of the house seems less important. Among the less privileged classes, the mode of reproduction of the primary social unit tends to favor the principle of conjugality. But again the difference with the southern regional systems is apparent, for we encounter a greater acceptance of joint residence of parents and married children in northern Portugal. It must be noted, however, that among the wealthier classes the principle of the house again makes its appearance. I am not referring here only to the practice of investing the oldest male child with the symbols of familial prestige, which is still common among aristocratic and wealthy bourgeois families. A more widespread symptom can be found in the way in which such families use their *quintas* as sources of identity.

A quinta is a secondary home in a rural area to which some landholdings are usually attached. Often these houses are rather old, carrying with them implications of aristocracy (even when the present owners have no genealogical claim to any title). It is common to find that at the death of the parents, children are loath to divide these quintas (Pina-Cabral 1990). In some cases even though the property rights had legally been handed over to one of the children as a result of formal inheritance, the others continued to use the quinta as a holiday home and as a place where they met on festive occasions to celebrate their familial links. If the agricultural holdings are potentially economically profitable, it is not uncommon to find that family companies were created so as to keep the property together, ensuring that it remains profitable (Pina-Cabral, forthcoming).

Over and above their economic significance, and as Jorge Dias had already perceived in the 1950s (1963), these quintas are an important source of identity among the bourgeoisie, for they are a central symbol of distinction. Even though in their daily urban life such people reproduce their primary social units in a syncopated fashion (that is, stressing the principle of conjugality), the appeal of the principle of the house continues to be strongly present.

3. FAMILY AND COMMUNITY RELATIONS

The next step in my argument, therefore, is to try to demonstrate that there is a relation between the modes of reproduction of the primary social unit and the modes of organization of neighborhood relations. I repeat that I am not claiming that there is a unidirectional causal link between both levels of social organization, but merely that an historically mediated relation can be seen to exist. Thus we must start by looking at the relation from the point of view of the family and then from the point of view of community. I hardly need to repeat that the only reason it is possible in this society to talk of the two levels as if they constituted separate, albeit interrelated, spheres is that there is no lineage principle in operation.

From the point of view of the family, and put in its simplest form, the relation can be formulated in the following terms: if the principle of the house is dominant at the level of the reproduction of the primary social unit, then the units of interrelation at the level of neighborhood relations tend to be houses; if, on the other hand, the principle of conjugality is dominant, then the relations of neighborliness tend to depend on the links which the spouses create.

Thus we have already found that in ethnographic instances in which the principle of the house has a strong presence, economic indigence is associated with the incapacity to reproduce a casa. One of the main reasons for this is that only those who belong to a casa, in the fullest sense of the word, can have full access to community rights—in terms of both political prestige and influence and economic assets (that is, when the community controls such assets, as is still the case in most of the northern region of Trás-os-Montes and many of the mountain villages situated in the area between the two northern provinces).

Characteristically throughout northern Portugal, there is an ambiguity about the meaning of the words casa and *vizinho* which precisely points to this sociostructural feature. As I have discussed this issue elsewhere (1986: 3–4), here I will only indicate that casa can mean both a building dedicated to dwelling and a household, in the sense of a full unit of community; vizinho, which means anyone who lives near me, can also be used in a different sense to mean each unit of community. In the latter sense, it excludes those whose primary social units do not live up to the standards which are expected by the community—that is, usually the landless. This is the sense in which in the village of Salto the community is divided into casas, on the one hand, and pobres, on the other, even though the latter comprise the vast majority of the people living in the village.

The egalitarian ideology which dominates the life of the communities of northern Portugal is based on the fact that these are conceived as aggregates of casas and that for the purposes of community rights all casas are equally placed. This applies to instances both where the community controls assets and has a semi-independent form of self-management (such as Rio de Onor) and where community belonging is less intensely felt (such as the parishes I studied in Alto Minho). The fact that some people never really manage to form a casa in the fuller sense of the term and that they therefore never achieve the full status of vizinho tends to be under-played by the shift in the meaning of the terms that I have just indicated. However, some such logic has been noted by the ethnographers who worked in both Minho in the late 1970s and early 1980s (Brettell 1986; Pina-Cabral 1986) and Trás-os-Montes (O'Neill 1984; Pais de Brito 1989). Without some reference to the principle of the house, it is practically impossible to make sense of many of the features of rural life in northern Portugal, such as marriage strategies, festivity organization, mutual aid systems, and community level politics.

Finally, it is the ideological centrality of the principle of the house that explains some of the processes through which the household links itself with its social surroundings in northern Portugal. Jorge Dias (1963) has already noted that godparenthood in northern Portugal assumes a lesser importance than in southern Portugal, for there is a tendency in the north to subordinate it to familial relations—typically, it is the grandparents and the elder siblings who perform this role. Similarly, most ethnographers have insisted that there is a tendency to subordinate extra-household kinship relations to community relations. There is no extensive logic of kindred cooperation because kinship relations beyond the link of siblingship tend to be subsumed under the logic of interhousehold relations.

One of the characteristic features of the areas where the principle of the house is dominant is the frequency with which we encounter *rodas, turnos,* or *vezeiras.* These are systems of communal labor use in which each unit of community is responsible in turn for undertaking a certain predefined task of communal interest. They tend to be symbolized by means of circular motion (Pina-Cabral 1986: 134–49). What makes them interesting to us at this stage is that the units of such systems are always casas (or persons as representatives of casas) and never individuals or couples. Furthermore, we have no evidence at present to support the claim that these systems are survivals from systems of community organization predating the state. On the contrary, the drift of the evidence today is that whenever strong communal interests have survived (and usually these are embodied in the communal ownership of pastoral land or buildings), new systems are readily invented to respond to changed conditions. William Kavanagh (1988: 136) reports such an occurrence in the area of Avila, in Castile, and Pais de Brito (1989) shows how the

25 April revolution was central in granting new vigor to the communal institutions of Rio de Onor.

By contrast, in southern rural Portugal, it is the principle of conjugality that governs the reproduction of the primary social unit, and even though the sense of belonging to a domestic unit may create a link between people, this is seldom a central logic of community relations. Indeed it is couples which form the units of neighborhood—that is what is meant by the insistence that they should live neolocally, a fact that has been so stressed by all ethnographers who have worked on Alentejo or Algarve. Only at marriage does "a man acquire the condition of full member of the community" (Cutileiro 1977: 136), but he does not acquire it for his own personal benefit. Rather, he shares the rights of membership with his wife. Therefore it can be said, as Cutileiro demonstrated for Alentejo (1977: 136), that communities are made up of conjugal units. Situations such as are common in northern Portugal, where households are formed by a group of unmarried siblings, are taken as deviant in southern Portugal.

Thus the links of neighborhood which make up community relations are interpersonal (or better still interconjugal) and not links between casas. Community life does not present the egalitarian aspect which is so characteristic of the north. As Cutileiro has put it, "The people who are bound to be recognized as neighbors are partly determined by the social group to which each one belongs" (1977: 181). That is, unlike in the north, stratification becomes a formative aspect of community relations. He stresses that "villagers are networks of social relations characterized more by a spirit of competition than of cooperation" (1977: 195). Of course there is a sense in which something similar could be said of the northern communities, only the central importance of the principle of the house as the basis of neighborhood and community relations means that such a network aspect is less easy to discern.

Network type relations, where godparenthood and the kindred become central processes of establishing preferential links, are the very stuff of community life in the south. This is reflected in the forms of community naming: house names, which are such an important point of reference in northern Portugal, play a very subsidiary role here; nicknames are far more prevalent, and these tend to be personal or attached to localized kindreds.*

*See Pina-Cabral (1984). I am grateful to Francisco Ramos for a paper on the subject which he read at ISCTE in 1988.

It has often been argued that such a type of community relations is the result of the greater stratification of rural society in
southern Portugal. I am convinced that this is not correct. Although
I cannot refute that the greater inequality in the access to land which
characterizes Alentejo considerably affects social structure, I believe
that the cast in which neighborhood and community relations are
shaped in southern Portugal cannot be explained by reference to
landed property alone. This will become apparent to anyone who
chooses to compare Cutileiro's monograph of a small town in the
latifundia region with Cristiana Bastos's study of the small mountain villages of northeastern Algarve, where property differentiation
does not play a major role.

4. REGIONAL TRADITIONS

I will summarize the argument so far in two points: first, there
is a correlation between patterns of community organization in Portugal and the principle of solidarity which dominates the process of
reproduction of the primary social unit; second, although the modes
of reproduction may vary within one single community and between nearby communities, they nevertheless exist within a regional
context. That is, they form an integral part of regional traditions. As
I have already expounded this notion (Pina-Cabral 1989b), I will
now take it for granted that the reader accepts that for the purposes
of ethnographic comparison, Europe can be divided into areas of
appreciable sociocultural integration which we shall loosely call sociocultural regions (see also Pina-Cabral 1989a).

If, then, we look at Portugal from the perspective of regional
patterns of community organization, we find that the differentiation
which we drew out, dependent as it was on the modes of reproduction of the primary social unit, is correct but insufficient. In fact,
regional traditions in community organization are dependent on all
sorts of historical factors, the complexity of which cannot be easily
recounted. And much though they be affected by the nature of family systems, they must be seen, in turn, as a powerful influence on
family organization.

The north/south divide in Portugal is one such regional differentiation, but within it other regional differences do occur. For ex-

ample, in northern Portugal, Orlando Ribeiro speaks of what he calls the "world of the parishes" (that is, the area of scattered settlement in the hills and plains of northern coastal Portugal) and the "world of the villages" (the area of dense settlement in the northern interior mountains and plateaus) (for a recent use of this distinction, see Pais de Brito 1990).

For those who know Portugal, this distinction may seem suspiciously similar to that between the provinces of Minho and Trás-os-Montes. But I stress that although there is a historical relation between both forms of differentiation, they are not coterminous, for they are based on different principles of classification. The first is based on sociocultural principles (i.e., different types of community organization) while the second is based on political principles (i.e., the existence of provincial political identities).

Even though Orlando Ribeiro chose to characterize these two regional traditions by reference to the style of rural settlement, his aim was to produce a classification which was far more significant in sociocultural terms that merely in settlement styles. The coastal world of parishes is not merely a region where rural settlement tends to be dispersed, for the process of community-building assumes other, more specific, features. Thus it is characteristically a world where community relations assume a segmentary aspect. A number of neighboring households join together to form a hamlet, which has a name, has a distinctive sense of identity, and controls a clearly outlined portion of territory. In turn, a parish is formed by the group of hamlets which are united around a church and a cemetery. Even though the parish constitutes the most visible level of community, it is not the most embracing level. Indeed the boroughs (*conselhos*) which are formed by a number of parishes around the nucleus of a small town are organically important levels of community to which a sense of identity is also clearly attached.

By contrast, the interior world of the villages is a region where the most characteristic type of settlement is the small village which is surrounded by a hinterland of uninhabited space which is controlled by the community. These villages (*aldeias* or *povos*) do not fit in the same way into the sort of segmentary pattern which ethnographers have used to describe Minho.* There is a binary relation be-

*I am grateful to Carlos Alberto Afonso for many interesting discussions concerning this issue.

tween the povo or *pueblo* (meaning the inhabited center) and the rural hinterland (the *termo*). Indeed village identity is more unitary—the relation between a people and its land tends to be absolute, contrary to the coastal regions of scattered settlement where the land is subdivided between the different subgroups of the parish—that is, casas and hamlets. Thus borough identity in the world of the villages is weaker than in the coastal area, and the state-imposed organization into parishes is practically irrelevant for community life. It is furthermore worth noting that joint communal action, as manifested by the decisions of an assembly of the people (the conselho), is far more characteristic of the world of the villages than of the internally more complex and divided world of the parishes.

5. CONCLUSION

I want to conclude with the claim that family relations are affected by these distinct traditions of community organization. The first time my attention was drawn to this fact was in the early period of my fieldwork in the Alto Minho in the late 1970s. An informant was telling me that during his military service in the 1940s, he had been attached to a group of engineers who were carrying out a cadastral survey in one of the border areas of Trás-os-Montes. He insisted that people there were much better than in his parish of origin, and he proceeded to explain that even though the soldiers were carrying out such a disagreeable task, when they got to a village, they were received as welcome guests. What surprised him most was that people readily opened the doors of their houses to these total strangers, fed them, gave them wine, and allowed them to sleep in their homes. In Minho, he said, people would be too evil and wary (*maus* and *desconfiados*) to do this.

Since then, I have learned to recognize that his opinion was quite correct. It is still to this day surprising to me to observe how differently the people form the world of villages and the world of parishes manage their domestic space. It should be stressed that we are not here dealing with traditions of hospitality properly speaking, for it is not only toward outsiders that such a difference in the management of domestic space is observed, but also toward community members.

Why is it that people who live in villages do not feel the same need forcefully to define an internal world of domestic privacy as those who live in parishes? My answer to this riddle is related to the very nature of the experience of community. The unitary nature of the experience of community which characterizes the world of villages gives the inhabitants a greater sense of shared fate and intimacy. As the village is surrounded by an uninhabited space (the termo), the villagers have a greater sense of interdependence. Contrariwise, in the world of the parishes, each house lives on its own, surrounded by its fields, and the various levels of community (hamlet, parish, borough) compete with each other in claiming the allegiance of the members of each casa. In short, different styles in the experience of community end up diversely affecting the way in which familial space is utilized by community members. Family and neighborhood are causally interrelated.

I am deeply indebted to João Arriscado Nunes for the many discussions we have had on these topics. I also wish to thank the students of the M.A. program in História das Populações of the University of Minho and the students of the course Antropologia Social II at ISCTE (Lisbon) (1989/1990) for the discussion of their work, which has provided me with a wide-ranging picture of family life in Portugal today and to which I might not otherwise have had access.

REFERENCES

Bastos, Cristiana. 1987. "Os montes do nordeste Algarvio." Master's thesis, Universidade Nova de Lisboa.

————. 1988. "The Northeastern Algarve and the Southern Iberian Family Pattern." *Journal of Family History* 13: 111–22.

Brettell, Caroline. 1986. *Men Who Migrate, Women Who Wait*. Princeton.

Castanheira, António. 1988. "Transmitir para manter: Transmissão e preservação do património numa aldeia do Barroso." *Meridies* 7/8: 941–68.

Comas D'Argemir, Dolors. 1987. "Rural Crisis and the Reproduction of Family Systems: Celibacy as a Problem in the Aragonese Pyrenees." *Sociologia Ruralis* 27: 263–77.

Cutileiro, José. 1977. *Ricos e pobres no Alentejo*. Lisbon.

Dias, A. Jorge. 1963. "Algumas considerações acerca da estrutura social do povo português." *Actas do 1. Congresso de Etnografia e Folklore (Braga, Junho 1956),* vol. 1. Lisbon

————. 1981 [1948]. *Vilarinho da Furna: Uma aldeia comunitária.* Lisbon.

————. 1981 [1953]. *Rio de Onor: Comunitarismo agro-pastoril.* Lisbon.

Iszaevich, Abraham. 1980. "Household Renown: The Traditional Naming System in Catalonia." *Ethnology* 19: 315–25.

————. 1981. "Corporate Household and Econocentric Kinship Group in Catalonia." *Ethnology* 20: 277–90.

Kavanagh, William. 1988. "Por turno: Sistemas rotativos de participación por orden fijo de familias en formas institucionalizadas de cooperación." In *Aproxiamación antropológica a Castilla y León,* ed. Luis Díaz. Barcelona.

Lisón Tolosana, Carmelo. 1971. *Antropología cultural de Galicia.* Madrid.

O'Neill, Brian Juan. 1984. *Proprietários, lavradores e jornaleiras.* Lisbon.

Pais de Brito, Joaquim. 1989. *A aldeia, as casas: Organização comunitária e reprodução social numa aldeia transmontana.* Doctoral thesis, ISCTE, Lisbon.

————. 1990. "O atlas etnográfico e a carta das fogueiras anuais." In *Homenagem a Ernesto Veiga de Oliveira,* ed. F. Oliveira Batista et al. Lisbon.

Pina-Cabral, João de. 1984. "Nicknames and the Experience of Community." *Man* 19: 140–50.

————. 1986. *Sons of Adam, Daughters of Eve.* Oxford.

————. 1989a. "L'Héritage de Maine: L'Érosion des catégories descriptives dans l'étude des phénomènes familiaux en Europe." *Ethnologie française* 4.

————. 1989b. "Sociocultural Differentiation and Regional Identity in Portugal." In *Iberian Identity,* ed. Richard Herr and John H. R. Polt. Berkeley.

————. 1990. *Os contextos da antropologia.* Lisbon.

————. Forthcoming. "Permanence et changement dans les rôles masculins et féminins au nord-ouest du Portugal." *Bulletin des études portugaises.*

Pina-Cabral, João de, and Rui G. Feijó. 1983. "Conflicting Attitudes to Death in Modern Portugal: The Question of Cemeteries." In *Death in Portugal: Studies in Portuguese Anthropology and Modern History,* ed. Rui Feijó, Hermínio Martins, and João de Pina-Cabral. Oxford.

Rowland, Robert. 1986. "Demographic Patterns and Rural Society in Portugal: Implications of Some Recent Researches." *Sociologia Ruralis* 26: 36–47.

MULTIPLE VOICES AND THE MEANING OF REVOLUTION: A COMMENT ON THE CONTRI-BUTIONS OF JOÃO CAMILO DOS SANTOS AND JOÃO DE PINA-CABRAL

Caroline B. Brettell

We forget that a society is made up of a multitude of voices. Too often, when the events of 1974 that overthrew forty-eight years of a political dictatorship in Portugal are discussed, it is from the perspective of those who were at the center of activity—the military men, the leaders of newly formed or reactivated political parties, the technocrats, etc. And yet, this so-called revolution has affected the lives of all Portuguese citizens both at home and abroad, and their interpretations of the outcome are varied and equally important. More than a decade ago, I observed that for the peasants of northern Portugal, the revolution was "Lisbon's Revolution" (Brettell 1978). At that time, factors other than political upheaval, and especially the post–World War II emigration to northern Europe, were bringing the most significant changes to their lives and their communities. In the ensuing years, revolution has yielded to a slower process of social and economic development, a fact that makes Portugal increasingly less interesting to political scientists who want to be where the action is—today, it is in Eastern Europe. But it is precisely these ongoing changes that are of interest to other social scientists and social critics (among whom I would include writers and artists) who watch how various sectors of Portuguese society are adapting to the mechanisms that have brought their country rapidly into the twentieth century. For many northern Portuguese peasants today, it is not the ongoing political confrontations in Lisbon that are of concern, but the fact that it is almost impossible to find day laborers during seasons of high agricultural activity. Fields are left uncultivated because the costs are greater than the rewards, especially when day

laborers are no longer satisfied with the kind of food that traditionally was offered to them for their day's work.

It is in the context of multiple voices and ongoing change that
the papers by Camilo dos Santos and Pina-Cabral must be viewed.
On the one hand, we learn about the intellectuals who were disappointed by a revolution that in their view did not go far enough, and
on the other, we are introduced to the social world of northern
Portuguese peasants, a world that is still rooted in ties of family and
neighborship.

It is not uncommon for literary intellectuals to stand outside
their social order and comment on it. This is precisely what Portuguese neo-realists have done in their expressions of disillusion with
the events of 1974. Many of these writers yearned for a major upheaval because their hope was for a totally new society (a "real"
revolution), while the goals of the armed forces were much more
pragmatic and immediate. Though these writers thought they were
the voice of the masses, they were really speaking for themselves.
The revolution was their myth both before and after it happened.

The replacement of dictatorship by democracy was important,
as was the ensuing political and economic restructuring of Portuguese society. But, as Camilo observes in passing, perhaps more
significant was the subtle change in Portuguese national identity
that was the forced outcome of the loss of the African colonies. For
the first time in centuries, Portugal has had to turn its back on the
Atlantic and look toward the Serra da Estrela and beyond for a new
world within which to shape a new sense of self.

If intellectuals and military men have had different ideas about
the meaning of revolution, politicians and peasants, even today, have
different ideas about what kinds of changes should be implemented
in the new democratic society that Portugal is building. These divergent interests became blatantly apparent to me during the summer of
1990 in a conversation with a friend who owns a farm and vineyard
in northern Portugal. My friend employs several workers. Recently
the Portuguese government has instituted mandatory vacation laws.
Justifiably formulated to protect laborers from the worst kinds of
exploitation, these laws are well adapted to those who work in factories or other members of the urban economic sector who would like
several successive weeks of holiday time each year. But they are not
well suited to the needs, interests, and world view of agricultural

workers who have no place to go and cannot afford it anyway. These workers would rather have time off during the afternoons so that they can work their own garden plots. My friend has had to strike an informal deal with his employees; in essence he reports one thing and does another in order to accommodate their preferences. Of course, the disjunction between the state and the populace that this particular problem represents is by no means unique to Portugal. In the United States, laws that prohibit home work, especially the production of items of clothing, discriminate against women, including numerous immigrant women, who find in this kind of activity a satisfactory way to combine income-earning with childcare and other domestic responsibilities. For many families in the United States home piece-work is a lifeline; they disobey the law.

The question of family and family economy brings me to the contribution of Pina-Cabral. This reminds us not only that a society is composed of a range of institutions (beyond political parties, unions, the European Parliament) that affect people's lives, but also that regional, local, and microlevel analyses are as important as those at the national, international, and macrolevel. Furthermore, depending on where we are in Portugal, local institutions and the guiding principles for social organization and social interaction are different. What is absent from Pina-Cabral's detailed analysis of these variations is the implications that they may have for processes of continuity and change. It is quite apparent to me that the three-generation *casa* of northwestern Portugal, a social unit well suited to the agricultural way of life of this region, has adjusted quite adequately to a world where not everyone is employed in farming. Many young couples in this region who are working in factories, as artisans, or, in the case of many young women, in education, continue to marry and move in with one set of parents or the other. In some cases this is still the result of economic constraints; but in others it represents an attitude toward family that has survived the introduction of a consumer economy and a new political order. If kin do not coreside within a single structure, they still tend to live in proximity to one another in a series of households that are linked through vertical (parents and children) and/or horizontal (sibling) relationships. Such relationships are often the basis for successfully coping with conditions of unemployment or underemployment that persist or have been aggravated by the road to democracy and

European integration and, as Pina-Cabral has demonstrated elsewhere, they are as characteristic of the Portuguese bourgeoisie as they are of the Portuguese peasantry. In this light, it is no wonder that the communal institutions of places like Rio de Onor have been reinvigorated by the events of April 1974. They are not archaic survivals but vital mechanisms for social living.

REFERENCE

Brettell, Caroline B. 1978. "Emigration and Its Implications for the Revolution in the North." In *Contemporary Portugal*, ed. Lawrence Graham and Harry Makler. Austin.

CONCLUSION: WHITHER PORTUGAL?

Richard Herr

The discussion noted in the Introduction to this volume concluded that the accomplishments of Portugal in the nearly two decades since 1974 can best be characterized as the achievement of democracy and a reorientation toward Europe. While the term "revolution" makes some of our authors uncomfortable, no one can doubt that the Portuguese world has been revolutionized in these decades. The coming generations of Portuguese people will live in a far different country from that of their ancestors.

What the country will be like in the future, the chapters in this volume help us to envision. On the one hand, we can predict that Portugal will maintain its own character within Europe. João de Pina-Cabral, looking as a social anthropologist at rural society, shows us that an underlying social reality has persisted through the rapid modernization that the country has been experiencing. The difference between northern and southern Portugal, which has always characterized the country, continues in the nature of the family and its relation to the community. In the south the conjugal couple is the "primary social unit." The units disappear when the couples die, while new units are continually taking their places. But in the north the *casa*, which consists of both a family and its property, is the primary unit; the individual is identified by the casa to which he or she belongs, which existed before the current members were alive and will persist after they disappear. So ingrained in much of Portuguese society is this pattern that high bourgeois families of the city preserve their rural estates as the holiday gathering places for the entire family, not just the current legal owners.

Another sign of underlying continuity is the strong identity of the Portuguese people with their region. By putting an end to the imperial dream, the revolution forced the Portuguese people to reformulate their identity. Manuel Braga da Cruz explains in his chapter that he has found through his surveys that a Portuguese person is more likely to be attached to his region than to either his town or his nation. This is very evident in the case of the Azores and Madeira. These islands were joined to Portugal before the origins of the overseas empire, and their separation from the mainland by hundreds of miles—only a small proportion of their inhabitants ever saw continental Portugal—has meant that over the centuries their inhabitants have developed strong feelings of individuality. The constitution of 1976 made them autonomous regions with their own parliaments and governments.

Braga da Cruz's figures indicate that most Azoreans are satisfied with their autonomy statute, but not all are, as José Guilherme Reis Leite, once president of the Regional Assembly of the Azores, makes clear. A resident minister of the republic, appointed by the president, has the power to review the constitutionality of the regional legislation. Up to the time of the conference that person had always been a military person and an outsider. The political role of the military had been eliminated at the national level, but in this symbolic fashion it continued at the regional one. Reis Leite speaks in favor of a constitutional revision to eliminate this office, analogous to the 1982 elimination of the Council of the Revolution. In 1991 the central government responded at least in part to the Azorean discontent by naming a civilian to the office.

The Azores resemble other European regional minorities that demand self-government—the Bretons and Corsicans in France, the Catalans and Basques in Spain. Except for the Azores and Madeira, however, Portugal does not appear to have a "regional problem" comparable to those of France and Spain. Despite the sociocultural differences noted by Pina-Cabral, everyone speaks the same language, even if there are regional accents. And yet Braga da Cruz finds that regional loyalty is strong also on the mainland, and that this is not a new phenomenon but a traditional sentiment. The entrance into the European Community may be giving this underlying reality of Portugal a new life, for the growing economic and political integration of the European Community is reducing the sovereign power that the European nations have traditionally enjoyed.

At the same time, a change in outlook is surely taking place. Braga da Cruz's figures show that regional and national identity are stronger among old and rural people than among young and urban ones. One may venture that attachment to the casa is also an old cultural trait that may weaken with the "tertiarization" of society and as Portugal becomes more incorporated into Europe. One is reminded of Pina-Cabral's observation at our round table discussion that a "process of transformation has manifested itself in the legal structure, the political structure, the economic structure, and also in the ways people live" (Introduction).

If democracy appears safely established, Portugal's membership in the European Community leaves open a number of issues. Nineteen ninety-two should complete the economic union of the Community. Although its results cannot be entirely foreseen, Goucha Soares notes that Portuguese leaders are less concerned by them than by the political reforms of the Community that are likely to follow. If the sovereign states are to lose their autonomy to the Community, the form that its political structure takes will have a great importance for Portugal. As a small country, Portugal is in danger of having less weight in an organization where each country no longer has a veto.

Portugal has a different card up its sleeve, however, when playing for stakes within the European Community. This is its connection with the Lusophone countries of Africa. Portugal's withdrawal from its African empire and its incorporation into Europe leave open the question of its proper role toward its former colonies. It has certain advantages over other European countries in these regions: its new democratic and European existence gives Portugal a new personality in dealing with them, to which are added the common official language and the long familiarity of the Portuguese with these regions. Jaime Gama, from his intimate experience as foreign minister, describes how divided Portuguese public opinion is on the role it should take. Nevertheless, he assures us, despite its turn toward Europe, Portugal will always look toward Africa as well as toward Europe. Current developments confirm his analysis. The recent Portuguese economic expansion has drawn many Africans to Portugal as laborers, while others come to attend the universities. Knowledge of the common language facilitates these migrations. Meanwhile the Portuguese government provides support as its former colonies struggle to establish democracies, and Portuguese entrepreneurs invest there with an eye to the future.

Goucha Soares sees international problems being presented by the European Community. Gama finds both dangers and potential in Portugal's relations with Africa, while Reis Leite shows that regional claims are producing tensions within the domestic structure. These are all challenges facing the country. Yet as Douglas Wheeler points out, Portugal's Third Republic has already lasted longer than the First, and the main threat to the First, from military intervention, now appears remote. Barring serious unforeseen developments, one can predict a successful future for this old country in its new democratic European existence.

INTERNATIONAL AND AREA STUDIES
University of California at Berkeley

Richard M. Buxbaum, Dean

2223 Fulton Street, 3d floor   Berkeley, California 94720

Recent books published by International and Area Studies:

RESEARCH SERIES

83. *The Contradictory Alliance: State-Labor Relations and Regime
    Change in Mexico.* Ruth Berins Collier. $18.50

84. *The Future of European Security.* Ed. Beverly Crawford. $23.50

85. *High Technology and Third World Industrialization: Brazilian
    Computer Policy in Comparative Perspective.* Eds. Peter B.
    Evans, Claudio R. Frischtak, & Paulo Bastos Tigre. $14.95

86. *The New Portugal: Democracy and Europe.* Ed. Richard Herr. $15.50

87. *Russia and Japan: An Unresolved Dilemma between Distant Neighbors.*
    Eds. T. Hasegawa, J. Haslam, and A. Kuchins. $26.50

88. Political Parties in Russia. Ed. Alexander Dallin. $10.95

89. *European Dilemmas after Maastricht.* Eds. Beverly Crawford
    and Peter W. Schulze. $22.95

90. *The Soldiers' Story.* Anna Heinämaa, Maija Leppänen, and
    Yuri Yurchenko, eds. $12.50

EXPLORATORY ESSAYS

1. *The Question of Food Security in Cuban Socialism.* Laura J. Enríquez. $7.50

2. *The Collapse of Soviet Communism: A View from the Information
   Society.* Manuel Castells and Emma Kiselyova $9.50

INSTITUTE OF INTERNATIONAL STUDIES
POLICY PAPERS IN INTERNATIONAL AFFAIRS

39. *Lessons of the Gulf War: Ascendant Technology and Declining Capability.*
    Gene I. Rochlin and Chris C. Demchak. $5.50

40. *Impediments on Environmental Policy-Making and Implementation
    in Central and Eastern Europe: Tabula Rasa vs. Legacy of the Past.*
    Peter Hardi. $6.50

41. *Flying Apart? Japanese-American Negotiations over the FSX
    Fighter Plane.* Gregory W. Noble. $7.25

42. *Beware the Slippery Slope: Notes Toward the Definition of
    Justifiable Intervention.* Ernst B. Haas. $6.50

43. *Industrial Policy Supporting Economic Transition in Central-Eastern
    Europe: Lessons from Slovenia.* Tea Petrin $6.95

INSIGHTS IN INTERNATIONAL AFFAIRS SERIES

1. *Confrontation in the Gulf: University of California Professors Talk
   about the War.* Ed. Harry Kreisler. $7.95

2. *Refugees: A Multilateral Response to Humanitarian Crises.*
   Sadako Ogata. $5.95

3. *American Intervention after the Cold War.* Robert W. Tucker. $3.95

4. *Crisis in the Balkans.* Eugene A. Hammel, Irwin M. Wall, and Benjamin N. Ward. $6.95

CENTERS FOR SOUTH & SOUTHEAST ASIA STUDIES
MONOGRAPH SERIES

32. *Scavengers, Recyclers, & Solutions for Solid Waste Management in Indonesia.* Daniel T. Sicular. $16.50

33. *Indonesian Transmigrants and Adaptation: An Ecological Anthropological Perspective.* Oekan S. Abdoellah. $14.95

34. *Thai Music and Musicians in Contemporary Bangkok.* Pamela Myers-Moro. $22.50

35. *In the Shadow of Change: Images of Women in Indonesian Literature.* Tineke Hellwig. $22.00

OCCASIONAL PAPERS SERIES

15. *The Penis Inserts of Southeast Asia: An Annotated Bibliography with an Overview & Comparative Perspective.* Donald E. Brown, J. W. Edwards, & R. P. Moore. $6.00

16. *Patterns of Migration in Southeast Asia.* Ed. Robert R. Reed. $19.50

17. *Bridging Worlds: Studies on Women in South Asia.* Ed. Sally J. M. Sutherland. $17.50

18. *Essays on Southeast Asian Performing Arts: Local Manifestations and Cross-Cultural Implications.* Ed. Kathy Foley. $14.95

LANGUAGE TEACHING MATERIALS

Introduction to Hindi Grammar. Usha Jain. $30.00

Hmong for Beginners. Annie Jaisser et al. $28.00

Devavanipravesika: Introduction to the Sanskrit Language. Robert P. Goldman and Sally J. Sutherland. $23.50

Teaching Grammar of Thai. William Kuo. $23.50

Tamil for Beginners, 2 vols. Kausalya Hart. $12.50 ea.

SINO-TIBETAN ETYMOLOGICAL DICTIONARY AND THESAURUS PROJECT
MONOGRAPH SERIES

1A. *Bibliography of the International Conferences on Sino-Tibetan Languages and Linguistics I-XXV,* 2d ed. Randy J. LaPolla and John B. Lowe $28.00